ENDORSEME

"Thanks so much, I've been following Mike since right after he published "Landlording On AutoPilot" and attribute most all of our success to his insights and techniques. I constantly insist and recommend that new Landlords MUST buy a copy if they want to have any hope for success in real estate investing"

Charlie—Charter Properties of Texas

In my opinion, by far THE BEST landlording book I've read and I've read a bunch. Mike, the author, goes into great detail about what to do and how to do it as well as what not to do when it comes to being a landlord. His ideas make sense and I hope to put his ideas to work as I'm setting out on my real estate investing future.

—James Stanton

"Mike Butler's 2nd edition is the Gold Standard for managing rental properties"

Fixer Jay Decima—Best Selling Author

"Without Landlording on Autopilot, I doubt I would have ever succeeded with rental properties. Mike's book guided my business every step of the way, and I owe a huge debt to Mike for his insights. This book is a MUST-READ for any current or future landlord."

Brandon Turner, Author of The Book on Rental Property Investing &
Co-host of The—BiggerPockets Podcast

"If you manage real estate, you need to read this book. Mike is the real deal and you can learn ways to manage that will make you money and improve your life."

—John Schaub

"I've been representing real estate investors for over a quarter of a century. And, I've been a real estate investor myself for most of that time. I read TONS of books on investing and attend every seminar I can find. Mike's method is simply the best resource on the market, PERIOD. I recommend Mike's Landlording On Auto Pilot book to ALL my new clients. And it is on my MUST RE-READ list every year. Each time I open it, I'm amazed at the knowledge Mike has in the business. SIMPLY THE BEST!!! Mike has made me and 1000s of other investors more efficient and more profitable."

—Harry Borders, Borders & Borders Attorneys

"Being a landlord can be a tough business, but Landlording on Autopilot gives you hundreds of tools, tricks, and tactics to make landlording enjoyable- and profitable! This book has literally saved me thousands of dollars and helped me streamline my landlording down to just a few hours a month. If you are a landlord, or ever plan to be one, read this book again and again."

—Brandon Turner, Author of The Book on Rental Property Investing & Co-host of The BiggerPockets Podcast

AWESOME!!! I own $100 million of real estate already-but learned a lot from this guy! Should be called Landlording StreetSmarts... great tip, *I read many of the books that come out, and should be considered a real estate veteran, not a beginner, as I own over $100 million of real estate in the Midwest, mostly apartment communities. I bought the book because of the title... and really learned a lot from this author. I highly recommend this to ANY owner or potential owner... large or small... you'll make back a thousand times what you paid for this book in the first year of running your own property!!!*

—J. Stewart. St. Louis, MO

This book is hands down chalk full of material for anybody that owns a residential property and is either thinking of renting or already renting. There are so many great points from how to introduce yourself to potential tenants, to using a door lock system so you aren't constantly buying new locks at the retail stores, to all the forms that you can use, to encouraging long term tenants. The list just goes on and on. A definite read that is straight to the point and super simple to understand.

—Jared Kluver

"What I Learned From This Book Will Make Me My First Million In My Sleep... Literally"

—St. Louis Investor

Great, actionable advice for running a rental portfolio like a well-oiled machine. Filled with tips and tricks to make the average landlord more successful, while removing themselves from the business.

—Sterling Fields

If you intend to be a landlord this book is a MUST have. Mike Butler does a superb job simplifying the business and how to deal with day operations. Without this book I would not have had the confidence needed to start my rental business.

I recommend this book to everyone who is starting out and want to take the guess work out of owning rentals. Only giving 5 stars because Amazon will not let me give it 10.

—David Chw

Best book on being a landlord - Ever! It doesn't matter if you've been a Landlord forever or just starting out, you must read this book. Fast paced and easy/fun to read.

—Jone Renee Zalk

"I have known Mike Butler for a long time now, and he is without a doubt one of the most knowledgeable people on the planet when it comes to being a successful landlord.

He knows how to get tenants, how to retain them, and you will learn how to create systems and procedures that will eliminate a lot of the typical headaches in this business. I highly recommend his book for anyone that has rental property whether you are brand new or you're a seasoned investor."

—Sharon Vornholt, http://LouisvilleGalsRealEstateBlog.com

I originally read this book in 2012. Having just read it again (tenant moving out) I was reminded why the book was so helpful the first time! Almost every situation I've come across as a landlord has been covered and remedied in Landlording on Autopilot!

—Travis Vizier

LANDLORDING ON AUTOPILOT

LANDLORDING ON AUTOPILOT

A Simple, No-Brainer System for Higher Profits, Less Work, and More Fun (Do It All from Your Smartphone or Tablet!)

SECOND EDITION

MIKE BUTLER

WILEY

Published by John Wiley & Sons, Inc., Hoboken, New Jersey.

First edition © 2006 by Mike Butler.

Published simultaneously in Canada.

For general information on our other products and services or for technical support, please contact our Customer Care Department within the United States at (800) 762-2974, outside the United States at (317) 572-3993 or fax (317) 572-4002.

Wiley publishes in a variety of print and electronic formats and by print-on-demand. Some material included with standard print versions of this book may not be included in e-books or in print-on-demand. If this book refers to media such as a CD or DVD that is not included in the version you purchased, you may download this material at http://booksupport.wiley.com. For more information about Wiley products, visit www.wiley.com.

Library of Congress Cataloging-in-Publication Data:

Names: Butler, Mike, author.
Title: Landlording on autopilot : a simple, no-brainer system for higher
profits, less work and more fun (do it all from your smartphone or
tablet!) / Mike Butler.
Description: Second edition. | Hoboken, New Jersey : John Wiley & Sons, Inc.,
2018. | Includes index. |
Identifiers: LCCN 2017058469 (print) | LCCN 2017059382 (ebook) | ISBN
9781119467939 (pdf) | ISBN 9781119467908 (epub) | ISBN 9781119467915 (pbk.)
Subjects: LCSH: Real estate management. | Landlord and tenant.
Classification: LCC HD1394 (ebook) | LCC HD1394 .B88 2018 (print) | DDC
333.5068—dc23
LC record available at https://lccn.loc.gov/2017058469

Cover Design: Wiley
Cover Images: Smartphone image: © Nastco/iStockphoto; Houses image: © jhorrocks/iStockphoto

Printed in the United States of America.

SKY10092029_112524

I am the Luckiest Guy on the Planet!
In Loving Memory

"Pretty Girl" Tammy Butler
September 12, 2004
Our phenomenal success in real estate investing is from the support, confidence, enthusiasm, encouragement, commitment, love, and sacrifice during 21 wonderful years with this "Pretty Girl" who allowed me to "break my chain" to invest aggressively and safely. Most investors can only dream of having a life partner and soulmate so perfect.

My Bride "Beth"
I am truly blessed and my little brother. Matt frequently tells me how lucky I am. He has been married three times and says he has never had anything close to the relationships I had and have today with Beth. I met Beth in 2008 after a boot camp. Beth married me in 2011. She makes my world and business ROCK! My best friend, life partner, and big sister to my daughters. They love Beth too.
Thank you, Beth, for everything you do!

I am the luckiest Guy on the Planet!

In Loving Memory

"Pretty Girl" Tammy Butler

September 12, 2004

Our phenomenal success in real estate investing is from the support, confidence, enthusiasm, encouragement, commitment, love and sacrifice during 21 wonderful years with my "Pretty Girl" who allowed me to "break my chain" to invest aggressively and safely.

Most investors can only dream of having a life partner and soulmate so perfect.

My Bride "Beth"

I am truly blessed and my little brother, Matt frequently tells me how lucky I am. He has been married three times and says he has never had anything close to the relationships I had and have today with Beth.

I met Beth in 2008 after a long time. Beth married me in 2011. She makes my world and business ROCK! My best friend, life partner and the big sister to my daughters. They love Beth too.

Thank you, Beth, for everything you do!

CONTENTS

SECTION II
BEFORE YOU GIVE KEYS TO YOUR NEW RESIDENT

SECTION III
GO 100% DIGITAL AFTER THEY MOVE IN

SECTION IV
MASTER THESE TO MAXIMIZE YOUR INCOME AND PROFITS

ACKNOWLEDGMENTS

I'm not a genius. I've learned a boatload of life-changing information from many experts in my life and real estate. I've taken these techniques and strategies from these folks and have tweaked and twisted them to fit into my program of life, investing, and landlording. I want to thank my family, mentors, coaches, business associates, and all of our tenants who showed me how to work smarter, not harder.

Thanks to my dad, mom, brothers, and sisters, who lit my fuse to achieve "more" in life; to be a superstar. Thanks again to my first wife, Tammy, who passed away in 2004, and our daughters, who kept this fuse lit, keeping me fired up to be the best I could be for myself and my family.

I also want to thank my wife Beth. I feel like the luckiest man on the planet because Beth is my life partner, best friend, my bride, she loves my daughters, and my daughters love her like a big sister. Plus, she jumped in with both feet to continue making our real estate business more efficient and profitable.

I owe a big thank-you to "Fixer Jay" P. Decima of Redding, California, who directed me to "Wild Man" Richard Narramore, senior editor at John Wiley & Sons publishers, who published both editions of this book.

Special thanks to all of my mentors, coaches, and business associates. I will miss a few and please accept my sincere apologies. I wish to thank—in no particular order—John Schaub, Pete Fortunato, Jack Miller, Jimmy Napier, Pete Youngs, Carl Fischer of CamaPlan.com, Ron Legrand, Brandon Turner of BiggerPockets, Inman News, Nick Sidoti, Jeffrey Taylor, and many more. From my hometown—Ed Melton, Jay Long, Chris McCarty, Chris Dischinger, Mark Lechner, Rue McFarland, my CPA Mike Grinnan, my attorney Harry Borders, Dick Vreeland, and old-timer Layne Smith.

ACKNOWLEDGMENTS

I'm not a genius. I've learned a boatload of life-changing information from many experts in my life and real estate. I've taken these techniques and strategies from these folks and have tweaked and twisted them to fit into my program of life, investing, and landlording. I want to thank my family, mentors, coaches, business associates, and all of our tenants who showed me how to work smarter, not harder.

Thanks to my dad, mom, brothers, and sisters who lit my fuse to achieve in my own life to be a competitor. Thanks again to my first wife, Tammy, who passed away in 2004, and our daughters, who kept this fuse lit, keeping me fired up to be the best I could be for myself and my family.

I also want to thank my wife Beth. I feel like the luckiest man on the planet because Beth is my life partner, best friend, my bride, she loves my daughters, and our daughters love her like a big sister. Plus, she jumped in with both feet to continue making our real estate business more efficient and profitable.

I owe a big thank-you to "Brother Jay" P. DeCima of Redding, California, who introduced me to "Wild Man" Richard Narramore, senior editor at John Wiley & Sons publishers, who published both editions of this book.

Special thanks to all of my mentors, coaches, and business associates. I will miss a few and please accept my sincere apologies. I wish to thank—in no particular order—John Schaub, Pete Fortunato, Jack Miller, Randy Napier, Pete Youngs, Carl Fischer of ChimFactor, Ron Legrand, Brandon Turner of BiggerPockets, Inman News, Mark Sipsey, Jeffrey Taylor, and many more. From my hometown—Ed Mellon, Jay Long, Chris McCarty, Chris the Ringer, Mark Leathers, Ray McFarland, my CPA Mike Gallman, my attorney Harry Sanders, Dick Weiland, and old-timer Larry Smith.

ABOUT THE AUTHOR

Mike Butler began his real estate investing career while working his full-time job as an undercover police detective in Louisville, Kentucky, investigating murders for hire, contract killings, and organized crime. Mike began buying fixer-uppers and renting them to make extra money versus working off-duty moonlight jobs like many of his fellow police officers.

Mike discovered very quickly that investing in real estate was to be the pathway to financial freedom for his family. He then exploded his real estate business by buying an average of 2.5 rental properties every week while working his full-time job! Mike did this for several years. Mike Butler knew he must have a brain-dead simple system for his booming business and developed his Landlording On AutoPilot System. It enabled him to own and operate over 75 properties while working his full-time job before making a huge decision to hire a "part time" office person to work 5 hours per week in his office in his basement.

Mike Butler's Landlording on Autopilot Systems allow him to consistently get paid over 100% of his rents every month. Mike started investing with less than a thousand bucks and has NEVER gone to a bank to buy an investment property nor has he ever used a private lender or hard-moneylender. Now Mike Butler works when he wants to—as a husband to Beth, Dad to Rachel and Melissa, an investor, speaker, author, coach, and consultant. Mike enjoys training and helping millionaires and future millionaires and is a sought-after featured speaker and trainer at real estate seminars all across America.

Mike's investing success has been featured in *Money* magazine's article "Can Real Estate Make You Rich?" and the *Wall Street Journal* radio network with over 170 syndicated radio stations.

Mike Butler is a two-term past president of the Kentucky Real Estate Investors Association, served three years on the board of the National Real Estate Investors Association, and is a supporter of The Home of Innocents, a great organization to help disadvantaged, abused, and neglected children.

ABOUT THE AUTHOR

Mike Butler began his real estate investing career while working his full-time job as an undercover police detective in Louisville, Kentucky, investigating murders for hire, contract killings, and organized crime. Mike began buying fixer-uppers and renting them to make extra money versus working off-duty moonlight jobs like many of his fellow police officers.

Mike discovered very quickly that investing in real estate was to be the pathway to financial freedom for his family. He then exploded his real estate business by buying an average of 2.5 rental properties every week while working his full-time job! Mike did this for several years. Mike Butler knew he must have a brain-dead simple system for his booming business and developed his Landlording On AutoPilot System. It enabled him to own and operate over 75 properties while working his full-time job before making a huge decision to hire a "part-time" office person to work 3 hours per week in his office in his basement.

Mike Butler's Landlording on Autopilot Systems allow him to consistently get paid over 100% of his rents every month. Mike started investing with less than a thousand bucks and has NEVER gone to a bank to buy an investment property nor has he ever used a private lender or hard-money lender. Now Mike Butler works when he wants to—as a husband to Becky, Dad to Rachel and Melissa, an investor, speaker, author, coach, and consultant. Mike enjoys training and helping millionaires and future millionaires and is a sought-after featured speaker and trainer at real estate seminars all across America.

Mike's investing success has been featured in *Money* magazine's article "Can Real Estate Make You Rich?" and the *Wall Street Journal* radio network with over 170 syndicated radio stations.

Mike Butler is a two-term past president of the Kentucky Real Estate Investors Association, served three years on the board of the National Real Estate Investors Association, and is a supporter of The Home of Innocents: a great organization to help disadvantaged, abused, and neglected children.

How I Owned and Operated 75 Rental Properties While Working My Full-Time Job as an Undercover Police Detective *(BEFORE Hiring a 5-Hour-a-Week Office Person)*

Hello fellow landlord investors; I'm honored to have the opportunity to share my investing lessons and techniques with you. Not all of my landording education has been pretty. I've also got honorary PhDs from both the "School of Hard Knocks" and my private high school diploma. If I help you get on the fast track to holding good solid rental properties, it'll be another notch on my belt of achievements. Before we get started here, I'd like to share with you a little bit about where I've been, what I've done, and where I am today.

Mom, Dad, and seven kids grew up in this two-bedroom home a few blocks from Churchill Downs, Kentucky

I grew up just a few blocks from the world-famous Churchill Downs, home of the Kentucky Derby. Our neighborhood consisted primarily of blue collar workers, where the definition of "successful" was to land a good job, at a good company, buy a home and get it paid off, and retire and buy a riding mower. In our neighborhood and church, I don't recall any doctors, attorneys, or CPAs. Those folks lived on the "other side of town." I was the oldest of seven kids, and we were raised with a good strong work ethic. Pop worked at a slaughterhouse and proudly identified his occupation as a "meat cutter." He'd let people know pretty quickly that anybody can be a "butcher." Mom stayed at home and did a great job of keeping everybody fed, healthy, and in clean clothes. We had no clue we were poor. We knew Dad worked hard and I admired him and wanted to be just like him. I played football for nine years and got a paper route delivering daily morning and afternoon papers the summer after the eighth grade. This paper route was passed on to my brothers and sisters for almost a decade and delivering papers allowed us to attend a private high school.

I worked for 10 years at Winn-Dixie supermarkets starting out as a bag boy and working my way up to Store Manager. In November 1982, I had the wonderful opportunity to get robbed at gunpoint, with a revolver nervously shaking centimeters (not inches) from my nose.

This event, along with catching shoplifters (some violent), sparked my interest in law enforcement. I took a pretty good cut in pay to become a cop. My starting salary was $17,000. I worked all the overtime I could get and worked "off-duty" jobs for extra income.

I was very intent on finding something to supplement my police pension down the road. I feverishly read the classified ads daily, especially the "Business Opportunity" sections. I wanted the "magic pill" too. I thought it might be found in vending machine routes or coin-operated car washes and Laundromats. There had to be a simple, easy way to financial success.

My goal or objective was to spend my time and energy (because I had no money) into something that would grow in value and income. My attitude was I could simply outwork everyone else, resulting in success. I was searching for something to grow and make money as an "ABSENT OWNER," a hands-off system. My gut instinct kept directing me to real estate and rental property, but I didn't have a clue how to get started, where to begin, PLUS I HAD NO MONEY.

In those days, HUD advertised properties for sale in our Sunday classified ads. I'd drive by these properties in my old Ford Ranger pickup and I thought I was learning my market by seeing how much HUD's asking price for the property was and trying to catch how much they sold for in just a few days or weeks. One Sunday in December 1989, a two-bedroom house on my old paper route showed up on the HUD list. I made an all cash offer "below their asking price" and had no cash. I just wanted the experience of going through the bidding process.

Low and Behold, My Bid Was Accepted!

Now what? We had about $1,000 in our police officers credit union savings account and I got pretty nervous. I went to the Louisville Police Officers Credit Union and got a loan on my Ford Ranger pickup, our old Monte Carlo, and an unsecured signature loan with auto-payments to be taken directly from my paycheck. This still wasn't enough to pull it off and do the rehab needed. I resorted to my last resource, cash advances on several credit cards.

We bought this house for $17,000, put $2,000 in rehab and completed it all in 13 days. I hauled trash and debris to my police sub-station dumpster at night. After renovating this little house, I went to Office Depot and purchased a generic rental application and lease agreement, and put a tenant in the property. (I was lucky. This tenant is still with me today in his third home with us.)

The short version of this story is that I refinanced this house by paying off all of those truck, car, signature loan and credit cards and ended up with $5,000 cash in my pocket PLUS we were making almost $200 per month positive cash flow!

Another pretty house, ready to go, went up for sale across the street. I repeated the same process without having to do any repairs except changing the locks. WOW! This was pretty awesome. Now, Tammy jerked my chain and said, "WHOA!" She was very wise and conservative and ordered me to ride it out for 12 months and see what happens because of the "too good to be true" jinxes.

After a year, we had over $6,000 in our "real estate savings account" and she let me off my chain. I continued buying rental houses. In the beginning, it was just simply a lot easier to buy stinky, broken, ugly houses in need of repair. I'd fixed them up and rent them out. People thought I was nuts. I was buying them at a good price; but I was NOT selling them. It seems like the rest of the world wanted the FAST CASH NOW. I was simply trying to build something that would double or triple my police pension in about 15 years.

Several interesting achievements were accomplished by accident.

1. I NEVER went to a bank to buy an investment property. I always bought the property first.
2. I NEVER used a hard-money lender or a private lender for financing.

We started off our first year with two properties, then two more the following year, and I set a goal of one house per month, resulting in 18 properties purchased. After this, I was going to set a goal of two houses per month (24 for the year). My good friend, local competition, and education partner, Jay Long, and I had the opportunity to see Brian Tracy in Florida during one of his annual real estate investor conferences. Brian Tracy did a presentation on setting goals and challenged folks to "Shoot for the Moon!" If you fall short and miss your goal, he'd ask: "Are You a Loser?" His answer: "NO, You're Not a Loser, You're Just a STAR!" Because of Brian Tracy, I adjusted my goal from 24 houses for the year to four times this ... 96 houses, and rounded it up to 100.

Thanks to Brian Tracy, I did 85 deals that year, resulting in over 50 rental properties purchased and added to my portfolio. Absolutely incredible! That sure blows the doors off my original aggressive goal. Getting this Buying Machine cranked up was a huge challenge. There were so many train wrecks and potholes in the details of the Big Picture. I'll share many of those in later chapters in this book.

Warning

In today's real estate market, do NOT focus on "quantity"; focus on "Quality." Each rental must support itself with a "Pay Me First Mindset." Your rental must put money in your pocket every month. When I got started, I focused on quantity and I was buying rentals that were marginal deals. You *cannot* do that today.

The crucial learning for me was that I had to develop super-efficient systems, tools, and resources in order to realistically have a shot at achieving my goals. I hired my first part-time handyman on rental house #5 and pretty much never swung a hammer again from that point forward.

I used my noggin in creating my effective buying machine, managing rentals, and keeping it all together from a very small office in the corner of our basement. My communication tools were a pager and a cell phone. My real office was on wheels, my police truck. Today, absolutely everything is done remotely using my smartphone, tablet, or laptop.

As a cop and an undercover detective, I developed pretty darn good people skills or communication skills. I had a special ability of getting bad guys and gals to tell me their side of their story, either tape recording it or allowing them to tell their story in a written statement. An admission of the criminal offense, taken properly and legally from a bad guy, is one of the best pieces of evidence in a criminal case. What's kind of weird here is the bad guys usually thanked me as they were led away in handcuffs. I retired in March of 2000 and still get calls from bad guys in prison and on parole. Their girlfriends and family members have quite a bit different attitude about me. I know this is true, even today, because two of my little brothers are police officers, too.

Tammy and I lived off of our police officer and nurse wages. We chose to let our real estate grow itself. One beautiful Saturday morning, I checked the voice mail messages on my pager and found it full with 30 messages. I retrieved all of the messages and began returning phone calls at 8:30 A.M. while sitting downstairs in our lower-level kitchen. From this oak table, I could see the pond and swimming pool out back, the ducks and geese, and an absolutely gorgeous spring Saturday morning. I returned these 30 calls watching my pager dance on the table with more incoming messages. Tammy brought me a tuna salad sandwich at lunchtime and I continued returning phone calls, retrieving and deleting messages from the pager, and calling more folks. At 8:30 P.M., I still had a list of 30 people to call and I just realized I blew an entire beautiful Saturday because of our real estate business.

This Was *Not* What I Wanted from Our Real Estate!

I wanted our real estate to give us a higher quality of life, not a noose around my neck.

At this point, Tammy and I made the decision to hire a part-time office person. What a huge relief! She pitched vacancies and did a lot of stuff in her five hours. Yes, if she got behind on something, she'd work longer.

We operated 75 rental properties, plus the rehabs, and the buying machine before hiring a part-time office person.

This book will show you exactly how you can accomplish this too and to do it all 100% paperless by going all digital, using today's technologies.

You'll begin with learning the "True Life Cycle of a Tenant from A to Z" to show you the fundamentals, attitudes, and some of the pitfalls. By showing you the big picture, and the rewards and benefits that come with real estate, I hope it gives you the motivation and desire to stick with it. I kinda compare this process as very similar to learning to ride a bike. You're gonna get banged up and dinged up a bit, but if you keep working it, you soon learn to fly, for the rest of your real estate career. Just like a bicycle, if you learned to ride one as a kid, as long as our old aching body will cooperate, you could jump on a bicycle and ride one today … with a little more pain, perhaps.

From there, we'll move to some procedures of putting your Landlording on Autopilot with a very detailed and thorough, in-depth, process involving your Rental Application and the process of screening tenants. Just imagine what your landlording life would be like if all of your tenants were "perfect tenants." That's your goal. That was my goal too, and I have conquered and achieved this goal over the years.

Imagine what your landlording would be like with those "perfect tenants." Almost all of your headaches and nightmares commonly associated with landlording seem to almost evaporate and don't exist.

Your life really can be awesome. The key is to set up landlording on autopilot systems from screening tenants to your move-out inspection when they leave.

The next section involves "polishing your system" and cranking it up to the next level where you can actually begin getting more than 100% of your rents.

And finally, you'll have the opportunity to get the complete set of forms used in my Landlording on Autopilot System in PDF and Microsoft Word format immediately available by downloading it from my website. Plus, you also get free online training videos.

Real estate has rewarded me in so many ways. Money is not my measure of success. Success is the road; it is the journey. With success (and money), we've been able to help more people than I ever dreamed possible with my job as a cop. I've met great, generous people from all over this wonderful country of ours.

We're blessed to have all of these opportunities in our world. It's up to us to take action and make it happen for ourselves and for our families.

Good Luck and Happy Investing and congratulations on getting your hands on my "Landlording on Autopilot" System.

Mike Butler

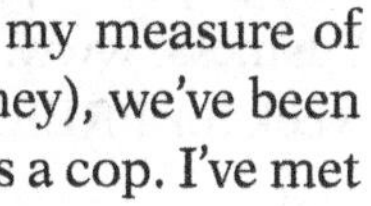

What's New in the Second Edition?

Today's technology is mind-boggling. With all of the free phone apps and other technology available for investors, there is absolutely no reason why you can't run your entire real estate business like I do, from your smartphone, tablet, or laptop from anywhere in the world, including cruise ships—all you need is an Internet connection.

PLUS, all of these technologies PROTECT YOU and YOUR BUSINESS BETTER because of the brain-dead simple, very accurate, and detailed documentation and recording of everything you do in your business—from buying rentals, to marketing, to managing your rental properties, move-in and move-out process, maintenance and repairs, paying bills, and everything else in between.

The second edition of *Landlording on Autopilot* is full of brand new proven strategies and procedures while bringing you the core fundamentals of the first edition. My goal is to bombard you with the newest information and strategies, allowing you to quickly advance to the next level. Work Smarter, Not Harder.

HEADS UP: I want to give you my no-holds barred insider secrets on how I run my real estate business in today's world. Please understand many of these technologies involve our favorite four letter *F* word—FREE; however, I am going to share with you some of the priceless, but not free systems and technologies to improve your efficiency and profitability of your business while giving you more time to Do What You Want In Your Life!

You will see a list of my recommended resources in the back of this book. I do not get one nickel for most of the products and services mentioned. I say this to let you know this is not a book designed to pitch products and services. It's designed to help you and your business. To drive this point home, you have my personal invitation to participate in several free Investor Training opportunities for you and your business. www.MikeButler.com/PowerLunch has Investor Training Webinars every week for FREE.

LEGAL WARNING!

It Is YOUR Responsibility to make sure you are in compliance with your state and local fair housing laws and landlord tenant laws.

All content and forms in this book are from my real estate business in Louisville, Kentucky.

I highly recommend you get your own copy of your local fair housing laws and your local landlord tenant law.

Odds are, Kentucky's landlord tenant law will not work perfectly in your town. Some of the major differences involve:

- Rent control
- Late charges
- Security deposit procedures and interest
- Eviction laws and procedures
- How many hour notice to tenant before entering

Residential Housing in the United States Is Sacred. You can prevent a boatload of expensive headaches by learning and having access to the rules and regulations your real estate business must obey.

Grab your FREE copy of your Landlord Tenant Law. Go online to http://askmikebutler.com/free-training/

SECTION I

YOU MUST HAVE THE RIGHT MINDSET FIRST

CHAPTER 1

Why Residential Rental Properties?

...because they are simple and easy when done properly.

"Imagine what your life would be like if you had 20 nice rental houses paid for..."

...and you could run your business from anywhere in the world using your smartphone, tablet, or laptop, as long as you have internet access! Awesome? Even Burned-Out Landlords Say "Awesome!"

This is exactly how I run my rental business in today's world. It is absolutely incredible how technology has catapulted my lifestyle allowing me to live exactly what I have dreaming about since my early teens.

How many businesses can you run from anywhere in the world? While smack dab in the middle of the ocean on a huge Royal Caribbean cruise ship, I can log in to my desktop in my office back home and drive everything just like I was sitting in front of my computer. This includes printing checks!

Now back to those 20 nice paid-for rental houses. Be Honest with yourself when you answer this question. Please do not allow yourself to be a "Debbie Downer" or "Negative Nancy" on *Saturday Night Live*.

But Mike...

- I don't want to wait 25 or 30 years to get 20 houses paid for.
- Been there, done that... I don't want Tenants and Toilets ever again.

Just answer the question. Would your life be awesome or miserable?

Even "been there, done that" burned-out landlords will admit their life would be awesome.

Now let's break it down into Fred Flintstone math. (Fred has only three fingers and this makes it really easy for me to cipher.)

1. Each Single-Family Rental House rents for $1,000 a month.
2. Subtract $500 for property taxes, insurance, repairs, and management.
3. This leaves $500 in your pocket every month for each rental house.

4. Now take the $500 profit on each rental and multiply by 20 rental houses equals…
5. $10,000 in your pocket every month!

   (Okay, here comes Debbie Downer, who says, "But what about vacancies, Mike?"… Great question. I do not factor in vacancies on single-family houses because the average life of a tenancy is over six years.)

A few years ago, I conducted a research study and asked investors, "How much money in your pocket, every month, would make you a happy camper?" I was shocked. By far, the number-one answer was $10,000. These surveyed investors stated that having $10,000 in their pocket every month would cover their cost-of-living expenses and allow them to pursue the passions in their life. In other words, that much would allow them to do what they want to do in life!

Wow! Just imagine waking up every morning and doing what you want! Sounds like living your dream.

This survey really opened my eyes to the real-world goals and objectives of mom-and-pop investors. In addition to true financial freedom and independence, most are not greedy or selfish. Most investors have a HUGE heart and truly enjoy helping people.

In my early years, I can't tell you how many times I heard "Money Is the Root of All Evil."

Odds are, you heard it too. And these words usually came from a poor person. Could this be their subconscious rationalization to convince themselves that poor is beautiful?

I say BALONEY! Let me tell you something here. GOOD People are GOOD People. Selfish, Greedy, Self-Centered, and Evil People will always be the same. Money has nothing to do with it.

I have discovered, assuming you are Good People, that you can help more people when you have money. Good People will be good people with or without money. Evil people will be evil people with or without money.

Personally, I truly enjoy and I am passionate about helping good people, who invest in themselves, to achieve true financial independence and freedom in three to five years and do it safely with the least amount of work, energy, and effort on their part. I enjoy being part of your real estate investing team to turbocharge and boost your results safely and quickly.

Here's what it boils down to: Would you like to make $10,000 per month and do what you want every day or make $50,000 or more per month and not have time to fart? (Just to let you know, I always set higher goals; a lot more than $10,000 per month.)

What about other investments, like stock, gold or silver, mutual funds, and so forth? Real Estate Investors invest in real estate primarily because they believe it is a real investment that they can control. You can see it, visit it, touch it, smell it, and show it off to friends and family. You can't do that with stock. You might be able to do it with gold and silver.

Here's the Biggie: Real Estate investments produce income for you. Because you own it, it puts money in your pocket and it has huge tax benefits—depreciation. Stock speaks for itself and it is an investment that you normally can't control. I am not a stock expert. Gold and Silver are being marketed as safe investments, but does owning them produce income for you? Nope.

Real Estate Investing 101: The Basics

Sorry, this may ruffle your feathers...

The BUSINESS Side of Real Estate is nothing more than a "JOB." In short, because you do stuff, you make money. For IRS purposes, your profits are taxed as "Earned Income" (not good) (see Table 1.1). Bear with me on this, as my goal is to show you the BASICS, not the complicated strategies.

This is no different from being a used car dealer. Why? How? The typical used car dealer goes to wholesale auctions to buy cars at a huge discount and then resells them at a higher price for a profit. Sometimes they fix them up (retail) and sometimes they sell as-is (wholesale).

To really help you to grasp this BUSINESS Side of Real Estate, let's use a real-world example that happens to many folks. People are living longer in the United States and abroad. There are many reasons to drive this point home.

Imagine something, anything in your life that would disturb or prevent you from doing your daily routine in your business. Especially in the health-related fields, any family member, close relative, or friend, who requires your assistance, bedside in hospital, feeding daily, helping around house, and so forth.

Perhaps it could be yourself or an immediate family member; an injury at work; a health crisis like cancer; a major accident of some sort; and the list could go on and on. I'm going to assume you want to be with your family member and loved ones to offer support and comfort.

If you are laid up in the hospital, or incapacitated, you will put the rest of your life on hold or hit the pause button, including your real estate business. Now what happens to your income? It *comes to a screeching halt* when you stop moving. Health issue; car wreck; whatever; whoever.

Real Estate Investors are unique, and we live in our own little bubble. Most of the folks around us, including coworkers, family, friends, folks at church, do not understand why we do what we do. They NEVER will. Get used to it. You can lead a horse to water, but you can't make them drink. Take me, for example. I am the oldest

Table 1.1 Real Estate Investing 101

BUSINESS	"INVEST"-ing
• TAXED as "Earned Income"	• TAXED as "Passive Income"
• Higher Income Tax Rate	• Lower Income Tax Rate
• Creates CHUNKS of CA$H Now	• BUY and HOLD—rentals
• Buy Low and Sell Now for Profit Now	• Direct Auto-Deposits
• Flippers (dolphins)	• Income Because You Own It!
• Wholesale	• HUGE Tax Benefits! (depreciation)
• Whole-Tail	• 1031 Tax-Deferred Exchange—defers Capital Gains Income Tax
• Retail	• Installment Sale Benefit
• Real Estate Agents	• Tax-Free Profit and Income for Life!
• YOU Do Stuff to Get Paid (JOB)	• (self-directed ROTH IRA)
• If You STOP Moving . . . No Income	
• NO Depreciation Benefit	
• NO Installment Sale Benefit	
• NO 1031 Tax-Deferred Benefit	
• Business Side is NOT Investing	

of seven kids and none of them, zero, nada, of my brothers and sisters are involved in real estate.

Because you are reading this right now, you are already qualified to be a great investor, and yes, you are a member of our "real estate investor bubble" world.

Investing in real estate is by far, the biggest common denominator of millionaires, multimillionaires, and megamillionaires and billionaires. Like you, I honestly believe Knowledge Is Powerful and your learning NEVER stops.

Do It Safely—Keep Your Job!

Odds are, you might have been raised just like me. In short, most folks are not raised with a silver spoon in their mouth. Most of us have been raised in a blue-collar neighborhood with the good old-fashioned blue-collar-job mindset.

Do any of these items sound familiar to you?

- *ALWAYS Pay Cash:* Never use Credit Cards because they are dangerous and will get you in trouble real fast!
- *AVOID Borrowing Money:* The only exception is the loan to buy your home. Your Home Loan should NEVER exceed one week's take-home pay.

- *Get Educated with a college degree:* No one can take this away from you.
- *Get a Good Job with a Good Company:* Safer, stable, and they have good benefits and pensions. (Ha! Not in today's world.)
- *ALWAYS Keep Your Job:* The thought of being unemployed or drawing an unemployment check was the tattoo of failure and being a loser in my world when growing up. It's easier to get a new job if you have a job now.
- *LIVE Below Your Means:* Now this one is a good solid foundation or cornerstone.
- *LEARN How to Do Things Yourself to SAVE Money:* For example, my Dad showed me how to change the oil in his truck so I could save money doing it myself on my truck.
- I lived and practiced these things that were brainwashed into my noggin. I made my Dad proud that I never drew unemployment and I always had a job *(until this real estate investing blew the doors off my police salary and pension).*
- The things mentioned here have been ingrained into our brains just like in caveman days. Believe it or not, these things are permanent and cannot be removed. We can hide them; we can do our darnedest to bury them in our brain... but they are still there.
- Here's an example: Do you mow your lawn or do you have someone else do it for you? Once again, I can do it myself and save $35 in today's market. You might agree with me on this one. Most folks do. FYI, I have NOT touched a lawnmower since the spring of 1996. I found it was not a good use of my time, unless I was pursuing the exercise thing.
- Okay, now for the big question. When do you pull the trigger to take control of your business, income, and lifestyle?

Rule 1—Etch This in Stone

Keep Your Job Until Your Real Estate Investing Income *Consistently* Produces MORE Income Than Your Job!

Let's use me and my job as an example. My full-time job as an undercover police detective paid me about $41,000 per year. (My wife was a critical care Registered Nurse, a full-time job with health insurance and benefits.) I mention my wife because of the benefits with her job, especially the Health Insurance. This is a HUGE concern and expense in today's world.

Because my wife's job took care of our family's health insurance, this made it a lot easier for me to transition into full-time real estate investing.

When Did You Pull the Trigger? You must note I honestly believed I had the best job on the planet doing this undercover police detective work! Fun, Adventure, Exciting, Helping People, and putting evil people in prison. Yes, it was time-consuming but I thoroughly enjoyed it.

My wife, however, was beating me up to retire early because my job was too dangerous. Long story short, some things got pretty serious and dangerous and she gave me an ultimatum—She was fed up with the fear and dangerousness of my job. She was going to leave with my girls if I did not quit my police job. She had been beating me up since 1996 when our real estate income skyrocketed. And it continued, and continued. Looking back, I'm going to guesstimate my income from real estate investments was more than four times my police detective salary. I retired early from my full-time job in March 2000.

I was absolutely terrified of retiring early. My job was part of "Who I Am." Perhaps I was going through some kind of identity crisis PLUS. I would NOT have a J.O.B. How could I function? Could I function? I did it and it worked out awesome for me and my family. I felt like I was on an extended vacation for life! You probably have some of these fears as well.

Maybe you hate your job. It doesn't matter. If you want to be responsible and still have the ability to function in life, you must make your transition from your job to full-time investor as obstacle-free as possible.

The number one obstacle is your INCOME. My personal opinion and recommendation is to NEVER quit your job until your real estate income is producing a lot more than your job income. In the past, I used to say don't quit your job until your real estate income matches or exceeds your job income. Because of health insurance, you must bump this income up a bit. Perhaps one and a half times or maybe double your job income. This will allow for health insurance expenses as well.

Please do not allow yourself to fall victim to the Saturday morning pep rallies from national expert gurus to drink their Kool-Aid, getting brainwashed into believing you can make more on one or two deals than your annual salary. Although I have not experienced this firsthand, my gut tells me I would not be able to function properly, efficiently, or wisely. My job was my "ROCK," my security blanket and gave me peace of mind and the confidence to pursue real estate investing until my results far surpassed my full-time job benefits.

Another way of looking at it might be to imagine yourself without your job . . . in my case, I would be freaking out how to pay the gas and electric bills, groceries, car insurance, and all of those other things I never worried about when I had my job. I was scared I would not be the same person without my job.

So, there you go. KEEP YOUR JOB until your real estate investing produces far more than your job income. Once you have confidently achieved this, you should be able to have a very smooth transition into full-time real estate investing.

Owning rental properties is very much a "hands off" owner-absent business you can run from anywhere in the world with Internet access.

Here's what you need to make this happen.

- Windows PC or MAC that can run Windows
- TeamViewer—allows you to access your desktop from anywhere
- Gmail with a Google Account

CHAPTER 2

The Life Cycle of a Tenant from A to Z

Much like the life cycle of a donkey is from A to Z, understanding the life cycle of a tenant from A to Z will give you a big advantage in running your rental business very efficiently.

If point A for a donkey is the conception of the egg and sperm, and point Z is the death of the donkey, we can apply this same basic concept to the life cycle of a tenant.

Point A

What is point A in the life cycle of your tenant? You might say when they get keys to your rental unit or when they sign your lease. Not true.

Point A is the moment you get notice of any upcoming vacancy of your rental unit.

- This could be purchasing another rental property. You know at that point you will have upcoming vacant unit(s), unless you inherit the existing tenant(s) with the purchase.
- Getting notice is also the moment one of your tenants informs you they will be moving out at the end of next month. If a great resident, find out why they are moving. Many times, you can simply move them to another one of your rentals. If you can't save them as your tenant(s), this is your point A for your next tenant.

Point Z

What is point Z for the life cycle of your tenant? Many investors believe this is when they have moved out or when you get the keys from them. Not true.

- Point Z occurs when this previous tenant owes you ZERO dollars. If you have followed and properly implemented the entire Move-Out Process, your tenant may still owe you money even after deducting their security deposit from the balance owed to you.
- In my system, within 30 days of their Move-Out Inspection date, my office prepares their final settlement report or move out report and sends it to this now-previous tenant by snail mail and email.
- If we owe them money, a check payable to this previous tenant is included with the snail mail.
- If they owe us money, they have 30 days to respond to pay in full or get set up a payment plan. If they play ostrich on their 30 days to respond, we then send their file to an expert collection company. Do NOT try to do it yourself. We use Morgan and Pottinger attorneys in Louisville, Kentucky. They have a national network with which they can find folks anywhere in the United States and get the tenants's wages garnished. They did this for me. Approximately seven years after a tenant moved out, they found him working in Wisconsin and garnished his wages.
    - How much does this cost? You can find high-quality and reputable collection attorneys who charge you court costs and filing fees to file the lawsuit against your previous tenant. That's it, no more fees until they get payment(s) from your previous tenant. At that time, they will deduct anywhere from 33% to 40% as their fee as you receive payments. Other than courts costs, you pay nothing else until they receive payments from your previous tenant.
    - Let the experts do your collections. NEVER do it yourself. Do you think if I tried to do collections myself that I could find my previous tenant from seven years ago, working in Wisconsin? PLUS, all of the headaches, negative stuff, time-eating efforts wasting your time trying to track down your previous tenant. This is why God created attorneys.
    - When should you use a collections firm?
    - A good collections firm will evaluate your file when you submit it to them for collections. The "you cannot get blood from a turnip" rule applies here. If it is really ugly and there is no obvious chance of getting a dime, then you are wasting your money moving forward on this previous tenant. A good collections company will tell you it is a waste of money to move forward.

Tip

All of your tenants who receive any kind of government assistance as their sole source of income are exempt from collections. Examples would be older folks living on Social Security checks, disabled folks living from their disability checks, and so forth.

Now you have a better understanding of the Life Cycle of a Tenant.

Your rental property business is just like a big, strong chain. Remember the old saying, "A Chain Is Only as Strong as Its Weakest Link?" The same applies to your rental business.

Let's visualize and fill in the links between Point A and Point Z (Figure 2.1). As you can see, you simply fill in the blanks between the beginning of their life cycle and the end of their life cycle.

Now just imagine one of your links is broken. It doesn't matter which one, but one is broken.

Suppose your rental application processing is broken. You could probably end up putting dirt bags in your rental unit.

What if your repairs and maintenance link is broken? Your great residents will get fed up and move.

FIGURE 2.1 Life Cycle of Your Tenant

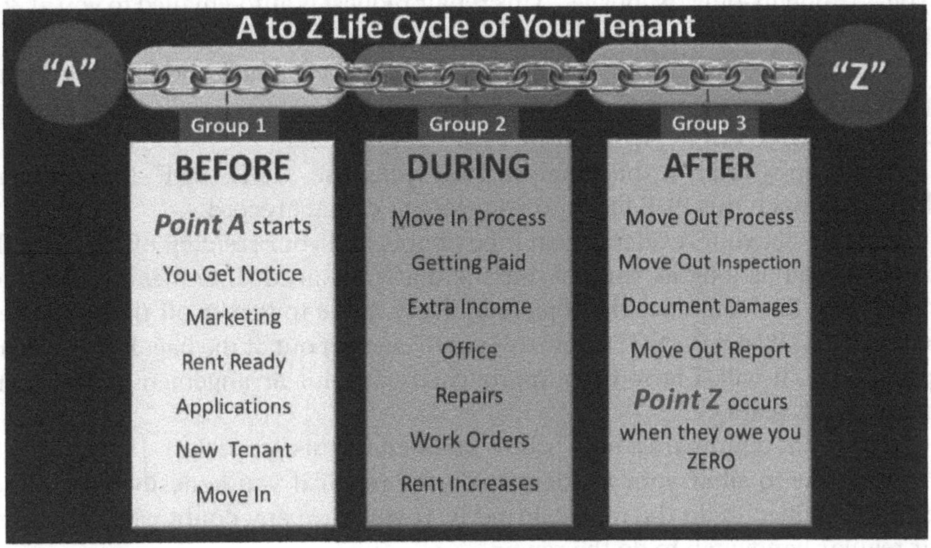

Move-In Process and Move-Out Process links are broken. Suppose you do a very quick move-in inspection without photos and accurate, verifiable, proof of the condition of the rental unit when they moved in. Unless you have a rock-solid, detailed move in inspection as evidence, you are wasting your time and money doing a move out inspection and photographing and documenting all of the damages caused by your tenant. If you can't prove these damages were not there when the tenant moved in... You Lose.

Each and every link MUST be strong and not broken if you want your rental business to run on autopilot.

Now let's get started working on these links.

Resources Needed

- Just your sharp noggin

A Few Landlording Ground Rules

1. NEVER Let Your Tenants Subtract Repair Costs from Rent

This one is totally preventable and causes many investors a ton of grief along with complicating repair expenses. Ultimately, this can affect your cash flow, income, and the value of your rental

Here's how it gets started. Things are rolling along just fine and you are living the good life. Then your resident, using your free website, submits a repair request on your "residents-only" webpage." This repair request is auto-emailed to you at 3:30 in the morning.

When you get up in the morning, you check your email and find this repair request from your tenant. It already has a date/time stamp on it. *FYI, excellent documentation!*

Next step, you print this email to PDF using the "CUTE PDF" free app, and upload and attach this PDF file in to your tenant contact record.

You contact your resident, even if by phone, and your resident offers to do the repairs for you as long as you pay for the materials needed. Somehow, this ends up as this... Resident does the repairs and you agree to take it off their rent next month. NO! NO! NO! Do NOT allow this cat to ever get out of the bag. If this has not happened yet, it will. I have been approached with this arrangement many, many times over the years.

To prevent nightmares, here is how you handle this properly.

It is okay to allow your resident to do the repair if you honestly believe they truly are qualified to do the repair properly. It you have any doubt whatsoever, get your regular handyman to do the repair.

So you believe your resident is capable of doing this repair properly. Simply tell them to do the repair, and send you the receipt for the material purchased. When they send you the receipts and billing, you will simply create a check made payable to them for the reimbursement of material for the work they completed and use the "Repair Expense" account in your bookkeeping.

FYI, if you are still curious why you should do it this way instead of deducting it from your rental income, here's some things to support the proper way to do it. First, you want to report and document all of your rental income. Doing it the wrong way reduces your rental income for this property. NOT Good. If you do it the wrong way many times, your cash flow, profit and loss, and tax summary reports would be all garbage. PLUS it lowers the value of your investment property, especially on apartments and commercial properties. PLUS, you would not be accurately documenting your repair expenses on this property. This too affects all of your reports as well. Always keep Rent as Rent and Repairs as Repairs and you won't go wrong.

Don't forget, once you let this bad cat out of the bag the first time, this resident will continue to try to reduce their income for repairs they claim they have done without your knowledge or approval. If things get ugly, just imagine them in eviction court telling the judge they did all of these repairs and they have deducted it from their rent payments. If your tenant can prove you did approve this one time... you will lose on all of the other phantom repairs made.

2. "Giving Your Resident a Project" Will Save You Time and Money

"Project": Is it a good word or a bad word in our world of real estate investing? Your mental knee-jerk reaction is probably BAD. Settle down for a moment and you will learn how you can benefit with BOTH your time and MONEY by creating projects.

Here is one of my real-world examples: How many times has this happened to you?

One of your great, long-term tenants contacts you with a request for a new carpet for their living room (not the whole house; just one room).

Do you have thoughts like:

- Think about how good they have been by not being a pain?
- Son of a #$#@, why now? I don't have time for this problem and spending more money.
- Perhaps a fear of not "giving in" to a new carpet may cause them to move, creating another vacancy?
- How can I play ostrich and buy some time to postpone this expense for another year?
- The carpet was new when they moved in. They don't need new carpet if they would take care of it properly.
- Thoughts switch to greed or "business"... "Hmm, upgrade with a new carpet could mean I up the rent."

Well, sit down and get ready to knock yourself in the noggin with a big stick.

Good Tenants are a rare breed today.

They are on the endangered species list. I think I saw it on the Discovery Channel.

Your Life versus Tenant Life

YOUR LIFE Do you have a busy schedule EVERY DAY. Putting out fires, "riding the bull," doing deals, paperwork, insurance, taxes, phone calls, messages, bills, payments, evictions, late charges, late notices, work orders, family, plus a job? . . . Sound familiar? I found myself in this rat race for many years. If this is not you, you are a rare exception. Stick to it.

TENANT LIFE (Perhaps as we view it), let's switch gears and step into their shoes. Watch late night TV. Sleep late. Coffee in the morning, Jerry Springer, soap operas, gossip TV, gossip phone calls, talk shows, pizza delivery is a meal, getting ready to wait for the mailman to arrive, two hours spent preparing a grocery list, . . . WAY TOO MUCH TIME ON THEIR HANDS!

Now let's go back to the carpet story.

Your knee-jerk reaction to this being another problem. WRONG.

You should view this as an OPPORTUNITY.

Especially with a good tenant, YOUR HOUSE is THEIR HOME. Do NOT forget this. It is a powerful tool for you.

When your good tenant contacts you with the carpet story, the absolute most dangerous act on your part is to go "check it out." This "good business" practice on your part simply puts a bullet right between your eyes of your tenant.

Your "good business" behavior is actually calling your great tenant a liar.

Your actions are saying, "I am not sure I believe you. Let me come over and check it out." Even with good intentions on your part, you just went 2 steps forward and 77 steps BACKWARD.

Hold on—there is more. . . . So you go check it out and you agree with your tenant. YUP, it is worn and could be replaced. Mentally, your tenant has their arms folded across their chest, saying, "I TOLD YOU THAT EARLIER, STUPID."

With good intentions on your part and a concern of SAVING MONEY. . . . You might tell your tenant something like . . . "Yes, I see you could use some new carpet. I will call my carpet guy and he will contact you to schedule putting in your new carpet."

This, too, is the KISS OF DEATH to your great resident.

Remember, you try to run an efficient rental business by using the same CHEAP carpet with all of your rentals, the same installer, and so forth. This really is a good business thing by putting systems into place on your tenant turnovers and vacancies.

Your KIND act and pride in showing your tenant you have a system in place to take care of their problem is a total disregard to the concerns of the tenant and you just SMACKED them square in the face with a 2 × 4 by reminding them that they are the TENANT who is RENTING MY HOUSE.

All of their thoughts about their HOME just evaporated with you bumping your gums about your system.

But wait a minute. You are trying to be a nice guy, a good landlord and property manager. Yes, this is true BY YOUR STANDARDS.

You are taking time out of your busy day, spending your money, to do something for your tenant in YOUR HOUSE. So when you get viewed as a greedy landlord, you remind yourself of your good intentions, good actions, spending money, all for not even one simple Thank You.

YOU are guilty of promoting the horrible US and THEM attitude as much as anyone else.

SWITCH GEARS and try this the next time.

When your good and great tenant contacts you with a request for new carpet in one room, turn it into a WIN-WIN situation for both your Great Tenant and yourself.

If on the phone, let the tenant bump their gums for a while. Use their FIRST NAME a lot when talking to them. It makes them feel good. After they make some noise for a while, here is how to make them want to stay forever.

Refer to your rental house as "THEIR HOME" and Give Them a Project.

NEVER go to their home to check it out. If they are a great tenant, you should believe them.

Tell your tenant you can help them out if they want the new carpet. Tell them they can pick out the carpet they want for their home and you will pay for THEIR carpet. All they need to do is get it installed. (Believe it or not, they almost always agree to this)... tell your great resident you can do this for them only if they will agree to stay longer. Tell them you can do this for them when they renew with a three-plus-year lease or rental agreement. Now this will definitely make it worth your while.

Instruct your tenant to go carpet shopping. Give them some places to go. There are carpet remnant stores and outlets in almost every town. Tell the tenant to be reasonable and give them good instructions... no gold-laced carpet allowed!

Even though you are a tightwad, you should not have to replace the pad. Your tenant is going to round up their own installer. Do not worry about the installer. Odds are your tenant will choose better quality carpet than what you normally install. By the time they move out, it really doesn't matter how it was installed because you will probably remove it and replace it again.

Now think about this in the big picture. Tenant contacted you with a request. You are a good landlord. You acknowledge their concern, and you give your tenant a PROJECT. In their mind, they are going shopping on your dollar to buy carpet they choose for THEIR HOME.

No more phone calls on your part and I bet the purchase of the carpet is CHEAPER than your system in the long run. I doubt if the cost of the carpet in this manner will be more than the expense of your installer and the carpet you usually install. And remember, your carpet installer absolutely HATES installing carpet in an occupied home.

If you have your carpet installer install the carpet you normally use for turnovers and vacancies, your great tenant will call this carpet that "nasty old cheap carpet." When you allow them to go shopping for carpet, your great tenant will call their carpet "My New Carpet" for years and years, just like you and I do in our own homes. We put expensive new carpet in my home in 2003 and I still call it new carpet today. Chew on that one for a minute.

Doing this the way most landlords would handle this, your tenant is reminded that they are a tenant living in your house. They will be sitting at home waiting for your system to do their thing. Your tenant has time to waste on projects to make them feel good. Give them TIME-EATING PROJECTS. Your Tenant will win and you will win.

This is a great program. Think about it from the Tenant's perspective.

- You did not challenge their request or call them a liar.
- Carpet Shopping Time has just become a priority and will be placed at the top of their list of things to do.
- Maybe they need transportation to go carpet shopping. Call family, friends, church people, to take them carpet shopping because their landlord is going to buy them new carpet.... Wow, good free advertising for you as well. And they are usually excited for this adventure.
- Spend hours at the carpet store listening to all of the BS stories from the salesperson. We hate it. They love it along with all of the attention.
- Maybe they need to think about it and return for a second trip or opinion or maybe go to three, four, or five carpet stores to help find the best deal. Yes, it sounds stupid, but this is a major project to them and they may really, truly try to find the best of both price and quality. (Haven't you seen co-workers who spend 60 hours of their time comparison shopping, researching prices on car tires only to discover their best deal is $12.25 a tire cheaper at XYZ tire store? Sound like they worked 60 hours to save $49.00. They worked for about $0.81 an hour!)
- You are giving the tenant an opportunity to instill pride in their HOME by allowing them to choose the carpet for their home. You will also become a hero and the best landlord in the world.
- Now they must consider a lot of stuff. Color, texture, quality, fiber, cost... wow, a lot of stuff they never dreamed of... is all an important part of their project

to install carpet in their living room. They had no idea how much stuff their landlord had to go through for carpet.

- Moving on, they finally make a decision on a piece of carpet. Now they make the salesperson write up some kind of bill and I recommend to have your tenant hand deliver the bill to your office. (This is another mini-project). If you do not have an office, have them email it, text it, or fax it to you.
- Once received, if you have an office, make the tenant return to your office to "pick up the check" made payable to the carpet store. (Again, another mini-project).
- With no office, simply log in to your online checking account and create a check made payable to the carpet store and click the button to mail this check to your tenant. Do NOT make the check payable to your great resident!
- Now the Tenant needs to make arrangements to get back out to the carpet store to purchase the carpet... another project.
- Don't forget about the installer... another project and a cost for the tenant. Now they have another project to research and will spend their time shopping for the best deal for a carpet installer.
- Still yet another mini-project involves making arrangements to schedule the installation, moving furniture, and so on.
- They do not mind all of these projects and time-eaters because all of these things we call headaches all benefit them. We despise time-eating projects. They love it and will probably seek an "attaboy" from you for the results of their efforts while thanking you for ALL OF YOUR HELP.
- You have really turned your house into THEIR HOME. They will be proud of their new carpet they picked out and all of the experiences of their project.
- QUESTION: If you delegate this project to them, how long will this carpet be labeled or referred to as "NEW"? I'll bet it will be called "NEW" for a lot longer than your old cheap builder grade carpet would be called new. If you used your system and installed your generic, run-of-the-mill cheap carpet, it will not last a year as being called NEW. Next year, it will be called "OLD CARPET" because it is over a year old.
- Now your tenant loves their home with THEIR NEW CARPET and their landlord is the best one around.

Yes, I dragged this out and made it painful. We do not have patience for *s-l-o-w m-o-v-i-n-g* stuff.

This is my point. We are in so much of a hurry and have no patience, we assume we are normal and everyone should be like us. WRONG. ***We, ME and YOU are the 1 percenters.***

We are the weird ones and proud of it. It is what makes us successful.

Use the same methods described here on almost any improvement request by a tenant. Do NOT use it on skilled or licensed trades like furnaces, plumbing, or electrical work.

It works great for requests for such things as painting, landscaping, or installing window air conditioners.

So slow down, be patient, and the next time you receive a request for something, use your creative abilities and TURN IT INTO A TIME-EATING, FUN, AND CHALLENGING PROJECT for your great resident. This reminds me of the Tom Sawyer story of whitewashing the fence and he was getting helpers to PAY HIM for the privilege of using his brush to have fun slopping the whitewash on the fence. Try it; You might surprise yourself and your tenant will THANK YOU.

To really nail it down good, drop them a note about how good a job they did or simply stop by with a positive attitude to see the results of their efforts.... NOT TO INSPECT. Let them bump their gums again and tell them they did great work on the colors and everything. They are decorating THEIR HOME. Help them feel proud and they will take care of it better and stay forever.

BUT, WHAT IF their installer did it wrong?

Don't take this the wrong way, but my answer is, "Who Cares?" Why should you allow yourself to get your panties in a wad because your great resident used a jackleg installer? I do NOT care if their jackleg installer simply rolled it out and stapled it to the floor. If my great resident is happy and thrilled to death with her new carpet... guess what? I am happy for them too.

Remember the big picture. What are you going to do with this "new carpet" when your great resident moves out down the road. Yup, odds are, you will trash it and replace it.

Now you have a great resident who has committed to another three years plus with your company. Awesome!

Do Some Research on Your State's Fair Housing Law

It absolutely blows my mind how most investor groups, clubs, and associations NEVER mention or train their members on Fair Housing.

FAIR HOUSING IS SO IMPORTANT, I have created a FREE Fair Housing Training Video you can watch any time 24/7. If you have anyone else helping you in your real estate, please make them view this Free Fair Housing Training Video because anything they say or do is treated as if you said it or did it. I am dead serious on this. Here is your link to view this short training video: http://AskMikeButler.com/free-training/. (It's only 19 minutes long.)

There are so many updates to Fair Housing since I wrote the first edition. Here is a bullet list of some of these major changes.

1. CALIFORNIA—My wife Beth recently attended a conference in Santa Barbara. A California attorney did a short presentation on Fair Housing and the ADA (Americans with Disabilities Act.)
   a. California has 16 Protected Classes!
      i. Section 8 is a protected class in California. This means you cannot refuse to rent to someone on the Section 8 program!
      ii. There's something going on about Convicted Felons as well.
   b. HUD's Fair Housing Laws list seven Protected Classes

      I have no idea why California has 16 protected classes when the rest of the country has seven or a couple more. Sixteen? Wow! Here is what we can expect. California sets trends that eventually trickle across the rest of America. We can expect some of these extra-protected classes in California could end up in your neck of the woods some day.
2. ADA—American with Disabilities Act Update

ANIMALS

I highly recommend you to remove the word "Pets" from your vocabulary. Replace it with "Animals."

   a. In the near future, online "service animal" certifications will be outlawed. This is good because right now, there are several websites where you can purchase a certificate, ID badge or card, and a vest for your animal for Only $50. It is all BOGUS and counterfeit. Unfortunately, Mom and Pop investors and some property management companies are falling victim to this huge scam.
   b. We recently had a rental application listing their "animal" as a service animal. Several years ago, I created an "Animal Application" for this very issue. My Animal Application must be completed by the applicant if they have an animal. This animal requires a mugshot and a side body photo of each animal. It also requires the name, address, and phone number of their Veterinarian. Plus, they also give us authorization to contact their Veterinarian to verify species or breed, age, and more.

If you are involved in residential housing in the United States, you must make sure you get yourself updated on all of the ADA updates and changes.

Fair Housing Laws and ADA, Both Federal and Local

This is SACRED territory. It goes hand in hand with the American Dream. The Federal Government and local governments across our country bend over backward to protect people and their homes. There are seven protected classes with the Federal Fair Housing laws.

From the HUD website

> *In General, it shall be unlawful for any person or other entity whose business includes engaging in residential real estate–related transactions to discriminate against any person in making available such a transaction, or in the terms or conditions of such a transaction, because of*
>
> 1. *Race*
> 2. *Color*
> 3. *Religion*
> 4. *Sex*
> 5. *Handicap*
> 6. *Familial Status*
> 7. *National Origin*

Many local communities are adding Sexual Orientation to their local fair housing laws. It's YOUR RESPONSIBILITY to know the rules and regulations if you wish to participate in this arena of renting property. I can't tell you how many times as a police officer, I locked somebody up for a criminal offense and they said, "I didn't know that was against the law."

There are a lot of other concerns involved with Fair Housing. Ultimately, it really does mean to be fair to all people. Here are a couple of examples of some things some investors may not immediately associate with Fair Housing.

Steering Trying to persuade tenants to go to a certain neighborhood or preventing them from going to a particular neighborhood.

Available Units Not showing all available units to prospective tenants or disclosing all available units.

Qualifying Standards You should have written qualifying standards for your property.

For more details and complete information straight from the horse's mouth, here's HUD's website for information on fair housing: https://www.hud.gov/program_offices/fair_housing_equal_opp/FHLaws, or go online to: https://www.hud.gov.

A MUST: Make sure this Equal Housing Opportunity is plastered all over your forms. Put in on your Application, Rental Agreement, Move In and Outs, and even the front door and wall of your office, and your website. In my town, this is a very huge concern of enforcement officers.

EQUAL HOUSING OPPORTUNITY

This logo is available for free on my website at www.MikeButler.com and you can get it free from HUD's website too.

ADA—Americans with Disabilities Act

Here is HUD's website for the Housing Concerns involving the Americans with Disabilities Act: https://www.hud.gov/program_offices/fair_housing_equal_opp/disabilities/inhousing or simply visit: www.hud.gov.

Some of the highlights involve "Service Animals," not "pets." Previously, you and I would think of dogs as pets, and if a person has a medical necessity for an animal of some kind, it can be labeled a "service animal" and not a pet. You might put yourself in a legal quagmire if you have a "no pet policy" and refuse to rent to an applicant who has a dog for medical reasons such as a "service animal."

Another highlight involves the applicant's or tenant's request and desire to make the unit "handicap accessible." For example, your tenant in a wheelchair wants to widen the doorways, lower the bathroom and kitchen countertops, and perhaps install a ramp. The ADA pretty much says you must allow your tenant to make these changes at their expense, providing they return your unit to its original condition when they move out. My experience has been great. Most of the time these residents do great improvements. As expected, many install a handicap ramp in front or rear. It's up to you to keep it or have them remove it when they move out.

The reason I bring this up now is that most rental agreements forbid the tenants from altering or making structural changes to the property. Once again, if this is a disabled person, you might be in violation of the ADA if you "stick to your guns" and forbid this request from your disabled tenant. Ignorance of the law is not an excuse.

Resources Needed

I highly recommend you to upload all Federal and Local Fair Housing PDFs into your electronic devices for quick easy reference, especially when you begin to delegate some tasks of getting your vacant rentals filled yesterday.

Resources Needed

Here's how you can make this happen without any paper:

- Gmail
- Google Voice and texts
- ACR cell phone app (All Call Recording)

A MUST: Make sure this Equal Housing Opportunity is plastered all over your forms. Put it on your Application, Rental Agreement, Move-In and -Outs, and even the front door and wall of your office and your website. In my town, this is a very huge concern of enforcement officers.

This logo is available for free on my website at www.MikeButler.com and you can get it free from HUD's website too.

ADA—Americans with Disabilities Act

Here is HUD's website for the Housing Concerns involving the Americans with Disabilities Act: https://www.hud.gov/program_offices/fair_housing_equal_opp/disabilities/inhousing or simply visit www.hud.gov.

Some of the highlights involve "Service Animals," not pets. Previously, you and I would think of dogs as pets, and if a person has a medical necessity for an animal of some kind, it can be labeled a "service animal" and not a pet. You might put yourself in a legal quagmire if you have a "no pet policy" and refuse to rent to an applicant who has a dog for medical reasons such as a "service animal."

Another highlight involves the applicant's or tenant's request and desire to make the unit "handicap accessible." For example, your tenant in a wheelchair wants to widen the doorways, lower the bathroom and kitchen countertops, and perhaps install a ramp. The ADA pretty much says you must allow your tenant to make these changes at their expense, providing they return your unit to its original condition when they move out. My experience has been great. Most of the time these residents do great improvements. As expected, many install a handicap ramp in front or rear. It's up to you to keep it or have them remove it when they move out.

The reason I bring this up now is that most rental agreements forbid the tenants from altering or making structural changes to the property. Once again, if this is a disabled person, you might be in violation of the ADA if you "stick to our guns" and forbid this request from your disabled tenant. Ignorance of the law is not an excuse.

Resources Needed

I highly recommend you to upload all Federal and Local Fair Housing PDFs into your electronic devices for quick easy reference, especially when you begin to delegate some tasks of getting your vacant rentals filled yesterday.

Resources Needed

Here's how you can make this happen without any paper:

- Gmail
- Google Voice and texts
- ACR cell phone app (All Call Recording)

CHAPTER 3

Before You Turn on Your Smartphone

Real Estate Investing Is NOT FIRE, Ready, Aim!

Just like any investment opportunity or business, you MUST do your homework before you pull the trigger or you could end up poorer.

One of my one-on-one mentoring students, who wants to keep his name private, had attended a Saturday morning pep rally in a big hotel ballroom hosted by a guru. He drank their Kool-Aid, hook, line, and sinker and enrolled in $30,000-plus coaching program. He found a big old house, similar to the Herman Munster house that had been chopped up into seven apartments. Before buying this money pit, he ran it by his coaching expert. Together, he and his coach "ran the numbers," and his high-dollar coach told him to do it. His coach said it was a killer deal.

This investor ending up buying this huge monster and it turned his life upside down. Trying to run down tenants to pay rent, repairs, fights, unauthorized occupants, and so much more. In fact, it was eating up so much of his time, he almost decided to throw in the towel and say piss on real estate.

It was at this time when he discovered me. He had purchased my book, liked what he read, and scheduled a one-on-one coaching session with me. Today, he vividly remembers what he was told at our very first meeting. Not only did he waste over $30,000 on this B.S. coaching program, he had also lost tens of thousands on a P.O.S. property. I told him to sell this time-eating and money-eating monster yesterday, even if it meant taking a loss. All in all, this experience was his biggest seminar in the school of hard knocks. Now he does all nice, single-family houses and life is good.

Today he's a multimillionaire, is unemployable, and enjoys a boatload of family time including coaching ball teams and more. In fact, he's taking his family on a two-month vacation traveling all over the United States for an adventure they will never forget. All because he learned how to "Ready, Aim, Fire!" instead of "Fire, Ready, Aim."

Here's your biggest challenge in this department. You must figure out how to find that line that balances Paralysis of Analysis against the Nike slogan "Just Do It."

Just to rattle off some things to learn before pulling the trigger:

- What town(s) to invest (property taxes, landlord friendly, and so forth)?
- What kinds of properties?
- Risks?
- Benefits?
- Take a few super-successful, self-made investors to lunch
    - Knowing what you know today, what would you do if you started now?
    - What are your biggest mistakes and include those you have seen before
- What is your goal for this year?
- What is your three- to five-year goal?
- Taxes and entity structure(s)
- Tax benefits?
- Asset protection and structure
- Rules, laws, and more involved with real estate investing
- Choosing the right system(s), tools, resources for your business

This list could go on and on, but you get the big picture here.

You must remember, there is no overnight "magic pill" for superstar success investing in real estate.

It does require some work on your part. Knowledge gives you POWER to make your efforts more efficient and profitable. There is no such thing as a free lunch.

EVERY single superstar investor that I admire and respect ALWAYS had Education as part of their annual budget for their business. No different from advertising, utilities, insurance, property taxes, and so on, they ALL had an annual budget for education to sharpen their saw every year. This includes newsletters, live training events, memberships, and mastermind groups.

This is how you can grow your real estate business quickly and safely. Learning from high-quality experts who have been there and done that. *(The main reason they are experts is because they have made more mistakes than anyone else...and this includes me, too.)*

Beginner Basics of Autopilot Landlording

You MUST keep the "Big Picture" in perspective. Just like Dr. Steve Covey reminds us and shows how we stay busy doing things "urgent and not important" and things "not urgent and not important," I hope to show you and keep you focused on his Quadrant 2 stuff, the "important but not urgent" things.

If you can keep the "big picture" in perspective, it'll really help you to have the patience along with the motivation to implement your systems to put your Landlording on Autopilot. A huge part of this process is attitude, philosophy, and understanding what YOU, the investor, really want from your real estate investments.

I screwed up many, many times during the first half of my investing career because I didn't have a clue about my ultimate goal. Sure, I realized owning real estate was good, but I operated with that Nike attitude of "Just Do It." So many times, I bought property and did things that did not move me forward toward my ultimate objective. Call it busy work, or a waste of time. Sure, it may have made some money or profit at the time, but some activities really steal our time from pursuing and achieving our investment goals quickly.

These beginner basics are the culmination of the many things I've learned from speakers and investors from all over the country, along with some tweaking of my own.

In short, one of my instructors made the following comment I've never forgotten:

"Are you stepping over dollars to pick up nickels?"

To achieve true financial freedom, you have to shake the blinders off your head. Blinders are those things horses wear on their head to prevent peripheral vision during horse races. Don't worry, you are not alone on this. We all have this big handicap, including me. You might have heard others refer to this same concept as your "comfort zone."

Let me give you an example. My dad taught me how to change the oil in his truck so I could learn "how to save money."

After I purchased my first home, my dad told me about my aunt, who was getting a brand-new dishwasher installed in her kitchen. This aunt asked my dad if Mike would be interested in getting her old, broken dishwasher. My dad gladly volunteered us to go get this broken dishwasher. Next step, my dad and me tore apart this broken dishwasher to see what was broken. After an hour or two, my dad found the broken part. Then we drove up to the HandyMan Appliance parts store and bought some kind of pot metal part for $12.00. We returned to my home, installed the part, and put the broken dishwasher back together. Altogether this took over six hours to do and I saved $12 or, to use my dad's mindset . . . I just got a "new" used dishwasher for $12.

Odds are, you were probably raised this way, too. Most self-made millionaires and multimillionaires were raised this way also. This whole idea of using your hands, your back, and trading your hours for dollars is WRONG!

What you have between your ears, up there in your noggin, is your true wealth creator. Remember this rule. Because you own it, it makes you money. This is a very hard thing for me to shake, even today.

Big Lesson Learned

Let me tell you about the time I paid $19,800 to paint five rooms in a house. True Story. Once upon a time in a town far, far away—Louisville, Kentucky—I bought my fifth rental house. Thinking I was smart and knew how to save money, I decided to paint all five rooms in this house on my off day. . . to save money. How much money? At that time, I could get these five rooms painted for about $180 in labor plus the cost of the paint.

I got up bright and early on my off day to make this happen early. I was in front of the paint store anxiously waiting the store to open at 7 A.M. I got my paint and made a beeline to the house. I pop open the paint bucket(s) and started slinging paint fast and furious using a roller. Everything is getting painted the same color. Walls, ceilings, woodwork, absolutely everything. My goal was to get the inside of this puppy painted in about five hours or less so I could go home and enjoy my off day with my family.

As you recall, I had a full-time job and I was also on the bomb squad for more adventure and fun. In those days, I carried a weird pager that let me know I had messages on my old answering machine. That machine had two audio-cassettes with TV Tuner Dials.

My pager started blowing up while I was painting these five rooms. I was not budging until I got all five rooms painted. PERIOD. No exceptions.

True to my own word, I did get all five rooms painted in less than five hours, locked up the house, and headed home. Once I arrived home, I kissed my wife on the cheek and told her I had to check the messages downstairs in "our office." (Our office was a piece of carpet scooted over in the corner of our unfinished basement, with a used desk, and some milk crates, and shoe boxes.) I turned the dial to rewind the audiocassette tape to begin playing the messages left on my answering machine.

My Dad was on there a time or two and my good friend and fellow investor Jay Long left a very excited message, too. Now Jay was a 23-year-old full-time investor who lived at home with his parents. His Dad paid for his truck and car insurance and his Mom did all of his laundry. *(I was married with two daughters and my wife was in nursing school.)* Jay's message was something like, "Hey Mike, remember the wholesaling boot camp we went to? . . . Well, it looks like it works and I just made $20,000 in about 90 minutes today." I had to call Jay right away because we were both pumped up about real estate investing and we were attending boot camps and seminars all over the country.

Jay proceeded to tell me about a lady who called from his classified ad in the newspaper. He told me she just wanted to unload her house and move to Florida next week to be with her daughter. Jay really did not like and did not want this big old house, but he made her a ridiculous offer and she said, "YES!" Jay's jaw dropped mentally. After gathering his composure, he then contacted a local investor who pays cash for investment property. Jay had this guy meet him at this lady's house and pose as Jay's contractor in order to do a walk-through and inspect the house. This local investor made Jay an "all cash offer" of $20,000 more than Jay's contract with the lady selling her house. It all happened and closed within five days.

I had all kinds of weird feelings for my buddy Jay. Yes, I was jealous, but I would much rather see him get this killer deal than some other lame investor in our town. Congrats to Jay.

Now It Is Time for My Jaw to Drop!

I then played the last message on my answering machine. It was from 8:30 A.M. the same morning. A lady called me because she knew I was buying houses. She stated she was moving to Florida next week to be with her daughter and she wanted to sell her house today. She also told me she would wait for my call until 12 noon and at that time, she would start calling the classified ads that said we buy houses.

OH NO!!!! This was the very same lady who sold her house to Jay! I was madder than a mashed duck. Sure, I probably belted a few choice words and said NEVER, NEVER, NEVER again would I swing a hammer, pick up a paintbrush or do any physical labor on an investment property again.

That paint job ultimately cost me $19,820 to paint five rooms in that house. Remember, I could have hired it out for $180. So dumb on my part.

Needless to say, I have never worked on any investment property since. Please learn from my School of Hard Knocks and I want you to do the same!

PART II—You MUST Identify Your Tools, Resources, and Your Team of Experts BEFORE you pull the trigger launching your real estate investing career. This does not mean you have to go balls to the wall spending a lot of money before you get started. But, you should know all of these things so you can grow your rentals quickly, efficiently, and safely.

Once you have made the big decision that real estate is your ticket to true financial freedom, here's my short list of the basic recommendations. If you have made this decision, it is okay to go buy a house to get your feet wet and see if you like it.

1. Office Operations, Bookkeeping, and Tax Time.
2. Join your local Real Estate Investment Association (REIA) group(s) to network, learn local laws, and find experts and resources.
3. Find Real Estate Investing Expert Attorney who owns investment property like you.
4. Find Real Estate Investing Expert CPA who owns investment property like you.
5. Find a Real Estate Investing Expert Insurance Agent who owns investment property like you.
6. Learn how to find honest, reputable handyman and contractors. Although I have not used them yet, I know many investors use the free service www.HomeAdvisor.com.

7. Make Quality EDUCATION a big priority in your business.
8. Take your time to create a company name you love. It will become your pride and joy. It must be very short and to the point. Also Create an Effective Slogan that clearly explains how your business can help your targeted audience. Example, my company name is VISTA and my slogan: "We Buy Houses! We Rent Homes!"
9. Business Cards must be effective.
10. SMARTPHONE—I personally prefer Androids and use the Samsung Note 8+. Make sure you load your desktop, tablet, laptop and smartphone with all of the great free apps for investors. Check with other investors and see what they are using and recommend. These are always changing. Today, you hold a very powerful database of information inside your phone. One I like is www.RedFin.com; another one is www.Zillow.com.

There are tons more free stuff, but this is kind of the basics to get you started. As you grow your business, you will have more things to implement. If you noticed, I did not recommend LLCs, corporations, partnerships, and so on. Why? Because these are not free. Get your feet wet first.

Resources Needed

To operate your business from your smartphone, here is what you need to make it happen.

- Desktop PC at home and turned on 24/7 with TeamViewer installed on all devices.
- Website: it must be effective and interactive.
- Your other electronic devices (tablet, smart watch, and whatever else).

CHAPTER 4

Never, Never Call Yourself a "Landlord"

This chapter will definitely ruffle some feathers. I'm gonna chop up some very sacred ground in the area of operating rental property. Hang in there, though, until the end to see the BIG PICTURE and where you fit in. It's your choice.

Let's get started with a simple, but very challenging issue.

"Landlord"

Just say the word out loud to yourself. Seriously, just do it. Just say "LANDLORD."

Is this a friendly word?

Is it a good word?

What kinds of feelings or opinions do you associate with this word, "Landlord?"

What do others, the public, think about this word, Landlord?

What does it imply?

My gut feeling tells me this word, "Landlord," is totally negative. The word simply sounds bad. It sounds evil, doesn't it? Remember, Eddie Murphy on *Saturday Night Live* did a skit similar to *Mister Rogers' Neighborhood* with a slogan or catchphrase of "Kill My Landlord! Kill My Landlord!" There's just a huge number of totally negative, bad, and evil connotations associated with this word.

Another misconception that's almost impossible to shake is "Landlords have deep pockets." It doesn't matter a hill of beans whether this "landlord" is an aggressive, honest, entrepreneur trying to do something good and positive in the neighborhood or town. This "Title" can touch some very sensitive, personal, issues. I know; it did with me too.

Stupid Move on My Part

Here's where I screwed up big time. I took pride in identifying myself as the

- "BOSS"
- "Owner"
- Their "Landlord"

The guy with the authority to make the decisions and call the shots. This also happened to come pretty darn easy and convenient because I was sort of already groomed for this as a "cop."

SOLUTION

This answer is amazingly simple. NEVER identify yourself as the Owner, real estate investor, or worse... "Landlord."

The simple answer is to identify yourself as the "**Property Manager**."

Or better yet, identify yourself as a person who works for the Property Manager. This powerful, stuck-in-the-middle position allows you a boatload of flexibility to dodge all kinds of bullets. These two words give you an easy out to avoid making rash "shoot from the hip" decisions that may be emotionally charged or you may regret later.

Don't freak out. In public, you can be the person who works for the "Property Manager" while behind the scenes you really still are the owner.

Here are two powerful examples to save you money and some grief.

THE LATE CHARGE STORY

Your phone rings:

TENANT "Hello <John>, this is Sally at 123 Main St. I know I'm late with this month's rent and I know it was due last Tuesday. My rent is $900 but Bill fell down while walking home from the bar last week and busted his head and hasn't been working since. I've got $900 now, but not enough for the late charge. It's okay <John> if you'll let us pay $900 to get caught up, right?"

Your NEW ANSWER "Wow, I'm sure sorry about Bill and your situation, Sally; however, I just work for the "Property Manager" and I do not have the authority to do what you want. There are rules and policies I've got to follow or I'll get in trouble. Only the "Property Manager," with approval from the owner, can make exceptions to the rules.

If legal in your town, I highly recommend you implement a "Daily Late Charge." In my business, rent is due on or before the first of the month. It is late on the 2nd. Our Late Charge is 10% of their monthly rent. On the third day of the month, our Daily Late Charges kick in. $5.00 per day.

Imagine, if you will, a tenant who has a $1,000 monthly rent due on or before the 1st of the month. They finally pay their rent on the 12th of the month. Here is what happens:

1. $100 Late Charge—Rent NOT received on the 1st
2. $50 in Daily Late Charges—$5.00 per day × 10 days

Your Daily Late Charges are POWERFUL because you can use them to protect your late charges. My resident manager does have some authority to waive some of the daily late charges, but never the 10% late charge.

Because the Property Manager does have some kindness in her heart, she agreed to waive your daily late charges. Most of the time, your great residents are happy with this and continue to gladly pay your 10% late charge.

Note

When you remove yourself from the face-to-face contact and go 100% digital, it makes you look more professional and actually protects you and your business more. No more painful long-winded phone calls.

THE LOCAL INSPECTOR

This scenario is just as valuable, perhaps maybe more. It doesn't matter if it involves a Section 8 tenant or a straight rental unit with a tenant.

Suppose you receive a notice or citation of some kind for a violation involving one of your properties. In dealing with local government agencies, we learned the easiest and simplest way to handle problems is to allow this individual at the government agency to believe they have the authority. Let the inspector believe they are all knowledgeable; they are the wizard; and they have the power. (Sounds pretty good, doesn't it?)

So, you've received your notice and you telephone the inspector or contact person listed on the notice or violation. Tell them you received this notice from them and you would like or appreciate any assistance of help they may be able to give you because you work for the "Property Manager."

(Some of our local inspectors, especially in the Section 8 arena, have "attitudes" toward investors and have made comments like they've made investor "so and so" wealthy because of their inspections. Perhaps they're jealous or envious of investors because they don't have the desire or motivation to get off their butt and become an investor, too.)

When you present yourself as the poor ole' person who just works for the Property Manager and is stuck in the middle between the tenants and those greedy old tightwad owner/investor/landlords, the inspector generally opens up and offers a helping hand, or at minimum, a helping attitude.

Here comes the great part. Having a conversation with you as this person who works for the Property Manager gives you the insulation and space to avoid having to answer or make an on-the-spot decision. You have no authority. Even as a "Property Manager," you give yourself the luxury and benefit of deferring all questions and all situations "TO THE OWNER." The owner can be yourself; it can be your spouse. As a "Property Manager" allows you the golden opportunity to PASS THE BUCK when placed in a tight spot unexpectedly. It also allows you the opportunity to avoid being the Bad Guy by making the Owner the Bad Guy.

YOUR BENEFIT is avoiding making a decision you will regret later. Most of these bad decisions are made from your heart and not your bank account. When you are not the landlord and you have zero authority because you work for the Property Manager, you are in a very sweet spot to say, "I don't have the authority to do that, but I will talk with my Property Manager and will get back to you."

Now you can schedule a meeting for tomorrow morning with yourself, your Property Manager and the Owner—all three at the same time—in your bathroom shower! Now you can chew on it. You can come up with a Plan A, a Plan B, and maybe even a Plan C that will make good, sound, business sense without caving in to the expensive school of hard knocks of letting your heart control your business decisions. If you get stuck, run it by one of your fellow investors.

Many times over the years this strategy of calling myself the person who works for the Property Manager has saved the day and saved me money. When my office manager stumbles into a hairy situation, she knows she can always dodge the bullet at hand by saying she'll have to "check with the owner first and get back to you."

When this occurs, it allows her the opportunity to research any information needed and to consult with me for a plan or plans of action. Sometimes she hits a bull's-eye and has the answer, and sometimes we discover the old saying, "two heads are better than one" and develop a battle plan or solution that is less devastating than a quick knee-jerk answer from a Landlord on the phone.

Education has always been a big part of my investing career. As part of our local investment group and a charter member of our local chapter of the National Association of Residential Property Managers, I've had the opportunity (or curse) to participate in meetings involving representatives and leaders of local government agencies involving housing.

Look how they play the game. NEVER will they commit to any plan of action while sitting at the table during the meeting. ALWAYS, ALWAYS, their knee-jerk answer to everything is to get with the "director," "the boss," or even the mayor to make sure a suggestion or plan can be put into action.

They always get back to us, but they never position themselves as having all the authority needed to make a decision on the spot. We should learn to do the same. As a Property Manager, we can submit a "proposal" to the owner for approval. This permits us, the owner, to chew on it, brainstorm, and run all of the "what-if scenarios" out to the fullest.

Always a "Property Manager," NEVER a "Landlord"

But, but, but...

My Tenants Already Know Me as Their "Landlord"!

Guess what? I had this very same experience. Your Solution is Simple. How do you eat an elephant? One bite at a time. Let's do it here too. Let me point out that you do NOT have to create any new legal entities, LLCs, or corporations to conquer this challenge. Almost every one of us began our real estate investing career in contemplating the name for our real estate business. After a while, you came up with the name for your Pride and Joy.

First, you could send a letter by snail mail, email, and text to all of your residents informing them that the XYZ Property Management Company has taken over and is their new Landlord. Let them know that all rent payments, repair requests, and all other correspondence shall be sent to the XYZ Property Management Company.

Sure, this can be brutal in the beginning, but stick to it and you will win. Your tenants will win, and you will also learn about those tenants who badmouth you when you were their landlord. I would also encourage your residents to go to your website when they need to contact the office. (Now you have set the stage to get a date and time, and in your resident's own words on all correspondence from them.) Also highlight that your XYZ Property Management's website is OPEN 24 hours a day, 365 days a year.

The transition is the hardest part. In fact, I still have many tenants today who knew I was the boss man or the "rent man" as some would say.

KEEP IN MIND, this chapter is NOT how to operate as a Property Manager. This is simply an article on how to present yourself to your residents and to be "perceived by others as a person who works for the Property Manager." We have two ears and one mouth for a reason. Use it to your advantage.

The small exception on this one subject and challenge involves your local landlord-tenant laws. If similar to ours, you cannot dodge the label "landlord" or "tenant." You must use these titles properly in all of your forms, especially when taking legal action, such as an eviction action.

The "Property Manager" title is simply a term to identify yourself and setting the stage to pass the buck and avoid the challenge of making a decision right now because you have the authority to do so. There are just so many benefits for you to calling yourself a "Property Manager" versus a "Landlord."

NIP in the bud any misunderstanding of the word and title "Property Manager."

First of all, this is simply a word, a title, for you to identify yourself to your tenants and others involved in your landlording business. In no way am I encouraging you to market yourself as a Professional Property Manager or anything close to it.

"Property Manager" in general, means someone who manages property for others FOR A FEE. Most states will require Property Managers to be a licensed real estate broker or an agent, at minimum. Don't freak out over this requirement if you're not licensed. Just understand and accept, because you call yourself a "Property Manager" you're probably not in a legal position to manage properties for others for a fee.

There is absolutely no problem with you managing properties you own. You could identify yourself as "landlord, Boss, Rent Man, Rent Lady, Landlady, Hey You, Mr. Smith," or anything you choose, including and preferably "Property Manager." Use the KISS Method, and Keep It Simple Stupid, and don't make it complicated for yourself.

Here's what I'm talking about. With all of the information today encouraging investors to protect your little empire, most of us implement some kind of asset protection program to protect and help with taxes as well. In my case, for example, I have a C corp., which is my "Property Management Company" and my "Dealer." My property management company manages property owned by several of my Limited Liability Companies. All of these are still mine. Therefore, I do not need to be licensed.

If I wanted to manage property for other investors and their entities of ownership, I would have to be a licensed real estate broker in my state to charge a fee for this service.

The point is, it is safe to call yourself a "Property Manager" if you manage properties you own and control.

NEVER call yourself a "Landlord" again. Now you work for the "Property Manager" and you must follow company policies and procedures. You do not have the authority to do squat.

Resources Needed

Here's how to go paperless and all digital:

- Gmail
- Google Voice and texts
- ACR – cell phone app – All Call Recording
- Interactive website with fill-in-the-blank forms

CHAPTER 5

Are Tenants Your "Customers"?

I frequently get to speak and train real estate investors all over the place. When teaching landlording, I always ask for a show of hand on who thinks "Are Tenants Your Customers?" Almost every time, about two thirds of the room raises their hand.

Then I asked them to help me say the famous retail slogan

The Customer Is ALWAYS Right.

Now replace the word "Customer" with the word "Tenant" and say this slogan again.

"The Tenant Is ALWAYS . . ." Uh-Oh?

Now they all have the "deer in the headlights" look. Confusion. Everyone is fast on their feet to say Tenants are NOT always right. So, if they are not your "customers," then what are they, relationship-wise?

May I suggest trying the word "Employees" on for size and see how this word fits:

- Good Employees—have responsibilities
- Good Employees—make you money
- Good Employees—you want to keep forever
- Good Employees—must be rewarded
- Good Employees—must have training
- Bad Employees—get retrained or fired . . . evicted!

Doesn't this look and sound more appropriate? We are only talking about having the right mindset. This has nothing to do with the legal or tax concerns. Just old-fashioned relationships.

Therefore, if you treat your tenants as employees, this means you are their employer or their boss. And yes, the boss has responsibilities as well.

Why the 1960s TV Show *Leave It to Beaver* Is Important

This old TV show is the best example of how to treat your residents in a typical rental property. If you own or operate A+ super-almost-luxury rental properties with top-dollar rents, you can bump this up a notch or two.

If you have never seen this TV show from the 1960s, just go to YouTube and search for *Leave It to Beaver*. You will find a boatload of the 20-minute shows. Watch a few of them and you will grasp what I am sharing with you. The *Andy Griffith Show* and *The Brady Bunch* are good examples as well.

First, think of Wally, Beaver, Eddie Haskell, and Lumpy or Larry as your tenants. Now imagine yourself as Mom and Dad, June and Ward Cleaver.

In these shows, you will see how Wally and the Beaver get involved in things that are not good. They find themselves in a pickle. Sounds like tenants, right?

These situations usually involve a conversation with Mom and Dad, June or Ward Cleaver. It is very important to watch how Ward and June treat Wally, Beaver, and their buddies. They do not raise their voice; they do not cuss; and always offer some guidance to solve and prevent their pickle of the day. Huge lessons learned and just good, old-fashioned family values.

In almost every situation when your tenant is in a pickle, you must let them know this pickle is "Their Problem." After they share their problem with you, then put on your Ward or June Cleaver hat and give your tenant some guidance in how to solve or remedy their pickle of the day, along with your simple version of "pickle prevention."

This also includes any repair request on your rental property. You must let them know "they have a problem" and you are going to help them solve their problem.

For example, they contact your office reporting the kitchen sink will not drain. When you contact them, let them know you have received their message about "their problem" of the sink not draining. Tell them you are going to help solve "their problem."

PLUS, use this same Ward and June Cleaver concept in dealing with every issue your tenant may have. Here are a couple of examples:

- Late Charges happen because of the tenant's behavior.
- Evictions—NEVER Tell your tenant YOU will file an eviction notice. ALWAYS tell your tenant that you, Wally and Beaver, will cause their own eviction because they have not paid their rent.
- With Negative Things, NEVER say, "I'm gonna . . . ." Replace it with "Wally, you are going to cause this or that to happen."

Your Rental Application Becomes a "Job Application!"

Try this attitude. The next time you give a prospective tenant your rental application, change your mindset and try to view this applicant as a prospective employee. Suppose you owned a manufacturing plant and it takes 43 people, trained properly, to operate the "line." For whatever reason, a position is vacant and you need to fill it quickly.

You hand out your job application, review it quickly, call the applicant with the good news and instruct them to meet you. You sign the papers quickly, perhaps on the kitchen counter or worse yet, on the hood of your truck, and point them to their station (your rental unit).

How will this new employee respond? What will they do? They will bring all of their past experiences and knowledge from their previous job(s) (rental units) and might try to do the best they can, giving them benefit of our doubt.

If they fail and perform poorly, whose fault is this? Perhaps they rented from very low-quality landlords; worked in below-average jobs.

While in high school, I got a part-time job as a bag boy at a Winn-Dixie grocery store. One would think this is a simple no-brainer job just sacking groceries. Absolutely not. They treated it like it was a level or two below brain surgery. I had to watch training videos, go through manuals, exercises, and practice, practice, practice in the back, out of view of customers before I graduated to performing the real job at the front of the store. I don't recall exactly, but I'm guessing I had at least a good 6 hours of training BEFORE I was cut loose to bag groceries.

How many hours do you spend with your qualified applicant, reviewing paperwork, responsibilities of both parties, you and the tenant, about your policies, BEFORE you give them the key to your INVESTMENT PROPERTY? You may have invested $50,000 or $100,000 or more in your rental property and because we (I've been guilty of this, too... you're not alone here) meet them in a McDonald's parking lot or at the vacant unit with an attitude of hurry up, sign here, give me the money, and here's your keys.

I can't tell you how many times when I got started I did stupid things like this. Perhaps I was in a hurry to meet Momma and my kids for supper and I thought by doing this real quick on the way home from work, I'd get an extra day's rent. I really don't have any real excuses for operating in this manner other than thinking and believing I didn't have time.

I was dumb and stupid. I'm giving the keys to a tenant who's gonna live in My Investment! We ought to spend at least six hours with them BEFORE they get the keys so we all start off on the same page together. We both should know what to do, and what the consequences are with failing to perform properly. This has made a huge difference in our operation.

This paper signing and procedures BEFORE giving them the keys, is referred to as RENT TALK. There is a chapter on this process later in this book. We allow a minimum of one hour to do the paperwork before a tenant receives keys to their home.

RENT TALK is an 11-minute video for your new and renewing tenants to watch. Think of it as "New Tenant Orientation." You can use it for renewing residents too. In fact, a few years ago, while viewing the Rent Talk New Tenant Orientation, an approved applicant politely told my resident manager this was simply too much for them and they made the decision, on the spot, to back out and not rent our unit. What a blessing! Wouldn't you rather have this happen now than to discover you've rented to a dirtbag after they're already in your property?

Having a mindset of Tenants as Your Employees allows you the opportunity to have Tenant Reward Programs. Tenants can earn discounted and FREE Rent with long-term, consistent performance on their part. This, too, is explained with the All-Star Program.

Don't keep this focus on tenants only. Spread it around. How about your own help? Office staff and maintenance staff should be treated as highly valuable employees. Your furnace person, electrician, plumber, roofer, lawn service provider, painter, carpet installer, carpenter, and so on.

Here is an absolutely powerful and CHEAP way to reward your employees. Most investors I know have had a job or still have a job today. For those of you who are "unemployable," go back with me for a moment to the days of punching a time clock.

What about the Holiday Season?

Your Opportunity to Shine as a Leader!

Think of the holiday season. From Thanksgiving to the end of the year, what happened to those folks (including myself) who have jobs in government or the corporate world? Holiday parties and more holiday parties were offered for the police unit I worked for along with invitations to holiday parties for all of the other police districts. It was almost a competition atmosphere about who could throw the most extravagant holiday party. The bragging rights for the best holiday bash usually went to the police district who had live entertainment, a dance floor, a huge hall, plenty of food, booze, beer, and even limousines! Sounds great, doesn't it?

Switch gears with me here for a moment. While I worked my full-time job as a police officer and observed all of the free holiday events for me and my wife, I happened to hit the pause button and reflect on the holiday happenings of those who are valuable to me in my real estate investments.

Remember my furnace person, electrician, plumber, garage killer, and so on? Most of these folks have mom-and-pop operations. (That's why we use them, because they are usually cheaper than the ones who have the full-page ads in the Yellow Pages.) What are they doing during the holidays and where are they going? Do they get invitations to any holiday bashes? I guess some do if their spouse has a job somewhere.

Here's what I do every year for my vendors, contractors, resident managers, including electricians, heating and air, plumbers, tree service, insurance agent, banker, attorney, window and doors, roofer, lawn service, pest control, concrete, my real estate agents in house, and the Sheriff's Deputies who serve the Set Out Warrants, and all those who are an integral part of my real estate business. For the last several years, I reserve the private lower-level banquet room at a nice, local Mexican restaurant for the Saturday before Christmas. We mail homemade full-page simple invitations to the Annual Vista Holiday Bash from 6 P.M. to 9 P.M. They can bring their spouse or significant other of the month. This banquet room also has a small bar and we include an open bar as part of this annual holiday event. We've never had any issues of anyone abusing the open bar. In fact, my experience is just the opposite. These folks are not used to the extravagant holiday bashes in their honor and are very, very appreciative of this event to benefit them for FREE. In fact, every year, they try to pay the bartender for their drink and are amazed when the bartender waves his hand and says, "No charge."

The restaurant has a buffet style of presenting the food on regular tables in raised foil pans and candles underneath to keep the food hot. Nothing fancy, pick and choose what you want and how much. From tortilla chips and hot cheese dip to beans, chicken, beef, and soft flour tortillas along with several vegetables and sauces. This covers almost everyone's food tastes, including vegetarians, making me "politically correct" again. Good music, fun, food, and drink set the stage for these folks to network and have a good time. I usually take the floor around 7 P.M. or so and introduce each and every vendor by name along with their product or service and a little light-hearted humorous story on each person. This is powerful. It allows each person, especially the guys, to be made proud and a hero. It also makes their spouses grin from ear to ear recognizing their man as an expert in his field. I'm fortunate to have a garage killer who has outrageous stories and he usually grows into the center of attention before the night is all is over.

As an additional bonus, my daughter has a friend who has a passion and is obsessed with Houdini. In fact, this kid changed his name to Aaron Houdini. I hire him for a very small fee and he puts on an outrageous inter-active magic show with everybody.

I also pretty much force my resident (office manager) and my Technical Services Supervisor, Bobby, to take the floor and make some comments. Nothing scripted, just take the floor, wing it, and say some good things. Usually, it's just good, old-fashioned "Thank you for all of your help and patience throughout the year." My intention is to make our resident manager and maintenance supervisor feel like they're "hosting" this event as they pretty much drive the entire operation on a day-to-day basis. As they take the floor and make their "heeby-jeeby" speech with a little stage fright comments, they're very proud and honored, (it shows) and their spouses just grin from ear to ear. You can't measure personal rewards and benefits like this in any bank account.

These folks come from all backgrounds and dress accordingly. My electrician starts talking about this annual event in June of each year and said his wife really looks forward to it, even though she's not much fun (his words, not mine).

Okay, now the bad news. This annual event cost approximately $800 TOTAL. That's right, room, food, booze, and tip for the waiter and bartender. Believe it or not, this is a nice restaurant just two blocks from my office. The rewards and paybacks can't be measured in money.

Your Benefit from the Annual Holiday Bash

Guess where YOU will be on their list of valued customers. I'm willing to bet Vista (my company) is probably at the top of their list. I might not be the biggest, but I'm probably one of their best.

We've had a rash of horrible storms and tornadoes recently and guess where my tree guy put me on the list of next in line? I didn't even have to call him. He called me at 6am asking where to go first! In addition to the great business relationship this kind of event promotes, it makes me feel like a million bucks to see the wonderful feeling of appreciation and value of the skills, trades, and workmanship of these folks. Several vendors told me no one has ever done this for them and their spouses before. This is a great way to let those who make your business successful know that you really appreciate them, their work, and relationship. Not only doing a good job for you, they're a walking, talking billboard for your business—by referring tenants, sellers, loan customers, and so forth.

Work on this one now and start planning for your own event for this holiday season. I'd like to hear how your event works for you. Here is a helpful list of those to consider.

Invite your banker(s), furnace person, electrician, plumber, carpenter, lawn service, resident manager(s), office manager, bookkeeper, CPA, attorney(s), siding and gutter person, tree service, pest control, roofer, insurance agent, highly valued real estate agent, auto mechanic, Section 8 inspector(s), helpful service clerk(s) at local hardware store, paint store, supply house, newspaper for your classified ads, your painter, garage killer, trash and junk hauler, and the person who lets you place your Dumpster in his rear parking lot for free, and those law enforcement folks who help you out throughout the year. Even if they don't attend, the simple goodwill invitation to your party is worth a lot.

This is just a small list to assist you in identifying those who might be important links in your strong real estate chain. So, remember, good employees are a good thing and make your life easier and more profitable.

Your Benefit from the Annual Holiday Bash

Guess where YOU will be on their list of valued customers? [illegible] my company is probably at the top or near the top. [illegible] the biggest, but [illegible] probably one of the best.

We've had a restoration [illegible] recently and [illegible] my [illegible] on the [illegible] and [illegible] in addition to [illegible] kind of event promoter. [illegible] feeling of appreciation and [illegible] of these folks. Several vendors told me no one has ever done this for them and their employees before. This is a great way to let those who make your business successful know that you really appreciate them, their work, and relationship. Not only doing a good job for you, they're walking, talking billboard for your business—by referring tenants, sellers, [illegible] customers, and so forth.

Work on this one now and start planning for your own event for this holiday season. I'd like to hear how your event works for you. Here is a helpful list of those to consider.

Invite your handyman(s), furnace person, electrician, plumber, carpenter, lawn care, [illegible] manager, [illegible] manager, bookkeeper, CPA, attorney(s), siding and gutter person, tree service, pest control, [illegible] insurance agent, [illegible] real estate agent, [illegible] mechanic, Section 8 inspector(s), helpful courthouse clerk(s), and all hardware store, paint store, supply house, newspaper [illegible] your [illegible] and [illegible] the person who lets you [illegible] his lot for parking for [illegible], and those [illegible] who help you [illegible] through the year. Even if they don't attend, the simple gesture of invitation to your party is worthwhile.

This is just a small list to assist you in identifying those who might be important links in your strong real estate chain. [illegible] remember [illegible] create a good thing that make your life easier and more profitable.

SECTION II

BEFORE YOU GIVE KEYS TO YOUR NEW RESIDENT

CHAPTER 6

Never Show a Vacant Unit Again!

Here's how you can allow prospective tenants to view your vacant rental without you being present and how you can get them to fill out an application at the same time.

1. For starters, you must be set up properly.
2. You must have an effective, interactive website with:
   a. Your vacant unit displayed with photos and details on your home page
   b. Online fill-in-the-blank rental application
3. Yard sign
4. Double-locking key lockbox (these have two locks built into them. The first lock secures it in place and it cannot be removed without the access code. The second lock holds the key. It has its own unique access code.)
5. Smartphone

This is the bare minimum to get started. Here is how it works.

A person drives down the street and sees your awesome yard sign in front of your beautiful rental. They are looking for a new home to rent. They stop their car and may get out of the car and walk around your rental home. They like what they see so far and look to your yard sign on how to contact somebody to see your rental.

In the old days, they would call the phone number. The landlord answers the phone, drops everything and treats this appointment like a five-alarm fire. The landlord busts his butt to go as quickly as possible to the rental to meet this prospective interested future tenant. Most of the time, the landlord arrives but the hoped-for tenant is gone. NEVER again use this system.

New Way. Your prospect takes a look at your yard sign to find a way to get more information on your rental. Here are several ways you can make this simple.

The Simplest Way

1. They call the number on your yard sign.
2. You answer the phone (I recommend a dedicated free Google Voice number) and quiz them quickly. You can even give them your basic qualifying standards such as:
   - Is your income three times or more the monthly rent?
   - You must have a favorable rental history.
   - You must have a favorable credit history.
3. If they pass your simple quiz, then ask for their name, cell phone number, and email address.
4. Then have them take two photos and text or email them to you.
   - **PHOTO 1:** have them take a clear, sharp photo of their driver's license or their valid photo ID.
   - **PHOTO 2:** have them take a "selfie" with your rental in the background. This proves to you they are actually in front of your rental.
5. Once you receive the required information, you can give the access code for your hidden key lockbox.
6. Now they can view the interior of your rental without anyone breathing down their neck or watching over their shoulder.
7. If they are interested and want to submit an application, you simply text them the link to your online rental application. You could text them something like:

   Here you go Ralph. Click this link to our online rental application: http://www.YourWebsite.com/application

Straightforward, simple, and it works.

To polish it and make it better, you can make them pay your application fee BEFORE they get your online rental application.

But Mike, What If They Trash My Rental or Steal Stuff?

Please STOP Your Attitude Now! Many investors are doing this all over America. It is simple and it works. Think about it. Do you really think after giving you their name, ID, phone number and email that they are going to trash your unit or steal stuff?

The odds of this happening are slim to none. It's the folks who do not contact you who you should worry about.

But Mike, they have my access code for the key? It's okay. Take a chill pill.

Now let's take a quick peek at the old way. Do you really want to wait for your fire alarm to respond promptly to show your rental when someone calls? Or schedule appointment times for an open house? The new system works.

This is how you can kill two birds with one rock. The first bird shows you how to never show a vacant unit again. The second bird is getting your rental application to them by using your online rental application on your website.

Here are some tips to make it even better:

Because I have a real office, prospects must come to our office and sign out a key. They complete a simple one-page Key Sign-Out form, which includes their contact information, including their current address. Then we make a copy of their driver's license or valid photo ID, and they must put up a $20 key deposit. The deposit is returned to them when they return with the key.

In my rental property system, I use Ernie Riddle's LandlordLocks.com and have a dedicated stainless steel cylinder used exclusively on the front door of vacant homes. They are given this key to see the inside of a home. If they do not return the key, we just made $19 because each key from Ernie only costs about a buck.

Okay, so you may be thinking, if they do not return the key, they have access to your vacant units. You are right. However, please remember they completed the Key Sign-Out and provided us a copy of their valid photo ID. FYI, I have never had any problems using this system. It works.

Next question about my system.

"But Mike, what if my rental is on the other side of town and it would be very inconvenient for them to travel to my office?"

My Answer is AWESOME! Why? Because I do NOT want tire-kickers or wannabes. It's very easy for them to sit in front of your rental, call you on the phone and make you jump right now to let them in to see the inside of your home. Baloney!

This system in my business makes them take a serious step in wanting to view this home. On my website, there is a page titled "F.A.Q." and it lists the answers to all of the Frequently Asked Questions. Here's the answer on "How to See a Home." Here's what they will see on my website:

How Can I See a Vista Rental Home?

You Can See a Vista Home ANYTIME YOU Choose!

Here's How:

1. Visit Our Office
2. SIGN Out a KEY!

That's It. Take your time, check out your potential future home, and with confidence, you can return the key, fill out an application and capture the home you want.

Question: When Can I See the Home?

Answer: Anytime You Want!

Question: How Can I See It?

Answer: This EASY-to-SEE-a-Home program has been designed for YOU! Have You ever checked out other homes and houses for rent while a leasing agent or landlord is standing there or following you through the home. Isn't this just absolutely nerve-wracking on your part?

You're trying to evaluate this house because it will become YOUR HOME! Don't you want to take your time, walk through the house, think about placing your furniture, rooms for your family members, laundry, yard size, neighborhood, and whatever else is a concern for YOU?

You should be concerned about making the right decision for this house to become your home. Vista wants you to make the right decision. Here's the Story:

How Your BIG Benefit Was Created

How to Make an Appointment to See a Home Before Submitting Your Application

Have you ever gone to see a home and found a landlord standing there watching you? Following you room to room, trying to listen to your comments, and "eyeing you up," evaluating you as a possible tenant? Isn't it horrible? Makes you feel like you have to walk through the house quick and get out of there, doesn't it?

Even worse, have you ever been told, "Meet me there at 5 P.M." only to find out that you and three other folks who want the same house are also there at 5 P.M.? Ugly, now you really have to go fast to beat out the others and you really might not like the house but simply got caught up in the excitement to BEAT the other folks.

Vista has a special program **JUST FOR YOU!**

Because you've been there and done that, Vista's "Key Sign Out" program has benefits JUST FOR YOU!

- Allows YOU to take your time.
- Check out your future home at your leisure.
- Imagine where you'll put your furniture, sofa, kitchen table and chairs.
- Check out the yard and the neighborhood.
- This might be YOUR HOME.

- We want YOU to make the right decision for you.
- It's not much fun feeling pressure with somebody breathing down your back or following you around room to room asking if you like it, being put "under the gun" to make a fast and quick decision.

If You Want These Benefits and More . . .

Check out your Home, Vista has 1 Simple Easy Step for You, . . . Simply sign out a key!

Now You got it straight from the horse's mouth to have a better understanding of this true benefit for you.

Give Us a Call Now.

We'll have your key ready for you to sign out.

Got a Quick Question or Short Message?

Simply TEXT: **502-896-2595**

Old School: Submitting the Application Is Your First Critical Step

These first couple of contacts with an applicant is so very critical. You must be on your toes. You must make sure you comply with all of the rules and regulations involved in this business. Not too much concern if you're doing this for yourself, but as you graduate into real, true, autopilot landlording, you will delegate this stuff to someone who represents you and your business. This can be a tad bit overwhelming at times.

I don't care where we get started here. Let's pretend we are at the vacant unit, showing it to a prospect and they acknowledge they wish to fill out an application. You pull out the one-page, two-sided simple, fill-in-the-blank Rental Application, and instruct your Applicant to:

"Please fill out this entire rental application completely and remember we need your signature and date on the backside too."

If an applicant wishes to leave your property with your application, don't worry. This is okay. I used to almost freak out and say, "NO, you can't leave with my application." This is what I was instructed to do by many gurus years ago. Once again. No need to worry. Here's what I've discovered. I will bend over backward to help good tenants. What I'm talking about is perhaps the Larrys' and Daryls' of the world. Just like the old *Bob Newhart Show* and his hotel maintenance crew, Larry and Daryl weren't very bright. They were still good people. You may find this a bit hard to swallow, but there are still many great, wonderful, people in our society today who cannot read or write and would still be EXCELLENT long-term tenants.

Their request to take your application with them to complete it at home just might be their way of concealing their inability to read and write. Knowing this today, I would never refuse to allow an applicant to take a rental application home with them.

Okay, back to the ones who can read and write.

Turning in the Application

You handed them an application form and instructed them in a calm voice to fill out the application completely. If you have an office, make a copy of their valid photo ID, and enlarge it so you can see more of it. If you're doing this at the house or while showing a vacant unit, use your cell phone camera and take a photo of your applicant, their valid photo ID, and both sides of their rental application. Many people are victims of identity theft and you don't want to get a trash bag posing as a responsible person.

When the application is handed back to you, quickly review the top section to make sure you can read their name, date of birth, Social Security number, and the phone numbers to contact them.

Here's the hard part:

Skip Everything Else, Flip It Over, and Make Sure They Signed and Dated It

Before parting ways with the applicant, we've encouraged a new, aggressive approach to prevent us from losing good applicants. In the past, we heard the phrase "Beware of the applicant waving cash. The odds are the cash they're waving under your nose belongs to their current landlord." Many times I've have worked up an application, called the applicant to let them know they're approved and then discover they've already rented another home. OUCH! Back to the beginning.

Now, when an application is turned in, we encourage them to put a **DEPOSIT TO HOLD** on to the unit. It must be close or exceed the dollar amount of the normal security deposit. The language on this form states the applicant puts up X dollars to hold this property pending the approval of their application. Once approved, this money will be used and applied toward the funds needed to start their tenancy. If they're not approved, the money will be returned to them within 30 days.

If they wish to receive their money sooner, we charge an $85.00 processing fee. If the applicant is approved and refuses to rent the unit, they'll forfeit the entire deposit on hold. The objective here is to prevent a good tenant from continuing their search for a rental unit while at the same time providing stiff consequences to the dirtbag trying to get one over on us by wasting our time hoping they can slide through the cracks.

Also, so they're not caught off guard, I inform the applicant of our 24-hour notice to perform when approved. How many good tenants have you lost because an applicant was approved, you made arrangements to do the rental agreement on Friday and your approved applicant becomes a no-show along with the inability to contact them by phone? Puzzled and frustrated, do you give them a couple of days? Do you rent to your next qualified applicant only to have the original approved applicant reappear and challenge your process. You can prevent this headache with a simple 24-hour-to-perform rule. Remember the small print on the backside of the rental application states that once approved, the landlord will use the phone numbers listed on the application to contact the applicant and inform them they're approved. This is the start of the 24-hour rule. Period. If no answer or voice mail, you may keep calling, but I sure would start working on my next application. Shoot straight with the new applicant. Tell them this other person is in front of them and they will have until 3 P.M. that afternoon to perform or your newest applicant can be in the driver's seat.

This next part is where a lot of landlords and professionals make major fatal mistakes. Do NOT worry about seeing blank spaces in the Rental Application.

An Incomplete Application Is WONDERFUL!!!

This Is Good and Very Powerful for You!

Before you start to "process" or work up their application, immediately make a copy of their application of the front page of their application. Even your little home version fax machines have a copy feature and many of the all-in-one printers can also do the same. Stop by your local Office Depot or Staples store and buy two cheap little rubber stamps. One is marked "ORIGINAL" and the other will be marked "COPY."

Stamp the original rental application submitted by your applicant with the "ORIGINAL" stamp. Perhaps stamp it in two places on the top and the bottom.

Stamp the copy of the rental application you just made with the "COPY" stamp and stamp it in several places on the front side. Now you can staple or paper clip the two together, placing the COPY on the top of the ORIGINAL. Do NOT write on the ORIGINAL in any way, shape, or form. Do NOT scribble on the original or fill in any blanks. Do nothing to the original and safeguard it, because it may turn into "evidence" to support your decision later. The stamped COPY version is now your Work Copy used to process this application.

Work through your application process using the work copy. You can write on it and fill in the blanks on the fields of information they failed to fill out. I get more worried about the 100% completely filled-out application versus an incomplete application. You can telephone the applicant and fill in the blanks on your WORK COPY, and not their original. (Remember, an incomplete application is a reason to disqualify.) I've found there are two types of applicants who leave blanks on their applications. The dirtbag professional tenant who's trying to get something over on you, and the plain, good old stupid person who doesn't know any better. I'll go out of my way to help qualify a good old stupid person because they usually end up being great long-term tenants. If you help the dirtbag professional tenant by filling in all the blanks on their original application, you're just making it more difficult for yourself to disqualify them. In fact, you're actually helping them become qualified.

So many Tenant Screening Services complain about this as one of their most challenging problems dealing with landlords and providing their services. Old J. R. Hutto with National Tenant Network (NTN) would give short seminars or classes to landlords and apartment owners telling them how difficult it is for him to pull or run a tenant check with an incomplete application. In fact, he'd instruct them to take a few extra minutes and help them to make sure every blank is completely filled out. J. R. is a great friend and good guy, and he was a little shocked when I told him this was the absolute worst thing a landlord or apartment owner could do. After explaining the process described earlier, he agreed, but I think he's reverted back to his original presentation because it's just easier for him and his staff.

Resources Needed

Tools Needed for "NEVER Showing a Vacant Unit":

- Yard Sign
- Google Voice number
- Cell phone
- Interactive website with your vacant unit photos and details on the home AND your online rental application.

Tools for old-school meeting them face-to-face:

- Clipboard with your rental application form.
- "Open Camera" cell phone app allows you to take low-resolution photos of your applicant(s), their valid photo ID, and a take-away photo of the application they submitted to you.
- "Square" or "PayPal.com" cell phone app—sign up for this app and they will give you a credit card scanner for free. You simply plug it into your earphone jack in your smartphone, click on the Square Icon on your phone, and you are ready to swipe their credit card and collect your application fee for each applicant.

You can also mix and match these things to fit how you want to run your rental business.

CHAPTER 7

A Rental Application Is Your Crystal Ball

When you process your rental applications properly, you will be able to see exactly what your rental unit will look like six months in the future.

For starters, there are two basic methods involving the rental application.

1. FACE to FACE when you are present with the applicant.
2. ONLINE where there is no face to face. (I like this one better.)

There are two separate distinct ways for you to handle these properly to CYA (protect your butt). Both methods have their dos and don'ts and we will get the "how to do each of them" later in this chapter. But first, some basics to know before you pull the trigger. Let's avoid Fire, Ready, Aim!

Your Rental Application Process Is by Far the MOST Important Link in Your Rental Business

YOU are relying on the information submitted on their rental application and the information you gather as the foundation for you to make a HUGE decision on whether to give them the keys to your precious and valuable investment property.

There Is No Free Lunch!

Rental business requires work. It's up to you to choose when—front end or back end. *(The front end makes your life 10 times easier and more profitable.)*

How many times have you heard someone say…

"Been There, Done That. NEVER again will I do rentals. I fix it up, make it nice, they tear it up, move out, and I've got to do it all over again. NEVER!"

And you just get to sit there and take it with no response to destroy their attitude and make you look like a genius. That sucks.

Here is your Brand-New Response to this person who hates rentals… and you get a little touché and a huge grin with it, too.

"I'm sorry you feel that way; but, who gave them the keys to your rental?"

This puts a good helping of "egg on their face" when they are trying to pretend to be an expert while implying you are dumb for pursuing rental properties.

I ABSOLUTELY LOVE THIS RESPONSE! It works! It'll make you feel great too!

Once again, when you learn how to legally process rental applications properly, you can weed out all of the dirtbags and get great quality residents like Mayberry's Aunt Bee, Sheriff Andy Taylor, and his son Opie.

I use a 6-point scoring matrix to process rental applications. Each applicant will receive a score for three areas or zones. The first is Income, second is Rental History, and last is a public records and credit check. Each area is scored from –3, being the worst, to a +3, being the best.

Any applicant scoring 6 or more is approved. A score of 4 or 5 can be considered. And a score of less than 4 does not qualify.

Compensating Factors: Should an applicant fall short of qualifying, we may allow them the opportunity to qualify by using compensating factors. For example, if they fall short on income and everything else is awesome, then we may require

- "LOCAL" qualified co-signer or
- Full year of rent paid in advance or
- Purchase an Option to Buy

With great residents in your rentals, you will NOT get all of the painful and expensive headaches most landlords' experience—all because they refused to invest in their business and get some high-quality training and education from a real-world expert.

When you do your right kind of homework on the front end, before they get keys, you drastically reduce the odds of having painful and expensive nightmares as many other landlords experience.

Just because they flash you a wad of cash to impress you, you must not let that influence your decision-making process. That cash they flashed to you is almost always the rent they did not pay to their current landlord.

To protect yourself, your business, your family, and your rental properties and assets, you MUST have a written policy on what it takes for an applicant to qualify to rent your property. AND you must follow your written policy to a "T."

HUD has "Fair Housing Police" whose job responsibility is find, cite, and charge rental property owners and property management companies for violating HUD's Fair Housing Laws. You must keep in mind these investigators must find violators to maintain their job security. My point is they will come up with very creative ways to trap me and you, along with the poor old mom-and-pop landlords.

Here's an example: An investor called me about getting charged criminally for Fair Housing violation. This investor has owned his 24-unit, two-story apartment building for over 15 years. He is the onsite, one-man show. He shows vacancies, does the apps, collects rent, does all of the repairs and maintenance, and all of his books.

Life was great until last week. Here is what he did to violate Fair Housing. Some lady drove into his parking lot and got out of her car. She was having a hard time using her walker, clanging and banging into stuff. She asked this investor if he had any vacancies. He replied, "Yes I do." She then asked him if she could see them. He said, "Sure." The investor then went to his first-floor vacant unit, opened the door and allowed the lady and her walker to take a look around inside this apartment. That was about it and she left, saying, "Thank you" to the investor.

The next thing you know, he gets a certified letter from HUD's Fair Housing Police. This letter informed him that he has violated HUD's Fair Housing Laws. He was shocked and all flabbergasted. If you get one of these letters, *YOU are Guilty Until Proven Innocent*. These investigators RECORD EVERYTHING and they got you by your $#%@ with their evidence. They use hidden video cameras, audio recording devices, and more.

Here is what he did wrong. The lady with the walker asked if he had any vacancies. He said, "I do." Then she said, "I would like to see THEM." The investor proceeded to show this lady the vacant unit on the first floor. Because of her appearance of having a hard time getting around with her walker, he assumed she would not be interested in any units on the second floor. This is where he screwed up. He did not offer to show her ALL of his vacant units. He only offered to show the unit on the first floor. This is where he did wrong. You must offer to show all of your available units or houses to be in compliance with HUD's and your local Fair Housing Laws. FYI, the investigators had already visited this investor on the same day asking if he had any vacancies and he offered to show them ALL of his vacancies, including the one on the second floor. All of this was recorded as well.

The investor threw up all over me and he kept saying, "This ain't right. This is not fair. I'm getting charged because I was trying to be nice and considerate to this lady and now they charge me with Fair Housing Violation? Ugh..." The end result?... I think he had a ton of legal fees and had to pay a $15,000 fine.

Brush up on knowing Fair Housing Laws inside and out. It is your Rule Book along with your local Fair Housing Laws and your local Landlord/Tenant Laws. You and your staff can have my free Fair Housing Training on my website.

Your Rental Application

Short, simple, to the point information you need. Do NOT try to have the most thorough and largest rental application in your attempt to get into the Guinness Book of World Records.

I like short, sweet, to the point questions on a simple-to-read one-page form. Just to give you a small sampling on some of the garbage on many other applications, many of them ask for the applicant's Bank Name, checking account number, savings account number and the balances in each bank account. You do NOT need this information. All you really want to know is if they have a checking account or savings account. If this is what you want to know, just make it a simple question.

- Do you have a checking account? _____ Yes _____ No
- Do you have a savings account? _____ Yes _____ No

This makes a lot of sense and keeps it simple.

Your rental application MUST be in compliance with all of your Fair Housing laws. Still today, I see many investors using rental applications asking for the name of their "Spouse." Big No-No. Some ask if they are married. Another big no-no.

My wife Beth, before I met her, tried to rent a house in Elizabethtown, Kentucky, with her best friend, Linda. The landlady told them both that she does not rent to two girls. She rents only to a single person or married couples. That's It. This happened in 2007! Wow! It's unbelievable that this is still happening today.

There is one exception to abiding by the Fair Housing Laws. If you own no more than three rental properties, you do not have to follow Fair Housing Laws. In my opinion, I think this exception was probably intended for an investor who owns a four-unit multiplex and lives in one of the apartments. This exception gives them more control on whom they will rent to. Now just because this exception exists, I highly recommend to follow all Fair Housing Laws because you will otherwise be lighting a fuse to a huge time bomb. Odds are, somebody is going to report you to Fair Housing Police. They will do their investigation and probably get charged for the violation. Now you have to get an attorney, legal fees start piling up along with the headaches and frustration.

Just follow ALL of the Fair Housing Laws and you will keep your butt out of hot water.

One more example. I always test my staff with mystery shoppers and it is all recorded. One of my previous leasing agents was a good friend from my days in the police department. She had taken all of the fair housing training and she knew it inside and out. My mystery shopper was a single mom with two girls. She is a police officer in Indianapolis, Indiana, and she is moving to Louisville because she was just hired by Louisville Police Department. Okay, sounds good so far.

Then my mystery shopper asks her this question on the phone: "Thank you so much for all of your help but can you please help me with one other concern."

My leasing agent replied, "Sure, I will give it my best shot. How can I help you?"

Mystery Shopper asks, "You know I am a single mom and I have two beautiful and precious daughters. I am very concerned for our family's safety. Can you please tell me what areas or neighborhoods I should avoid?"

Here Comes the Big Boom

Unbelievable. My leasing agent replied, "Legally, I can NOT tell you what areas or neighborhoods are dangerous and bad. However, as a friend, I can tell you to stay away from XYZ neighborhood, the ABC area, and the STP subdivision."

Me and my mystery shopper recorded this call and I was shocked. My entire real estate business can be jeopardized from this phone call recording. You can guess what I did next. The next morning a little meeting was arranged. I asked my leasing agent if she understood the fair housing laws. She was proud to say she knows them inside and out. I then gently asked her about the Indianapolis police officer transferring to Louisville. She said she remembered the call from the day before. I asked my leasing agent if she told this applicant to stay away from this neighborhood and that neighborhood. She told me, "Heck no, Mike, I would never do that because it violates fair housing laws."

I asked her again. She denied saying it. Then I produced the phone call recording and nothing else was said. On her own, she packed up everything from her desk and left the office. She knew how important fair housing laws are and she knew I had a zero tolerance policy on this. I have not seen her since. Sad.

You must be careful when you have folks helping you and your business. It does not matter if you pay them or they work for free. It does not matter if they are an independent contractor with a signed agreement. Anything and Everything anyone says about your rental properties is legally treated as if it came out of your mouth! Not fair, but true.

Even your handyperson, folks doing your rehabs or tenant turnovers, frequently have folks stopping by to check out your rental and they ask these people about renting or buying your rental property. Please train them properly with constant monthly reminders to not say anything about your property. My folks are trained to say this when someone stops by and asks them a question or two. "I don't have a clue. Just go to the website shown on the yard sign or you can call the office number displayed on the yard sign." This will keep you out of trouble as well.

The Rental Application Form

First, you can use my simple, one-page, double-sided rental application form (see Figures 7.1 and 7.2). It's the very same rental application form used in my business. It works. I have tweaked it a little here and a little there over the years as things change with Fair Housing laws and more.

As a bonus, all of our members get my online rental application already built in, done for you with your free Investor OnCarrot website.

Here is an image of my rental application form, both front and back. In a booming rental market today, we charge $40 application fee per applicant. You should also require an application on every adult who will occupy your rental. The reason for this is because you must know who will be living in your rental. One of the easiest examples to get this point across is convicted sex offenders. In my town, two property management companies were sued for allowing a convicted sex offender in their rentals. Both of these convicted sex offenders attacked and assaulted victims who resided in the same apartments. Both of these property management companies lost in court and had to fork over millions and millions of dollars to the victims. Always get an application on every adult who will be living in your rental. Only the financially responsible rental applicants will pay an application fee, not the adults who will be living with them.

This one-page rental application has literally hundreds of hours in its creation. Even back in 1989, one of my goals was to reduce pages of paper. Back then, many rental applications were several pages with a lot of info you really don't need. My goal was to get my rental application down to one piece of paper, printed on both sides. This allowed me to always have them with me in my used $1.00 American Tourister brand brief case used for all of my real estate business activities in the field. My simple, one-page rental application was also printed on a pastel-colored paper, like a light beige or light blue.

Here are some red flags to look for when some applicants are trying to feed you B.S. on their application.

FIGURE 7.1 Quick review of the Front Page of Your Rental Application

Date: ________ Time: ________ Address Applying for: ______________________ Rent:$ __________ Last Name: ____________________

RENTAL APPLICATION $35.00 Per Applicant (Each Adult MUST Apply)

Company: ____________________ Phone: ________________ Fax ______________ Website: ______________

ONLY CLEAN & RESPONSIBLE PEOPLE WHO PAY RENT ON TIME MAY APPLY with valid Picture ID

First Name: **MI:** **Last Name:** Jr.,Sr

SSN: Date of Birth: Phone: Is this your phone:

Cell Phone: Email:

List Your Addresses for the Previous 5 Years

Current Address: City, State, Zip:

Owner/Manager: Phone: Monthly Rent:

Moved In date: Why are you moving:

Previous Address: City, State, Zip:

Owner/Manager: Phone: Monthly Rent:

Moved In date: Moved out date:

Previous Address: City, State, Zip:

Owner/Manager: Phone: Monthly Rent:

Moved In date: Moved out date:

Employment and Income

Current Employer: Address:

Position: Phone: Hire Date: Hours worked per week:

Gross Wages:$ (__month __week __hour) What other income & source:

2nd Job Employer: Phone: Income$ __week __mon __hr

Are You on Section 8: If Yes, Have You had your briefing: If yes, I have a ____ BEDROOM Voucher

How Long Will You Live Here: __ 1 yr __ 2 yr __ 3 yr + Your Attorney's Name:

Is The Total Move In Amount Available Now: Have You Broken A Lease: Have You Ever Had Bed Bugs:

Are You a Convicted Felon: *(if yes, explain backside)* What kind of animals do you have: Weight:

How Many Evictions Have Been Filed On You: What may interrupt your income or ability to pay rent:

If Accepted The Following People Will Be Living in My Household

1.) Adult [ ]Yes [ ]No 4.) Adult [ ]Yes [ ]No

2.) Adult [ ]Yes [ ]No 5.) Adult [ ]Yes [ ]No

3.) Adult [ ]Yes [ ]No 6.) Adult [ ]Yes [ ]No

Credit References

Lender	Purpose of Loan	Balance	Monthly Payment	Do You Have A Checking Account:
1.)				Do You Have a Savings Account:
2.)				Do You Own Real Estate:

EMERGENCY CONTACTS Including Help To Pay Rent

NAME	ADDRESS	PHONE	RELATIONSHIP
1.)			
2.)			

.LIST All Vehicles & Trailers of your household: ______________________________

HOW DID YOU FIND THIS HOME: (friend, yard sign, etc.) ______________ Your Requested Move-In Date: ______________

Do You Want Rent with Option to Buy or Rent to Own ________ How Much Cash Do You Have: $____________

FIGURE 7.2 Back Page of Your Rental Application

Other Comments or Explanations You feel may be helpful: ______________________________

____
____
____
____
____
____
____
____
____

Check Each If Interested:

[ ] **"Pay Day Plan"** allows you to have your monthly rent payment made every two (2) weeks.
[ ] **"Simple and EASY Auto-Pay Plan"** makes your rent payments more convenient for you.

This agreement made this date by and between ________________, property manager for the Owner, hereinafter "Manager" and the below signed, hereafter "Applicant". The Applicant shall pay to the Manager non-refundable fee upon the execution of this agreement in the amount listed on application to cover the administrative costs, expenses, and time of the manager to verify information submitted by the Applicant. Applicant authorizes the manager, it's employees, agents, or representatives to make any and all inquiries necessary to verify the information provided herein, including but not limited to direct contact with Applicant's employer, landlords, credit, neighbors, police, government agencies and any and all other sources of information which the Manager may deem necessary and appropriate within it's sole discretion. The Applicant represents to the Manager the application has been completed in full and all the information provided for herein is true, accurate and complete to the best of the Applicant's knowledge and further, agrees if any such information is not as represented, or if the application is incomplete the Applicant may, at the Manager's sole discretion, be disqualified. The Applicant provides the information contained on this form. Manager is not liable to the Applicant, his heirs, executors, administrators, or assigns for any damages of any kind, actual or consequential by reason of the verification by the Landlord of the information provided by the Applicant, and Applicant hereby releases the Manager, it's agent(s), employees and representatives from any and all actions, causes of action of any kind or nature that may arise by virtue of the execution or implementation of the agreement provided herein. This property requires a Security Deposit equivalent to one month's rent. This property also requires a $100 administrative fee that must be paid in full before any rental agreement is made. Due to new laws and insurance requirements, all animals must submit an animal application. Animals shall not weigh over 30 lbs and shall not be on the list of CDC dangerous animal species. Animal deposit(s) are in addition to security deposit. Applicant, once approved, must obtain renter's insurance prior to entering into any rental agreement. Manager will contact the Applicant by the contact information listed on this application. After giving Applicant notice of approval using the contact info on application, Applicant has 24 hours from time of approval to fulfill rental agreement by producing all monies required and signing all rental agreement papers. If Applicant fails to perform within 24 hours of Manager's approval, Applicant may be disqualified and Manager may rent this home to the next qualified Applicant.
Our required standards for qualifying to rent a home are simple and fair. They are:

- All homes are offered without regard to race, color, religion, national origin, sex, disability or familial status.
- Each adult occupant must submit an application.
- Your gross monthly income must equal approximately three times or more the monthly rent
- A favorable credit history; however, bad credit will not prevent you from renting a home.
- Be employed and be able to furnish acceptable proof of the required income, or pay rent in advance.
- Good references, housekeeping, and property maintenance from your previous Landlords.
- Limit the number occupants to 2 per bedroom.
- Compensating Factors can include additional requirements such as double deposit, rent paid in advance, option to buy, or approved co-signer(s) for applicants who fall short of above criteria.

Applicant authorizes release of all information to ________________ and duplication of this form.

APPLICANT: ______________________________ **DATE:** ________________

NOTE: One Application Per Adult

EQUAL HOUSING OPPORTUNITY

OFFICE USE ONLY, Do NOT Write Below This Line

Date Received: ____________ **Time:** __________ **Received By:** ____________ **Paid Application Fee:** [ ] Yes [ ] No

Viewed This Home/Apt: [ ] Yes [ ] No **Deposit To Hold:** $_________ **Copy of Photo ID:** [ ] **Source:** ______________

Current Address—Owner/Manager

I frequently find applicants who try to hide the real owner/manager. These folks will enter the name of friend, family member, or co-worker to help them out. Here is how to figure this one out.

1. Go online to your county's website regarding property taxes. This is free in most counties. Search by property address and you will get to see who is paying the tax bill. You may also check any other websites in your town that offer this same information for free.
2. What if the owner of record is an LLC? Simple. Just go to your state's Secretary of State website and do a business records search. This will show you a lot of information, including the registered agent and more. In my state, I can view their articles of organization along with who the members are involving this LLC, partnership, corporation, and so forth.
3. Does any of this information match the name entered in the owner/manager field on their rental application? If not, here's what to do next. Review the entire application submitted and see if the owner/manager name and phone number has been entered anywhere else on their application. You won't believe this, but the most frequent is to see the same name and phone entered in the Emergency Contact field. Many times they will also enter the relationship to your application. I know you are thinking this is crazy, but this really happens a lot more than you could ever imagine. For example: They submitted Steve Gunn as the owner/manager and listed in the Emergency Contact field, you will see Steve Gunn, his phone number, and his relationship... good friend, uncle, brother, ex-husband, and so forth. I am not kidding here. So now you are thinking, who in their right mind would do something like this? Remember me telling you I have hundreds of hours in developing my rental application form? This is one of the huge benefits for me and you. There's a ton of psychology from my police detective days along with real-world experience in not only what questions to ask, but in what order, and in the specific words to ask these questions. You will a big, black, horizontal bar several times on the front page of the application. I call these "brain breaks" and they work! These big black lines with white text in them causes the applicant's brains to switch gears so to speak. These black bars have titles, which triggers their brain to forget what they just wrote down and now they are entering a brand-new zone of information regarding the title of this zone. I do not know why, but it works and it is a great tool for your real estate business.

When You Suspect a Phantom Owner or Manager

Have you received applications where you suspect their current landlord is a relative or friend trying to help them rent your place? If your gut feels this, here's a good method to expose the dirtbag.

1. Make sure you have your smartphone app ACR (All Call Recording) turned on.
2. Set it up properly on your cell phone because when you finish this phone call, you will save it and upload it to the folder for this applicant.
3. Make a phone call to this suspicious character your applicant is trying to say is the owner/manager. Do NOT ask them if they are the owner/manager/landlord for your applicant's name. This is exactly what they are prepared for in order to help out the applicant.
4. First, ask for the First Name only for the suspect Owner/Manager. For example, if Steve Gunn is listed as owner/manager, call the number and ask for Steve Only after they identify themselves as Steve, then ask "Steve, I am calling about the house you have for rent…" *(you will know the house or apartment from the current address listed on the application).* Steve will almost always respond, "I don't have any house for rent." I reply "Gotcha' and thank you, Steve" and hang up. Always save this phone call recording for your evidence trail. You and I both know in owning rental properties, we always try to fill our upcoming vacancies BEFORE your tenant moves out. But let me answer your Debbie Downer and Negative Nancy comment or question. You might be thinking, "But Mike… what if the owner or manager does not know his tenants are looking to move?" You are absolutely right, but here's the bottom line. It may be true his tenant(s) are planning to move out and they have not given notice to their owner/manager/landlord. This does happen in our world. But the big thing here is to remember, YOU are processing this rental application. So, ask yourself, do you really want a tenant like this applicant. One that B.S.'s you on their application, and one who does not let their landlord know they are moving? Now you've got it!

   They were expecting a brain-dead simple call with a question like

   "Hey, I am calling for APPLICANT NAME because they filled out an application to rent one of our properties."

Come on here, you are sharper than this. Put on your Columbo Hat. Be creative, but legal, and think about how you can get this suspected phantom landlord to fall into your trap.

Employment Zone

Repeat same as before. See if their boss's name and number appears anywhere else on their application. If a knucklehead reports they are self-employed and cannot produce original pay check stubs to verify their reported income, ALWAYS get a minimum of the two most recent bank statements for their checking account. This should show their income as deposits to support their reported income. If they do not have a checking account, they obviously can't produce anything to verify their income. When this happens, if everything is looking good so far, you could request this applicant to pay a full year of rent up front or you may consider a LOCAL qualified co-signer. NEVER allow an out-of-town co-signer because should things get ugly, it will cost you a lot more to pursue collections on a person not in your town.

APPLICANT who does not live in your town: Great Question, Mike! This does happen and a lot more frequently than decades ago. Here's what to do:

1. Let's Go Googlin', as George W. would say. Enter their current address in the Google Search field, including city, state, and zip code.
2. If a valid address, you will see the search results. Click on the MAPS tab and you will see everything about this address. If the Google Van has driven down this street, you will see a picture of the front of the house on the left side along with a detailed map on the right side. Using your computer, you can even drive down the street. Depending on the date of the Google photos, many times you will see the same vehicles sitting in the driveway as the vehicles listed on their application and you can get a good "feel" on how they will maintain the lawn or yard of your rental. This is great for out-of-town applicants because you can see if the neighborhood they live in today is similar to the neighborhood of your rental.

Here's an example of when the neighborhoods do not match. Here's your rental.

Here's where they live now.

Or what if they live here?

Why You Can Apply This Very Simple System to Everything You Do in Your Rental Business

"How many times have you had bedbugs?"

This question speaks for itself.

Section 8

Note

I no longer participate in the Section 8 program. They are very difficult to deal with in my town and cause you a ton of grief; no rent payments for the first two months and constant headaches and frustration. I had participated in my local Section 8 program since 1991 but as of three months ago, I will not accept any folks on the Section 8 Program.

Warning

If you have rentals in California, Section 8 is a protected class. Check your local fair housing laws.

If you don't participate in HUD's Section 8 program, you can remove this line from your application and skip over this section entirely. When I got started, it was a necessary evil. Section 8 in many markets pay top-dollar rents in low-income neighborhoods. The federally subsidized housing program is well-intended and is actually a good program helping many families in America today. I have many families on the Section 8 program who are as good or better than many of our straight rent tenants. The problem is not with the families. Section 8 has a bad name because it is operated by a government agency, allowing us, the taxpayer to see our taxes at waste.

Many landlords are frustrated and fed up with how the program is operated by local agencies along with allowing any family, including the worst of the worst dirtbags and tax-eaters to participate and benefit from the program. I had a pretty shocking experience a couple of years ago in my town. Our local Director of Housing, who is also ultimately in charge of our local Section 8 program agreed to meet a small committee of leaders from our local investor group. I was president at the time. Perhaps a dozen or so of us attended this meeting. These were not necessarily mom-and-pop operators. Our representatives included the past president of our Board of Realtors, and both large, medium, and small-size Property Managers.

Many in our group had been told by Section 8 leaders that if a family screws up, they'll get booted out of the Section 8 program. Our folks discovered some of these families who screwed and got booted out were actually back in the program. To our amazement, the Director pretty much told us they go to the back of the line and are given a new tenant number and are allowed to open a new file with Section 8. His justification for this was simply, "Where else can these folks go for housing?" He pretty much acknowledged the Section 8 program will take everybody. Dopers, criminals, drug dealers, tax-eaters, and all of the lowlifes' in our society.

This is not fair. Many good, wonderful families who need and have earned having some help are lumped into this group of bad families.

So, what can a Property Manager do? Before jumping into the Section 8 program in your town, contact other landlords and get their feedback. How do you find them? Go to your Section 8 office and ask for a list of available properties. They'll give you the list along with the phone numbers on whom to contact. Many Section 8 offices have available properties listed on a website, allowing you to let your fingers do the walking.

By contacting other landlords in your town, you discover the pitfalls, the pain-in-the-butt factor, and problems with the operation and your participation in the program. Here is one good rule of thumb I've discovered. The smaller the town, the better the program. If you live in a huge city, you'll probably find many complaints and horror stories. If you live in a small town, you'll probably find they run a pretty good ship with a helpful attitude toward landlords and tenants.

The line on my application about the Section 8 program is designed to "Cut Through the Bull NOW." Applicants come from all walks in life. Some are sharp and some are not the sharpest tool in the drawer, to put it nicely. Years ago, many times we've worked up rental applications involving a Section 8 family only to learn they were merely on the list waiting to be contacted to actually begin the program. Our waiting list at the time was over a year.

This is not the families' fault. The Section 8 representative gave the family some packet of information explaining how the program worked and tell them they can shop for a home of their choice. This is what they did. So we learned the hard way. Today, as you can tell on the application, we ask:

Are You on Section 8?

If Yes, Have You Had Your Briefing? The briefing is the meeting where a Section 8 representative gives misleading information to new participants on the details and the process of the program. They leave this meeting with a very large envelope and packet of information.

If Yes, I Have A ____ Bedroom Voucher Once again, because of the misleading information given to participants during their briefing, most families leave their briefing and begin their search for a home. At this time, the Section 8 Program is a Voucher Program based on the NUMBER OF BEDROOMS. There are changes in HUD coming down the pike where the Voucher Program will be terminated and local agencies are going to have the authority to manage the program as they feel best for families and their community.

ADDITIONAL PROVISIONS I created an ADDITIONAL PROVISIONS addendum to include and become part of every Section 8 Rental Agreement. I took it a step further, and had a HUD certified Section 8 Representative approve my additional provisions form acknowledging the date and time of his approval and put their name, title, and the date they approved your additional provisions.

HOW LONG WILL YOU LIVE HERE? __1 year __ 2 years __ 3 years + I'm not in the hotel business. I want all of our tenants to stay forever! It just makes everything so much easier. There is a big subliminal message being communicated to the applicant with this question. What do you think most check? For single-family houses, almost all will check the three-years-plus box. Why? Because they believe it will make them look more favorable over an applicant who checks the one- or two-year box.

"Your Attorney's Name?" Kind of speaks for itself. What if you see one of those ambulance-chasing attorneys who advertise on the Jerry Springer show? 'Nuff said.

Is the Total Move-In Amount Available Now? Many times, they will say no or they expect to have enough money the following Tuesday.

How Many Times Have You Broken a Lease? This is a pretty generic question. Nothing fancy, but it does force them to think about being responsible. It's also another opportunity to capture another piece of ammo for your team in the qualifying process. The majority of applicants will answer this question NO hoping to convince you they're responsible. If you discover they have broken a lease in the past, this could be deemed false information on their application.

Are You a Convicted Felon? Do NOT Ask "Have You Ever Been Arrested?"

Today, this is a very hot potato. There can a huge amount of liability for Property Managers if not handled properly. For example, here's a real story from my hometown. A large, nice apartment community on the taxpayer side of town had a resident tenant who was a victim of a burglary, rape, and robbery. The onsite managers were made aware of this crime and the perpetrator accessed the victim's apartment through the sliding glass doors on the first-floor patio.

- Unfortunately, a short time later, I don't recall if it was days, weeks, or even months, but the bad guy struck again. Almost the exact same behavior repeated again.

- The second victim, along with the entire apartment community was never notified of the first criminal offense that took place. The second victim, upon discovery of an earlier recent criminal offense with no warning from the management, initiated and pursued a civil lawsuit against the apartment community management and owners and whoever else could be tagged.
- The result was a huge multimillion-dollar judgment against the apartment community and others awarded to the victim. This sent shock waves not only locally, but throughout Apartment Associations on a national level.
- Don't freak out and make this real complicated for yourself. Remember, my very first tenant was a convicted felon and he is still with me today. If they answer this question YES, I've found the majority of the good folks who've screwed up in their past, have a huge desire to explain their past. The applicant who writes YES with no explanation needs further research.
- If they check YES, you have several resources at your fingertips. Once again, the Internet allows you to let your fingers do the walking from your home or office. Get online and check out your local Sex Offender Website. I recommend you should do this on all applicants anyway, especially if you have multiple units.
- Depending on their conviction, the offense, when it occurred, their performance since then, can all play a factor in working through their application later. A convicted felon is not a good thing, but in my state, a third conviction of DUI is a felony.

How Many Evictions Have Been Filed on You? *THIS ONE IS HUGE!!!* I Repeat, This One Is HUGE because your applicant has trouble reading the question properly. For some reason, I assume because every other rental application on the planet asks:
"Have You Ever Been Evicted?" This seems very routine and comfortable to them. They answer the question

> *"How many evictions have been filed on you?" (as if the question were, "Have you ever been evicted?").*

Even while working up the application process and when the applicant is confronted about the false information they submitted on their application involving the discovery of three filings of starting the eviction process from a former landlord, the Applicant who answered this question ZERO or None will almost always respond, "But I've never been evicted!"

Fortunately, that's not the question. Read the question again if you need to. Again, this question puts another bullet in your gun, gives you some more ammunition to protect you. This entire application and process is designed to help me, designed to help you, the investor.

"What Kind of Animals Do You Have?" Do NOT ask, "Do you have pets?" This phrase almost automatically implies the landlord does not accept animals and your applicant will almost always answer this question with a "No." The first question implies it is okay to have animals. From the tenant's perspective the question "What kind of animals do you have?" implies a pet-friendly landlord versus "Do You Have Pets?" implies and sends a message to your applicant that you probably have a No Pets Allowed policy. Many folks unfortunately treat animals better than many treat their kids. It's also another opportunity to bump up your cash flow by increasing their rent perhaps $25.00 per month per animal in addition to an animal deposit.

If they have animals, the applicant MUST complete our Animal Application Form.

What May Interrupt Your Income or Ability to Pay Rent? Don't laugh at this one. I've had applicants write, "I'm losing my job in two months." Some write remarks such as, "If I get sick, die, or in a bad car wreck." I've also discovered scheduled serious income zapping surgeries. Other things listed have been, "I'm getting divorced after we move."

"If Approved, The Following People Will Be Living with Me" Household composition is the next section. You cannot use the word "family" or "children." Think of those words as lighting fuses to cause you trouble. If you're doing it, STOP IT NOW. Substitute the phrase "How many people are in your household?" If they answer and respond about children and spouses, you're in good shape because they volunteered the information. You did not ask it. Yes, it does seem like a play on words; however, the fair housing mystery shoppers (investigators) looking for landlords who violate the federal laws will call and record your phone conversations. Be aware.

Notice on the application in this section, there are simply 6 numbers with a line or space for the applicant to write down names. Many times, without asking, because of everybody else's rental applications, the applicant will write

1. Shelly Smith, girlfriend
2. Tommy, 6-year-old, son
3. Sally Jones, 12, daughter

If your applicant completes your application in this manner, you're okay. Just do not instruct them to tell you anything about the relationship of those who will be living with them. This would or could violate the Familial Status of Fair Housing. It's the application process that's so sensitive and critical with fair housing. Once qualified and approved, you can require names, ages, date of birth, and relationship of all those who will be occupying your unit. The important thing is to remember how critical the application procedure is involving fair housing.

Credit References

This one is simple. It's used to simply help us identify other monthly payments the applicant is responsible for. Most of the time, we'll see car payments, and credit card payments, and student loans. I'm not the least bit interested in taking up space on my rental application for lenders' addresses and account numbers. Phooey on all of that. You can still get a lot of insight into your applicant by what they write in the blank. Suppose you see car payment and student loan? Not too bad, but you sure would consider and factor in the dollar amount of their monthly payment(s) against their income and your rent.

Suppose you see an Alrenco payment for TV and a Pawn Shop payment? Hmm? Totally different, isn't it?

Do You Have a Checking Account? Just a simple yes or no question is all I need. Many applicants do NOT have a checking account or savings account.

Do You Have a Savings Account? Moving on down the list. More applicants have checking accounts than savings accounts. If an applicant has BOTH a checking account and a savings account, you may have a pretty good responsible application in your hand. If you notice, I don't ask for bank names or bank account numbers. It's simply a waste of time and takes up valuable space on my one-page Rental Application.

Do You Own Real Estate? Once again, another lead generator for the investor/landlord still looking and searching for deals. I have stumbled and tripped over many good deals here on this one question. Just a thought, perhaps you might like to trade some rent for a property?

Emergency Contacts

This section includes the phrase "**including nonpayment of rent.**" Nonpayment of Rent is an emergency to me and I'm letting them know my definition of an emergency. I also include this phrase right above the emergency contact information section in our rental agreement. This is powerful and allows you to contact these folks if they get behind on their rent. Yes, your tenant might throw a fit the first time you contact them, but you remind them they instructed you to do so on both their application and rental agreement. Usually, the Emergency Contact for applicants is someone they respect, admire, and hold in high regard. Many times, it's a parent, a favorite uncle or aunt, a reverend, or some other relative.

When they do screw up and drag their feet on paying their rent, I send a copy of their late notice (Seven-Day Pay or Quit Possession Notice in my town) to their Emergency Contact(s). Most of the time, Mom or Dad coming after them with a skillet is 10 times more powerful than an attorney, a court paper, or a Sheriff's Deputy.

After perhaps some embarrassment, I've found this to be a powerful tenant-training tool. They will make sure rent is paid on time to prevent their emergency contacts from being notified. I recall one tenant in particular where the mother would go off and attack and slap her son over his irresponsible actions. We need more moms like her. Don't think you have to do this all the time. Just the first few is usually enough to get them trained.

LIST Vehicles and Trailers Your Household Will Possess Many towns have local laws, ordinances, and/or regulations regarding the number of vehicles allowed on a property. Many have strict laws regarding vehicles that don't operate and where and how they can be stored.

How Did You Find This Home? (Friend, yard sign, and so on) This is self-explanatory and helps me to track my advertising and marketing along with referrals and referral fees earned from those advertising and pitching homes for us. I also use the word HOME for apartments. Remember our slogan is WE BUY HOUSES! We Rent Homes! *Homes* have an emotional, warm, fuzzy feeling, or at least that's what I've been convinced.

Your Requested Move-In Date Don't get fooled here. Responsible applicants might write in a date three, four, or five months down the road. Irresponsible tenants will write NOW or Yesterday.

Do You Want "Rent With Option to Buy" or "Rent To Own?" What's wrong with asking this on an application? It sure is a great opportunity to encourage and promote the "long-term relationship" with your tenants. Offering an avenue to homeownership is pretty appealing to many tenants. Some prefer to remain tenants and NEVER own their home.

How Much Cash Do You Have? Very seldom does an applicant get their feathers ruffled about this question. Most answer the question, I believe, pretty honestly. I've seen this question answered with "None Now" to $25,000. It can sometimes get you pumped up a little if a large number appears here.

Other Comments or Suggestions This small section allows the applicant to explain anything they want, to vent, to blast their current or previous slumlords, or to write anything they choose. Interesting stories have been scribbled in these few short lines. One in particular, I recall, detailed the ongoing lawsuit the applicant had with her current landlord over mold and mildew under her kitchen sink.

Back Side of Rental Application

Here are some excerpts from the Fine Print on the Back Side:

> *"The Applicant represents to the Landlord that the application has been completed in full and all the information provided for herein is true, accurate, and complete to the best of the Applicant's knowledge, and further agrees that if any such information is not as represented, or if the application is incomplete, the Applicant may, at the Landlord's sole discretion, be disqualified."*

This is excellent for you by saying false information or just an INCOMPLETE APPLICATION is enough reason for the Landlord to disqualify the application.

"The Applicant provides the information contained on this form."

This means the person signing this form, the Applicant, is the same person who completed the application. This removes any opportunity for someone to say, "But my brother filled it out for me."

"This property requires a Security Deposit equivalent to one month's rent plus $100.00 and must be paid in full before any rental agreement is made."

Simply put, now you can use this one rental application form for ALL of your rental units both Single Family and Multi-Family. By keeping your Security Deposit MORE than a month's rent, it gives you the opportunity to hold a carrot in front of them saying, "You've got to play by my rules to get this back when you move out."

"Animal FEE(s) (deposits) are in addition to security deposit."

"Applicant, once approved, must obtain renter's insurance."

This speaks for itself, but Renter's Insurance is your first line of defense in your asset protection program. Suppose your resident has a grease fire while cooking bacon naked on a Sunday morning. Without Renter's Insurance, your insurance will have a claim and repair your property. With Renter's Insurance, your Tenant's Renter's Insurance will have the claim, leaving your insurance as clean and slick as a whistle.

"and Landlord will attempt to contact the Applicant by the phone numbers listed on this application."

This doesn't say MUST contact. It says, once approved, the landlord will ATTEMPT to call the Applicant using the phone numbers the applicant provided on the application.

"Applicant has 24 hours from time of approval to fulfill rental agreement *by producing all monies required and signing all rental agreement papers. If Applicant fails to perform within 24 hours of Landlord's approval, Applicant may be disqualified and Landlord may rent this home to the next qualified Applicant."*

This is HUGE. I can't tell you how many times an applicant was approved and pulled a "No Show Jones" on me. This caused the 24-hour rule to solve this problem.

Also require your newly approved applicant to immediately pay a deposit to hold fee equivalent to at least one month's rent. This will be forfeited if they pull a No-Show.

Required Standards for Qualifying to Rent a Home

Our required standards for qualifying to rent a home are simple and fair. They are:

- All homes are offered without regard to race, color, religion, national origin, sex, disability, familial status or sexual orientation.

  This is the Fair Housing thing.

- Each adult occupant must submit an application.

  When it comes to adults, don't give your applicant an opportunity to house a criminal or dirtbag, or a threat to the community into one of your properties.

- Your gross monthly income must equal approximately three times or more the monthly rent.

  This is a starting guideline. In the old days, I was raised where your rent or house payment should never exceed ¼ of your monthly income, or one week's income.

- A favorable credit history.

  Don't hold your breath on this one. Odds are, your Applicant wouldn't be here if they had good credit because they could buy a home. There is such a thing as "good bad credit" and "BAD, bad credit." We also tell folks, "Bad Credit will NOT prevent you from renting a home."

  Example of GOOD Bad Credit All kinds of medical tragedies and collections associated with the medical tragedy. This is an example of "GOOD bad credit."

  Example of BAD Bad Credit In reviewing their credit report, you see collections on local utilities, judgments and garnishments from previous landlord(s), and evictions.

  See the difference?

- "Be employed and be able to furnish acceptable proof of the required income."

  This is pretty simple . . .

- Good references, housekeeping, and property maintenance from your previous Landlords.

This is your silent sleeper. Your knuckleball. Your curveball. Your home run with bases loaded. It allows to use your "stealth strategy" to do a housekeeping check on their current residence. DO NOT Blare this phrase out loud everywhere. As you can see, it is contained in the fine print on the back side of the application.

- "Compensating Factors can include additional requirements such as a local qualified co-signer, rent paid in advance, or purchasing an Option to Buy for applicants who fall short of preceding criteria."

  This is the landlord's weasel clause allowing us the opportunity to make exception to the qualifying standards set forth in our application.

- "The Applicant authorizes release of all information to Vista Properties, Inc."

APPLICANT: ____________________ DATE: ______________

The applicant signs the application and this back page becomes your AUTHORIZATION TO RELEASE INFORMATION signed by your applicant. If your applicant has scribbled some sensitive information in the comment section, simply cover it up before faxing this page to an employer and previous landlords. Note HUD's EQUAL HOUSING OPPORTUNITY LOGO is everywhere.

Housekeeping Check

Your Final Step BEFORE Approval

Today you have two methods of doing this.

1. The old-fashioned way of showing up unannounced at your applicant's current residence.
2. Now you can do it online. Social Media can be used in many ways. As long as what you are looking for is available for the public to view, you should be okay using it as another resource to gather information when processing an application. You can use this for both local and out-of-town applicants. I am a little familiar with Facebook and it is unbelievable what some people put on their Facebook page. There are many other social media things that probably do the same thing. I am just not there yet.

A housekeeping check is your best screening tool. This is your last and final step before approving an applicant. This is done with no phone call, with no notice to your applicant. If you are going to do this in person, you must do this step unannounced. If you tell them about this in advance, it defeats the entire procedure and you would be wasting your time.

This Is Your Crystal Ball

It shows you exactly what your rental will look like in six months or so.

After working up their application on your work copy paper and on the phone—get out of the office! Your final step before approving them is to ride by and see where they live now. If it's ugly, tall grass, cars in the yard, no need to stop. If it looks okay from the street, then stop and knock on the door. You need to verify they actually live in this pretty home. Here's how it goes:

If the outside looks acceptable, stop by and knock on the door and ask for your applicant by name BEFORE you identify yourself. Many times, the person who answers the door says, "They don't live here. They live over..."

Step 1: Ask for the Applicant's Name—Is Deborah home? Only after they say, "Yes, I am Deborah," do you identify yourself and say:

"My Property Management Company sent me here to do two things:

1. To verify you really live here.
2. To see how you take care of the place."

I used to do this housekeeping check myself. "However, I've discovered how to pass this task off to my maintenance supervisor. He now does the housekeeping checks. Here are his guidelines. After stepping into Applicant Deborah's living room, ask yourself:

Q1. "If Sally fixed me a bologna sandwich, would you eat it?"

If Answer: NO, not approved.

If Answer: YES, go to Question 2

Q2. "Do you want to clean up behind Deborah when she moves?"

If Answer: NO, not approved.

If Answer: Yes, approved.

Let's say my maintenance supervisor discovers a horrible pigpen, animal-infested, urine-smelling house, and he answers his questions NO. Make sure you get good exterior photos of their residence if these photos support their horrible housekeeping.

My experience has been these folks simply never call anymore because they got the message. But if they do call and inquire about their application, this is the ONE Exception where I will GLADLY disqualify an applicant for being a dirty, filthy pig!

There have been some occasions when an applicant just didn't get it. They didn't have a clue they were simply pigs. On a couple of these, I did have the gazoongas to tell them on the phone they were just too dirty, and they were pigs. I even had one of these applicants try to file a complaint telling the Fair Housing complaint taker she was disqualified for being too dirty. I got a chuckle because he was not allowed to file her complaint because "dirty people" are NOT a protected class and we had this properly noted on our application.

Remember the top of the rental application reads

"ONLY ***CLEAN*** AND RESPONSIBLE PEOPLE WHO PAY RENT ON TIME MAY APPLY, with a valid Photo ID."

Dirty people are NOT a Protected Class . . . *yet*.

CHAPTER 8

Never Disqualifying an Applicant Keeps You Safe

If you NEVER disqualify an applicant, it sure is harder to get a complaint. Nobody, even "dirtbags" like rejection. Those folks who are thorough and document everything and cross their t's and dot their i's can still get slammed on discrimination complaints. Please understand, even if they've done nothing wrong, other than disqualify an applicant, the disgruntled applicant can cause havoc to the landlord with a formal discrimination complaint. It doesn't matter if it is valid or unfounded, it will still be treated with a full-blown, expensive, time-consuming, and very intense investigation. The investigation is conducted by some government agency and unfortunately, it seems they have an attitude of "You're Guilty until Proven Innocent."

Don't get me wrong. I was a government employee, too, and as a cop, I witnessed many tax-eaters use the System to their benefit as well in the criminal court system.

Another good, solid, SAFE procedure to implement is how you process your applications. Do NOT get caught in the trap of reviewing all of the available applications in front of you and choosing the best one. This system could be considered illegal, because if you have more than three rental units, you must rent your unit to the first qualified applicant.

So, what is a qualified applicant? Now, we're right back to the basic challenge of having a "system" or a policy or a procedure. It's safer to have it in writing too, like right on the backside of our rental application.

You MUST you have a simple, fair, legal, and written policy on how you process applications. The no-brainer procedure is good, old-fashioned, first in, first processed. How do you protect yourself or CYA for this procedure? You must document the DATE AND TIME their application is submitted. At the bottom of the backside of our rental application is a block for you to write in the date and time this application was submitted.

Now, if you're at an open house showing a vacant unit with six applicants present, you have a system to properly and fairly document the submission orders of your applications.

With this system, you MUST process one application at a time. For example, suppose you got six applications at an open house. They now include documentation establishing the chronological order they were received.

Application 1 is processed first. It is run through your entire application process without sneaking a peak at any other applications. If Application 1 meets your qualifying standards, they are approved and become your next tenant. If they fail in some area or get disqualified for whatever reason, only then may you move on to Application 2. The application process for this available unit continues in this pattern. If you operate in this manner, you should be pretty safe with processing applications fairly and having the documentation and evidence to prove your actions.

Additionally, when processing applications, use your application worksheet to keep things simple. Document everything you do with a date and time stamp.

If You NEVER Disqualify an Applicant . . . You Will Reduce Your Odds of a Discrimination Complaint

The simplest method to achieving this goal is to always present a challenge or hurdle to the applicant that prevents you, the application processor, from moving forward with their application. Boomarang it and put the ball in their court. You should have a friendly attitude by offering a helping hand or guidance showing possible solutions to fixing or curing their newly discovered problem.

The APPLICANT needs to take action to correct THEIR problem *you found for them*. You project an attitude of helping them by explaining to them how they can work through this obstacle. Being friendly, in your best Ward or June Cleaver voice, you will show a sincere and caring concern to help your applicant(s) Wally or Beaver. When you give your unqualifiable applicant a couple of big hoops to jump through with asking them for a date they can get this done, it almost always happens that they tuck their tail and run. This gives you the liability-free position of not having "disqualified a person for housing."

If you insist on disqualifying an applicant for whatever reason, NEVER do it over the phone or in person. Always do it in writing so you have proper documentation. Make sure your letter is in compliance with your Qualifying Standards following all Fair Housing Laws.

For example, let's say a horrible applicant, Tim Smith, has no chance—ZERO, of renting a unit from you for reasons 1, 2, and 3. I'll telephone Tim explaining I need a little bit of his help in working up or processing his application.

Mike: "Is this Tim Smith?"

Tim: "Yeah, this is Tim."

Mike: "This is Mike with Vista Properties calling about your application for the house at 123 Main St."

Tim: "Okay."

Mike: "Tim, while working up your application, I see your current address is 123 Main St., right?"

Tim: "Yes."

Mike: "Okay, and before that, you lived at Mountain View Apartments and before that you lived with your Mom and Dad . . . Right?"

Tim: "Yes, that's right."

Oh NO!!!!! Now Tim has sparks blowing out his ears because he is now acting like Chris Farley in the movie Tommy Boy. *Inside his head, he is probably cussing himself big time because he screwed up. Tim did not want to put Mountain View Apartments on his application because it got ugly with the landlord while he was there.*

Mike: (in your best Ward Cleaver voice): "Well, Tim, I am not sure if you knew this or not, but the folks at Mountain View Apartments filed an eviction notice on you. Did you know that, Tim?"

Tim: "No, I got all of that worked out."

Mike: "Well Tim, if this is wrong information, I can HELP you get this fixed. Do you want to get this fixed because the way things are right now, you are going to have a very hard time trying to rent a good place. You got an ink pen or pencil handy, Tim?"

Tim: "Yeah, I got one"

Mike: "Great, now write down this number, Tim . . . CI-2018032271. Okay, you got that, Tim?"

Tim: "Yes, I got it."

Mike: "Tim, please read the number back to me . . . . (He did not write it down.) Now Tim, here's what you need to do. Keep that number; it's important and take it with you to District Court. Explain to them your situation and what's going on and they'll help you, too. You need to get this case and number removed from your record and then you can move forward with your application. How long will it take you to do this, Tim?"

Tim: "Uh, oh, a couple of days."

Mike: "Okay. Here's what I can do for you, Tim. Do you have my phone number here at Vista?"

Tim: "Yes."

Mike: "When you get this done, give me a call right away and I can get right back on your application, but in the meantime, I'm gonna have to put it on the shelf until I hear back from you. I've got to move on to the next application until you get back with me."

Tim: "Okay."

I can't tell you how many times conversations have been similar to this one. Remember, the question on our rental application is "How many evictions have been filed on you?" This is not what Tim read. He assumed the question was "How many times have you been evicted?" and he answered ZERO. He also would never put Mountain View Apartments on his application because of the ugly experience there.

After pulling his credit report, it was discovered we found perhaps another address and an eviction filing. At minimum, this sets the stage for false or incomplete information on his application.

The simplest and easiest way to NEVER disqualify a tenant is to offer them a helping hand. Give them an out, give them an example or course of action on their part to fix their problem. Another example could be a bad landlord reference. Do not go into details, but explain there's a problem with their rental history and THEY CAN FIX THEIR PROBLEM with a letter from that landlord explaining their situation and how it was resolved. If THEY do this, it will allow you to move forward with processing their application.

I've found by implementing this into our application process has removed a lot of liability on our part because very few applicants actually get "officially disqualified." They just get "parked on the shelf" until they contact us showing they've resolved their issue.

Enjoy!

Resources Needed

Your cell phone

Cell Phone App "ACR" – All Call Recording

CHAPTER 9

Why March 31st Is a Wonderful Day!

Who started this stuff you gotta rent your properties for 12 months or for 1 year? Are you in the hotel business? I'm not. I want my great residents to stay forever! Chew on this and start doing this now.

From now on, all of your single-family properties, your rental agreements or leases with tenants will be for a minimum of 36 months, with all of them expiring on March 31st AFTER completing 36 months.

For example, a new tenant moving in on December 10 will complete a lease with an "anniversary date" (lease expiration date) of March 31st, three years down the road, which would give you a 40-month lease! Don't start crying or thinking like a tenant saying nobody will do this. You're nervous and jumpy because you're not used to seeing it.

Keep in mind, you've been "grooming" your applicants and tenants for this all along with these subliminal ticklers:

- On your rental application, you asked "How Long Do You Want to Live Here? ___ 1 year ___ 2 years ___ 3 years (odds are they already checked the 3-year box)
- Your Resident Rewards ALL STAR PLAN offers Rent Discounts including a free month of rent upon successfully completely 36 consecutive months with no late payments and no rental agreement violations. They can only redeem their free month of rent when they renew their leases for another three-plus years.
- You pitched to you new tenants they have access to below market rent because you offer long-term housing, whereas other landlords usually do the short 12-month rental agreements.

Sometimes tenants ask a question about an expiration date of March 31 when moving in on December 10. We just kindly remind them "Do you really want to move again right before the holidays, during the school year, and in bad weather?" This usually prompts a big thank you for looking out for their concern. Besides, March 31 is a better time of the year.

From our perspective, March 31 is the day before April 1. Not too far ahead of when school lets out for summer vacation.

Many tenants do have school-age kids. Responsible tenants usually begin their search for a new home when? When will Aunt Bee on *The Andy Griffith Show* begin her search for a new home to rent?

How about 30 to 60 days BEFORE they want to move?

What kind of tenants do you find between Halloween and January 1? I bet there are not many responsible tenants looking to move in this period.

How many tenant turnovers do you want to deal with? Ideally, you really want to almost shut down during the cold, holiday winter season. If you have tenants moving out during this time, it just causes more work for you and it is just ten times harder to find a great tenant.

I like to say finding great residents like Aunt Bee is as easy as "Shooting Ducks in a Barrel." However, you want to do this when the Barrel is Full of Ducks, not when the barrel is empty. When the barrel is empty, you can find any "cream of the crap" because it is all crap.

Now, imagine looking at a page displaying a calendar with all 12 months. Looking at this calendar, what are the worst two months of the year when the barrel would be completely empty—meaning everything is crap. Your answer is November and December. Would Aunt Bee ever consider moving in these months? Heck, NO! She is focused on holidays, baking, and hunkering down for the winter.

Then, looking at your calendar, pick the two months when the barrel is stuffed full of ducks. Your answer here is March and April for many, many reasons.

Also, responsible families with kids begin their search a month or two before school is out for the summer.

I've found this also coincides with when tenants get their tax refund checks and it allows me the opportunity to pounce on doing Rent with Option to Buy for extra income.

It also works wonderfully well for all of our current tenants. Responsible families do NOT want to move during the school year. Therefore, a current, responsible tenant will be encouraged and feel very compelled to renew their rental agreement to keep from having to move in March and jerking their kids out of school. Not a 12-month lease, but another brand new 36-month lease!

There are many reasons to have your leases expire on March 31 after their third year. It just makes good CENTS.

Remember also, with our Resident Rewards ALL STAR PLAN, tenants can get their 37th month absolutely FREE providing they sign a new 36-month rental agreement.

Resources Needed

- Nothing needed here. Just a good understanding on how this can make your life easier.

CHAPTER 10

Your Digital Cookie-Cutter Move-In Process

Always remember to use the June and Ward Cleaver approach with your communications with all of your residents. This is your biggest tip along with using their first name every other sentence, to help you keep the right mindset.

Always Remember Your Residents Cause Their Own Problems

NEVER threaten them that YOU are going to do something ugly like file an eviction notice. Instead, gently remind them, just like Ward Cleaver would talk to Wally or the Beave, that THEY will cause their own immediate eviction.

This is another way to think of yourself as a person who helps them Solve Their Problems. That is why your 11-minute Rent Talk video is so powerful.

Now it's time to tee it up and get your approved applicant graduated to Active Tenant in your program.

Today, you can truly go 100% paperless. This is what we do in my office today. 100% paperless! Everything, absolutely everything, is done with digital paperwork and files. Just like when you go to the Doctor, they have you sign on their electronic pad and some will even take your photo using a webcam. Why can't you do the same? You can! Now is the time.

Tools you can mix and match to go paperless if you have an office or if you meet your tenant at your rental unit or you can do it all long distance. You get to decide how you want to go paperless.

The information shared here applies to "manila file folders" and true hard copy paper.

Now you replace those old-fashioned hard-copy files by scanning them and uploading them into their proper digital folders in your computer. Everything will be digital. PDFs for documents; JPGs's for photos, audio recordings, videos, forms, and whatever else.

Before your "Sign the Papers" meeting; instead of printing all of your documents on your printer, you simply print all documents to PDF.

Using your tablet or smartphone, you open each PDF, and using a free smartphone or tablet application, your new resident(s) can watch your Rent Talk video, and initial and sign every PDF you have prepared. Once everything is signed and dated, save and upload them into your new resident contact record in your Tenant Tracking file.

1. Prepare a "goodie bag" and a package for your New tenant to keep all of their papers together. Be professional and take pride in your business. Look how many homeowners, when they attend their closing, they receive a nice Century 21 bag or a Re/Max bag to keep all of their important papers together. You don't have to get custom-printed bags or folders. I use plain old colored paper pocket folders from Office Depot. Inside the pocket folder is a place pre-punched to insert your business card. This works just fine and costs less than a dollar. This professional attitude will carry through in many things you do in your business. Your goodie bag could contain such things as:
   - Your peel and stick calendar.
   - Refrigerator magnet
   - Coffee mug
   - Welcome flyer or page
   - Utility, phone, cable, Internet contact information
   - Community packets (THESE ARE FREE from your local chamber of commerce or travel agents)
   - SCHOOL information
   - Coupons, and whatever else you can come up with
   - Key tags with your logo, slogan, and website on both sides
   - Zip-It tool—to unclog drains, (a cheap, plastic tool that works)
2. Have your Office In-House New Tenant Move-In Checklist in your tenant's file folder to make sure you dot your i's and cross all of your t's.

   Use your "OFFICE Only: New Resident Move In Checklist" form—Free for you
3. Once approved, your applicant must immediately pay your Deposit to Hold. How much? I recommend at least a dollar amount equal to one month of rent. Their deposit will be applied and used for the funds needed to complete the

move in process. Should your approved applicant not perform within 24 hours as noted on your rental application, then your approved applicant will forfeit their deposit and you will move on to the next application for your rental unit.

4. You can complete the move in process without paper, using your smartphone or tablet because these two devices allow you to use your finger to sign and initial documents. You prepare all of your documents for your new tenant(s) in PDF format with fields to sign and initial where needed. You can do this face to face or you can do it remotely using today's technology.
5. To do your move in process face to face, you can plan and schedule a 60-minute appointment for the indoctrination of your new tenant. Let them know it will take no more than two hours. If you get done in less time, you'll look like a hero. Tell your tenant what to bring:
   a. Certified check from a local bank for the amount of funds needed to sign the papers and get started. Tell them exactly how the check should be. (Never take a personal check when starting a tenancy and do your best to stay away from CASH for safety reasons.)
   b. Full Year Renter Insurance Policy PAID for. If they don't have it handy, let them know you can contact their insurance agent right now to email/fax a declaration page or proof of insurance to your office. I highly recommend to try to help your own insurance agent by letting him/her have your tenant as an insurance customer. It will make your insurance agent happy and it will help keep you in more control of the big picture.
   c. Every responsible party who is signing the rental agreement must be present. If two adults, both must sign and complete your starting process before they get keys.
   d. SECURITY DEPOSIT: make sure your procedure is in compliance with your local landlord/tenant law. In my town, we must have this money separate and it also goes into a separate bank account, (not an escrow account) used exclusively for security deposits. (As a licensed real estate broker in my state, I'm required to have an ESCROW account for being a broker AND I'm required to have another bank account used exclusively for the tenant's security deposits.)
   e. ANIMALS: if animals are involved, they must have already completed an Animal Application Form complete with a mug shot and body shot photos.
6. When your tenants arrive, think of them as NEW EMPLOYEES. Don't tell them this; just THINK this way. How would a new employer greet you if you were a new employee?
7. Give them a clipboard with your "New Resident Welcome Checklist." To go paperless, this form will be displayed on your smartphone, tablet, laptop or desktop. Have your new tenant initial each step as you work through your new

tenant move in process. Your "New Resident Welcome Checklist" accurately documents every step in your move in process. It Protects You. In today's world, if you have an office, you might want to consider video recording this entire session. (just use the webcam on your computer)

8. FIRST—Make Every New Resident and Renewing Resident WATCH your Rent Talk Video. It's an eleven-minute video that clearly explains how you run your business. It is used by thousands of investors, landlords, and property managers all over the world!
9. Then go over your RENTAL AGREEMENT OR LEASE AGREEMENT in detail, line by line. BITE YOUR LIP. YOU MUST DO THIS to properly train your tenant like he is your new employee. I would highly recommend recording this process to document exactly what you said and vice versa.

Here is the first page of my rental agreement (Figure 10.1):

Things to note:

- Annual 2.9% Cost of Living increase in monthly rent is clearly spelled out on the first page. The effective date and the new rent for the next 3 years. No Need to worry about sending any 30 day notice of increase in rent, it's already done for you!
- Bi-Weekly Payments are huge. Encourage your new resident to get on your Bi-Weekly payment plan. This is NOT a TWICE a Month. BIG DIFFERENCE. You will get an EXTRA Month of Rent using the Bi-Weekly Payment Plan. Think about it for a moment. There are 52 weeks in a year. Bi-Weekly means every two weeks. This gives you 26 payments every year. Hmm.. 12 months in year, now you have a 13 month year!... you are welcome.

It's YOUR responsibility to TRAIN them and get them started out on the right foot. Don't get lazy on this part. Do it right. Ask them if they understand and make sure they do.

Use the "Welcome New Resident Checklist Form" to have your new resident initial each and every step involved in your move in process. Make them initial each page.

Make them sign each form properly and date them properly.

STEP 1: RENT TALK 11-minute video is a must for every new and renewing resident. It is powerful and clearly communicates how you run your business. Think of it as "New Tenant Orientation."

Your MOVE IN Inspection must be properly completed and signed.

MOVE IN INSPECTION FORM: The purpose of the Move In Inspection Form is to properly document the condition of the property at the time the tenant moves in. It is intended to serve a twofold purpose. Its purpose is to protect the interest of

FIGURE 10.1 Rental Agreement

Rental Agreement – Single Family House

Manager/Agent for Owner (Landlord): **TENANT(s)** (PRINT FULL REAL NAME):

Vista Properties, Inc. 4012 Dupont Circle, Suite 203 Louisville, KY 40207-4810	Name: ______________________ SSN: ___ - ___ - ___ Name: ______________________ SSN: ___ - ___ - ___
Website: http://VistaKy.com Email: Homes@VistaKY.com TEXT: (502) 896-2595	Rental Address: ______________________ City, State, Zip: ______________________ County: __________

Check One:
☐ Basic Rent Package ☐ Custom Rent Package ☐ Deluxe Rent Package

1.) **TERM:** Tenant(s) agrees to rent the Premises while abiding by the terms and conditions of this rental agreement. This rental agreement shall begin on ______________, 20___ at 12:01 a.m. and shall end ______________, 20___ at 11:59 p.m. at which time the premises shall be vacated returning possession to Landlord unless otherwise authorized by the Landlord in writing.

All terms start on the first day of the month and end on the last day of a calendar month. Upon expiration of this Rental Agreement and if Tenant remains in possession of the rented premises with the consent of the Landlord, a new month to month tenancy shall be created between Landlord and Tenant which shall be subject to all the terms and conditions. Sixty (60) days written notice served by either Landlord or Tenant on the other party is required to terminate this rental agreement.

__________ Package	= $	________
__________	+ $	________
Animal(s): __________	+ $	________
__________	+ $	________
__________	+ $	________
TOTAL RENT:	= $	________

$25.00 Additional Rent per Approved Animal

Easy Payment Direct Deposit via ACH

[ ] Bi-Weekly Payment Plan*

[ ] Monthly Auto Pay Plan

MONTHLY RENT:$ __________ SECURITY DEPOSIT: $ __________ ANIMAL FEE: $ __________ Trash Can Deposit:$ __________

* Bi-Weekly Payment Plan: if selected, Tenant acknowledges each bi-weekly payment of 50% of one month's rent + $5.00 admin fee ($__________) shall be scheduled via ACH to occur on the same day every other week. The rental agreement term shall be adjusted to a two week period and paid in advance.

Annual Cost of Living: effective the 13th month of this rental agreement and annually thereafter, rent will adjust 2.9% due to cost of living. This protects the Tenant from unexpected large increases in rent.

Your first annual rent adjustment effective date is ________, 20___ and your new rent will be $________ per month

Your second annual rent adjustment effective date is ________, 20___ and your new rent will be $ ________ per month.

Your third annual rent adjustment effective date is ________, 20___ and your new rent will be $ ________ per month.

2.) **Security Deposit:** To secure the property of Landlord from damage, Tenant has placed with Landlord a security deposit in the amount set forth above. This deposit will be utilized as a fund for repairing damage to rented premises.

FORM LeaseResidential_1703 - SFH Page 1 of 18 Initials:______

both the Landlord and the Tenant. Many states require the Move In Inspection to include existing damage or items in need of repair along with the cost at the time of the needed repair.

PHOTOS are a MUST with Your Move In Inspection Form. You MUST include good Move In Photos to accurately document and prove the condition of your rental before they move in. This includes photos of anything damaged or in need of repair before they move in.

CAUTION: Remember, in today's world, you will have a hard time trying to collect from a tenant on damages when they move out if you cannot prove their liability. For example, when you open the doors to the cabinet below the kitchen sink and you find all kinds of water damage, gunk, and funk from a leaking drain, you could have a very hard time trying to collect for this tenant-caused damage if you do not have a photo to support this area was bright and clean when they moved in.

Unfortunately, many investors are lazy with their move in inspection and photo documentation, but yet they blow a gasket when their tenant moves out leaving many tenant-chargeable damages.

Here's my "let the dust settle" and "real world" reality checks. I honestly believe no one Move In Inspection Form is the ultimate, absolutely perfect, landlord-safe, tenant-proof form. I believe any competent attorney who had a passion to attack a Move In Inspection, could attack the very best form and chew it up, causing the landlord to lose her case in court. I really and truly believe this. Remember, it's ultimately up to a judge.

Therefore, if I can't really incorporate a bulletproof form, why not use the next best thing, which is the simple KISS METHOD, a simple one-page fill-in-the-blank Move In Inspection Form. I admit it's not perfect; however, I used it in perhaps thousands of move-ins and move-outs, including very few involving a court, and have never been challenged on either form. PLUS, those tenants who end up in collections after their tenancy with cases going to court with judgments, garnishments, and more... not once, knock on wood, has my Move In Form or Move Out Form been challenged.

If it's worked 999 times out of 1,000, I'm sticking to it. Although this is titled Move Out Inspection, our Move In Inspection Form is identical. Only the title at the top is different. When a tenant moves in, we include digital photos of the property both inside and out, and there are about nine photos to a page. We use the Windows Fax and Picture Viewer to put nine photos on a page and we'll hand write the property address, the date, and allow the tenant to sign and date each page. This can be done in our office without having to travel to the property again.

On the Move In Inspection Form, unless it's a newly renovated or rehabbed property, we mark everything good and draw a line on the left column with "All Good." The Good boxes are checked down the left column as well and we instruct the tenant to look the property over again and odds are, they're gonna find some small things when they move in.

We ask them to please call us within seven days of the small things they discover, and we'll add them to their Move-In Inspection Form and we'll also send someone out to make any needed repairs we may have missed. This has worked fine for us.

Ask them for their current phone numbers and congratulate them on their new home.

1. With single-family homes, we'll instruct the tenants on transferring utilities and we'll document our request to terminate service on our Utility Log.
2. LEAD-BASED PAINT: Houses and residential rental property constructed before 1978 requires landlords to give tenants the EPA Publication: "Protect Your Family from Lead in Your Home." BEFORE they rent your property. You're also required to give them this pamphlet again if you ever do any repairs to their unit or a common area where a painted surface of more than two square feet may be disturbed. Not many landlords are aware of the two square feet requirement.
3. RENTS DUE ON THE 1st. Period.
4. ANIMALS: Use your Animal Addendum form to document the number and type of animals. There are 10 species of dogs forbidden because of insurance company regulations.

We've been informed and have seen other landlords' property insurance get canceled when an insurance representative has found these animals on the insured property:

1. Pit Bulls
2. Rottweilers
3. German Shepherd
4. Husky—Alaskan Malamute
5. Doberman Pinscher
6. Chow
7. Great Dane
8. St. Bernard
9. Akita
10. Wolf Hybrids

And they continue to add more animals.

Providing your tenant does not have these animals, we charge $25.00 per month additional rent per animal along with a nonrefundable Animal Fee of $100.

SERVICE ANIMALS and EMOTIONAL SUPPORT ANIMALS There is a new federal law in the works to outlaw online "Service Animal" certifications. There are two websites that charge about $50 or so to fill out their form and they will email you a "Service Animal Certification" with an ID number. THESE ARE BOGUS! Many landlords and property managers fall victim to this scam.

You must use some of your Columbo sixth sense common sense. For example, if you have an applicant who completes your animal application and it looks like a Pit Bull with a logging chain around it's neck chained up to a tree... odds are, they are trying to B.S. you. They will even produce a "Service Animal Certificate" and ID number. All of this is Bogus.

Here is your simple solution WITHOUT disqualifying them. Tell them they must give you a copy of their Renters Insurance Policy where the insurance company has the animal listed as additional insured or covered.

I have done this many, many times. Take a wild guess how many have produced a Renters Insurance Policy with the animal covered. ZERO!!!

Just saying, keep moving forward.

Resources Needed

Rent Talk 11-minute Video—New Tenant Orientation

Free cell phone apps allowing you to get digital signatures on all of your PDF forms

I also recommend you have some kind of Welcome to Your New Home goodie bag

If you meet face to face, it could be a real goodie bag

If done remotely, all digital, you can still create a goodie bag of some sort with links for coupons, discounts, free things to help with their move and so forth.

- Smartphone app—"Office Lens" allows you to use your cell phone camera as a scanner to create PDFs of your signed documents.
- Smartphone app—"Open Camera" to take photos of your new tenant and their valid photo ID. Open Camera allows you to take a lower resolution photo than "Office Lens."
- Always get a short video from your new resident and ask them this question, "Can You Tell Folks What It Is Like to Rent a Home from My Company?" Encourage them to be upbeat, positive, and fun. Make a 30-second video recording you can use for two big reasons

1. To put on your website
2. To save and attach it to their Tenant Contact Record in their Tenant Tracking file. This is good documentation to support they were completely satisfied when they moved in—this is important in case they change their attitude and things get ugly.

CHAPTER 11

Transforming Your Rentals into Tanks and CA$H COW$

"Quality of Your Property Parallels the Quality of Your Tenant"

You can always put a bad tenant in an "A" quality rental. It is almost impossible to put an "A" quality tenant into a Dumpster.

When building your rental portfolio, you want to make them as maintenance-free and headache-free as possible. From below the foundation to the tiptop of the chimney or roof. The less maintenance, repairs, upkeep, and headaches you have, the easier it becomes for you to put your rental business on autopilot, allowing you to work smarter, not harder, and pursue your passions in life.

For starters, if they are available in your town, try to acquire houses built after 1978 because this will automatically remove you and your business from all of the risks associated with lead-based paint. Unfortunately, some towns like Philadelphia, Boston, Baltimore, and so on, have most homes built back during caveman days.

Next up, unless you are buying brand new rentals, try to "cherry pick" newly built (after 1978) houses with open floor plans, maintenance-free exteriors AND energy-efficient windows, doors, insulation, and more. Depending on your climate, utility bills can be huge and I have seen many great tenants move because their utility bills were outrageous.

Energy Efficiency

ENERGY EFFICIENCY is critical in today's market, both for heating and for air conditioning. How can you make your rentals more energy efficient?

- Add more insulation in the attic and in the crawl spaces.
- Ensure all windows and doors are airtight.

- NEVER try to repair or replace storm windows. Replacing the entire window is your best bang for your buck. My Dad loved storm windows, but they are not good today.
- Squirt "Spray Foam' insulation in aerosol cans to seal up underneath cover plates on light switches and electric plugins. Carefully inspect the entire house for any cracks and holes where air and critters can come into or exit the house. Inspect dryers, vents, pipes, and drains underneath the kitchen and bathroom sinks and laundry hookups.
- You might find this shocking, but in my town, I still see many homes with ZERO insulation in the attics and exterior walls.
- Properly evaluate what method is best to heat and cool this house along with the most efficient way to heat hot water. Prices keep dropping on tankless water heaters. They are not there yet, but I do expect to go tankless sometime in the near future.

Plumbing and HVAC

PLUMBING and HVAC seem to be at the top of the list of repair expenses over the year. Therefore, let's see what you can do to minimize your plumbing expenses first.

- Do not use the cheap $17 toilets that look like a coffee can sitting in the bathroom. Go ahead and invest a tad bit more and get a good quality, high-rise toilet. It will pay for itself in short order because they can flush bricks and gravel. Yes, I'm exaggerating just to get my point across.
- Faucets—both kitchen and bathroom. My good friend, Chris McCarty, turned me on to the Moen brand kitchen and bathroom faucets. They cost about $64 each, but the neatest thing of all about them is they all use the same easy-to-replace cartridge. There are no stems, washers, and so on. This makes for very inexpensive repairs without having to run to the hardware store to get parts. Thank You, Chris!
- HVAC—furnace and air conditioning—don't swallow hook, line, and sinker on buying the most-energy-efficient, gold-plated system. These are okay to put in your home and in my home. But when it comes to your rentals, the biggest killer of your HVAC system is not keeping it clean and not changing the air filter monthly. Your forced air and HVAC, must BREATHE! If it can't breathe due to a clogged-up air filter, or dirty, clogged-up fins in the A Coil or outside compressor unit, including heat pumps, your HVAC will not run efficiently. Not only does this cause higher utility bills, it also causes extra stress on your system and this will cause it to blow up a lot earlier than you expected. Then you have

FIGURE 11.1 Example of Oversized Pad for Outside AC Unit

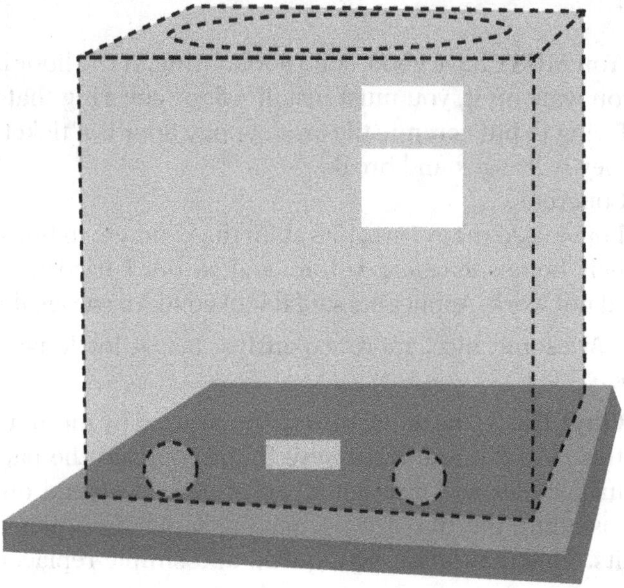

to replace the entire system. You must teach your new tenants how to change their air filter monthly. You must instruct them on how to cut the grass next to the outside compressor unit and to keep it clean and weed-free. Get together with your HVAC company and the simplest solution for your outside unit is to get an "oversized" pad. How oversized? How about a six-inch minimum on all sides (see Figure 11.1). This will allow your resident to just roll their lawn mower wheels on this pad and not have to worry about any trimming edges and so forth.

- BOTTOM LINE on HVAC for Rentals – install the cheapest system. Both cheap HVAC and super expensive energy efficient systems can be destroyed in ruined from a dirty air filter and/or not keeping the system clean.

Floor Coverings

If your house has hardwood floors… refinish them! Hire a good handy person who can rent a floor sander from Home Depot and it will cost you a bit more than carpet, but it will last longer than three or more carpet replacements. But Mike… my hardwood floors have stains, cigarette burns, or patched-up pieces. You can fix these cheap! For cigarette burns or stains, after sanding, take a capful of bleach and pour it carefully onto the stain. Let it sit for a day and dry. Then move forward with staining and finishing. I used to think the same way when I saw stains, burns, and chopped up pieces I thought totally ruined the hardwood floors. Here are some floor covering considerations:

Subflooring You MUST have good, solid subflooring. If the floor is spongy or gives in a lot when you walk on it, you must install a floor covering that will work in this environment. Trying to put ceramic tile on a spongy floor is a ticket for an expensive mess because they will crack and break.

Staining Concrete

In Texas, I have seen many investors stain the concrete in houses built on slabs. They market their homes as allergen free, and so on. I tried it in one of my slab houses and it did not work. Applicants said it looked like a garage floor. Keep Testing.

Ceramic Tile Awesome nice, more expensive, last a lot longer, and requires a skilled installer.

Peel 'n' Stick Vinyl Tile One of the most popular used by mom-and-pop investors. We have used this over the years and have found to avoid the paper-thin cheapest tiles. Get the thicker tiles and also get a can of glue to spread on the floor with a trowel before installing the tile. Always use the same vinyl tiles pattern for all of your rental units. This makes for easy, quick, and simple replacement when a tile gets damaged.

Hardwood Flooring Installing brand new hardwood floors seem to have gone by the wayside unless you are updating your home or a high-dollar luxury home to retail.

Vinyl Planking Vinyl planking is all the rage today. Avoid Pergo because it is basically a bunch of sawdust glued together (particle board) and when it gets wet, it soaks up water and falls apart just like wet noodles. Higher-quality vinyl planking has been installed in my office and looks awesome! It is very durable as well! It looks like hardwood floors. However, there is one big drawback. If a plank gets damaged, you will probably have to remove all of the flooring to get to the one damaged plank. This sucks. The good thing about the true high-quality vinyl plank flooring is it is free floating floor. We have had below-grade apartments get flooded and the vinyl plank flooring was not damaged at all!! Decent quality vinyl planking costs about $2.50 per square foot installed, not per square yard.

Sheet Vinyl Sheet vinyl still has a place in today's world. Not only is the stuff cheap, about $1.00 per square foot, but a good installer can do a whole room in about 30 minutes! We use this only on our low-income neighborhood houses and apartments.

CARPET To get the biggest bang for your buck using carpet, it's best to avoid "seams" at all costs. Why? Because your carpet installers HATE SEAMS. They are time-eaters and a major pain in the butt for them to install. Glue Tape: heat the carpet with the installer's iron and it takes a longer. If you can make arrangements for one standalone piece of carpet in each room in your rental, your carpet installer can stop by on the way home and do four rooms as shown in cartoon in just an hour or two! (The shaded areas shown in Figure 11.2 could be tile.)

Tip

NEVER install carpet at the front door. Always put some kind of entry foyer–like tile or vinyl planks for folks to stomp and wipe their feet on when entering your rental house.

Cabinets I prefer using solid oak, raised panel cabinets for kitchens, bathrooms, and laundry rooms. AVOID using glued particle-board cabinets. Avoid using the white cabinets too. My favorite cabinets to use are manufactured by Sunco. These have solid oak fronts and raised panels and they are built with real plywood, not particle-board. Make sure you get them prefinished, as they will look good for decades. Don't get the unfinished, and worse yet, do not paint them. A 36-inch kitchen sink base cabinet can be had for $184 at eBarnett.com, which was recently

FIGURE 11.2 Look Mom! No Seams!

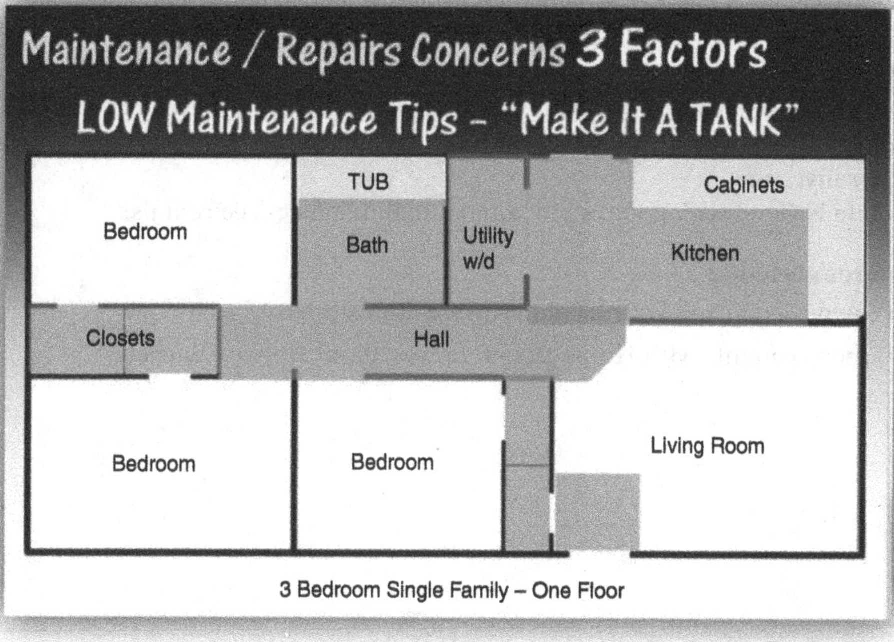

bought by Home Depot. Go to their website and sign up for free and they will send you a huge almost 3-inch thick catalog. www.eBarnett.com is the wholesale supplier for contractors, hardware stores, hotels, property management companies, and much more.

Bathrooms In older homes, just remove the old-school medicine cabinet and the light fixture above it or on the sides. Replace the medicine cabinet with a $17 mirror (18" × 24") from Home Depot. Then install a three- or four-light bar above the mirror. If the bathroom(s) do not have a closet, you can install an above-the-toilet cabinet with double doors, a shelf and a towel bar built-in. My good friend and investing expert, Brad Grayson, takes it one step better and says to never put this cabinet above the toilet. Install it on a wall anywhere except above the toilet. He says this remove any opportunity for something to fall out of this cabinet and end up clogging up the toilet. Great point, Brad!

Garbage Disposals NOT!!!! Remove all garbage disposals in all of your rentals. They are job security for plumbers and guaranteed future expenses that are 100% totally preventable. How can you prevent this expense? Remove the garbage disposal. The name of this device "Garbage Disposal" actually encourages your tenants to put all of their garbage into it. Guess where all of this garbage ends up? In Your Drain Lines! Do NOT waste your time trying to train your tenant on how to use a Garbage Disposal.

When building your rental portfolio, always make sure you target rock solid, structurally sound properties. Not all houses are built the same in quality or workmanship. Remember the old Johnny Cash song about him bringing parts home from the Cadillac plant? Same thing applies here. Some neighborhoods in my town are well known for having very cheaply built houses that could never have passed any building codes back in the day. But they are here. It's okay to buy these and wholesale to other investors.

Life Is Good with good, solid, almost-maintenance-free rentals.

Resources Needed

- Open accounts at your local hardware stores
- Open accounts with Home Depot, Lowes, paint stores, eBarnett

SECTION III

GO 100% DIGITAL AFTER THEY MOVE IN

CHAPTER 12

How to Consistently Get Paid Over 100% of Your Rents Every Month

This is not a typo. It's a true statement and you can get these results too. Before starting, let's clear up the definition here so we're both on the same page.

First of all, what exactly is rent? When traveling and teaching to groups, I ask, "We need an honest landlord with more than 15 units." After we identify our victim for education (the honest landlord with at least 15 units), this "led to slaughter in front of their peers" landlord is asked...

"Of all the rent owed you over a 12-month period, how much do you really get?"

Amazingly, the majority of folks put on this hot seat answer honestly. By far, the number one answer is 85%. Asked if they're guesstimating or do they really know, they embarrassingly admit it's only a guesstimate. Keep in mind that this question deals only with rent owed over a 12-month period. It includes tenants who slow pay, don't pay, get evicted, and so forth. It does NOT include lost rent on vacant units. If you know how to get rent on vacant units, I'll be the first to sign up for your class.

Therefore, if you have 10 units renting for $800 a month (all occupied = $8,000 month), over 12 months you should get $96,000. Based on the question asked here, most investors believe they're getting 85%. This means you're getting only $81,600 of the $96,000 owed to you. $14,400 in missing income is not good for the home team. Almost a month and a half of YOUR rents... Poof!... gone! Adios!

Now, some good news. Let's take the same scenario of $96,000 in annual rents, but at the end of your 12 months, you've got $105,600 instead of $81,600! I'm not kidding. Not only $9,600 above what was owed you, this would be an increase of $24,000 in 12 months if you operated like most investors! The $14,400 shortage + the $9,600 over = +$24,000 improvement in cash flow! Would you want $81,600 on the RENT INCOME line on your Schedule E or would you rather have $105,600? Not a difficult choice, is it?

These are not pie in the sky numbers. This is an example of an investor with only 10 units renting for $800 month. Let's nip in the bud any argument involving vacancies. If you want to argue a vacancy factor, no problem, let's use an investor with 12 rental units at $800 month rent and has 2 units vacant monthly. The numbers would still be the same. Got it?

Failing to Plan Is Planning to Fail

"Shoot from the hip" seems to be the system of choice for most investors who try to focus only on benefits without effort or hassles. Although you might be guilty of micromanaging by doing everything yourself, it's really not the best for you in the long run. Starting off this way to learn the business is great, but you should have a plan to graduate.

Implementing proven systems into your real estate investing business can "TurboCharge" your results in several areas. Not only in the financial department, but proven systems can literally quadruple the quality of your life, allowing more time for yourself, family, and hobbies (and yes, more time for investing if you choose to do that).

Proven Systems Are Time Savers, Money Makers, and Good CYA Programs

Here are some good solid tips to get your systems in operation. If you want excellent results, you must have good systems. If you want to quantum leap your investing results, you MUST learn how to "Work Smarter, Not Harder." This doesn't mean become lazy. It simply means using more of the gray matter between your ears instead of using your back and arms trading hours for dollars.

For example, are you painting and cleaning up property because you have time and honestly believe you're saving money? Don't feel bad if you're doing this, because I did it too when I got started. A lot of this has to do with your own comfort zone. We're simply too scared to take on a big risk and honestly believe we're saving money by swinging a paint brush or fixing stuff.

Go ahead and say, "Easier said than done," but it's true. Look at successful investors in your town. Do you see them painting or working on properties? NO. Many of them started out this way, but they quickly learned how to become "business owners."

Even McDonald's or your local grocery store won't turn a new hire loose without proper training. Why in the world would you turn one loose in your expensive investment?

How Do You Treat Your Real Estate Investing...as a Hobby or a Business?

This challenging question seems to separate the "girls and boys" from the "women and men." Here are some of the characteristics of each:

If you treat your real estate as a hobby:

- You're a micromanager.
- You're "hands-on."
- You're involved with repairs and maintenance.
- You buy weird things to save money.
- You knock on doors to collect your rent.
- Worse yet, you travel to get partial payments of rent when summoned by your tenant(s).
- Allow tenants to call you at home and/or cell phone.
- You go to court—God created attorneys to do this for you.
- You physically help with your own evictions.
- You show your own vacant units.
- You cut grass to save money.
- You have trouble "getting to the next level" because you feel so overwhelmed.
- You lose the desire to "get to the next level" because you believe your workload will only get worse.

When you treat your real estate as a business:

- You have a "business owner" attitude.
- You're "hands-off" and use "systems."
- You assign or delegate repairs and maintenance.
- You NEVER knock on doors for rent.
- You've trained your tenants to pay rent with ACH, online payments, or mail payments.
- Tenants never call your home or cell phone.
- Tenants don't know the owner.
- You never go to court, (that's for attorneys).
- You never physically participate or even show up at your own evictions.
- You never show your own vacant units.
- You never cut grass.
- You have no trouble "getting to the next level" because you have time to achieve objectives.

Once again, take a look at the successful investors in your town. I mean the serious successful investor. It doesn't matter what town you're in; there's a common trait among most of these people. They act like "business owners" because they are. They put themselves in a position to continue networking, learning, and "being close to the action." They don't go to court, paint houses, collect rent, cut grass, or help set out evicted tenants. They have systems in place to handle this for them. They also seem to have time for fun. Most have a hobby for fun. It may be golf, hunting, boating, music, or any number of things outside of real estate.

They may have double, triple or more number of properties than you, yet they seem so laid back, happy, and free of stress. I'm not promoting or encouraging you to buy more properties; I'm pointing out the importance of having your own "business system." It will make your life and investing so much easier and efficient. With a good, solid, proven business system, you can easily graduate to your next level or objective because you'll have the time to focus on achieving your objective instead of cutting grass or doing repairs.

Here's a no-brainer: Remember the earlier scenario of 10 units at $800 month? Picture yourself implementing a good system to produce a $24,000 swing in your annual income from real estate. That's $2,000 a month! Here's an example of working smarter and not harder. With $2,000 extra per month, you could hire a full-time handyman at $500 week, or how about a 20-hour part-time handyman at $250 week and a 20-hour part-time office manager at $250 week. Don't do it now; just start thinking in this manner.

When I started, I wanted aggressive, safe, growth. My question was, "How many houses would it take to pay for a 20-hour per week handyman?" Keep in mind, Tammy and I lived off of my police officer salary and her nursing salary, allowing our real estate business to grow. In the beginning, I didn't like unclogging toilets, so we hired a 20-hour a week part-time handyman pretty darn quick.

Work SMARTER, Not Harder!

Implementing good systems, especially PROVEN systems, can offer you tremendous benefits right now and in the long haul. A good property management program educating and training tenants from day one. You MUST explain in detail the tenant's responsibilities and the consequences for failing to perform properly.

You don't have to be a dominating dictator or an arrogant king. Remember, you play the role of a "boss" training a new hire employee. You explain company rules, regulations, and policies UP FRONT. It's so much easier doing the education part on the front end, because on occasion, you'll have a new hire (new tenant) who decides your rules and policies are just too much and they choose to move on. Wouldn't you prefer this now instead of later? Good employees can be rewarded, get birthday cards, and so on.

While schooling your new hire tenant, explain the process for making monthly rent payments. Tell them right now you don't knock on doors. They must mail their payment before the 1st because rent is due on the 1st and is late on the 2nd.

"It Doesn't Cost You Anything to Ask a Question"

SHOOT FOR THE MOON...

If You Fall Short, You're NOT a Loser...

You're Just a STAR.

Stop squawking. Imagine a tenant blasting you over your late charge and your daily late charges. This sets the stage for you to be a nice guy. You politely and professionally remind your tenant of their big tutorial session explaining the rules when they came on board; however, just this one time, you might VOID the daily late charges to show them you're a nice guy, making them feel better. Now the tenant thinks they've won and you're a fair person; however, you still got your 10% late charge nailed down tight.

Consider your daily late charges gravy or icing on the cake. It's your first line of defense to protect your 10% late charge. If you're thinking this is difficult, you need a bit more training yourself. Remind yourself "Business Owner" is your role.

Well-trained tenants frequently mail in their rent along with the 10% late charge BEFORE they receive their late notice. This will really make you feel good about your system because it's PROOF that it's working.

There's a lot more than late charges to get 110% of your rent. In fact, late charges are only 1.3% of our income received. Where does the rest come from? Investors have boatloads of money falling through their fingers they can't even see!

For example, how many times has this happened to you? You've scheduled an appointment for a repair and your service person phones you reporting nobody is home? What do you do? Do you phone your tenant and accept some lame excuse like "I forgot?" This is THEIR FAULT. Train your tenants to abide by the rules of your system. When this happens, charge them $85.00 for a missed repair appointment and stick to it. Do NOT void this charge. If you void this charge, you just enabled and trained your tenant that it's okay to behave this way!

Document tenant chargeable repairs and have them sign your work order form acknowledging the same. Now you have written documentation, "evidence" to support your claim of a tenant chargeable repair such as a ham hock bone in the toilet when the tenant dumped their bean soup in your toilet (a true story).

Another powerful source of extra income for you is implementing a good, solid, move out inspection process without having to worry about receipts, labor costs, and material costs. Set up a program giving every tenant the same set of instructions and a price list for failing to follow your instructions.

For example, you can charge $6.00 for a lightbulb. There were lightbulbs when they moved in and you expect working lightbulbs when they move out. Your tenant may scream "But I can get four lightbulbs at Walgreen's for only 99 cents!" Your answer is, "That's my point. We want you to go Walgreen's and get those lightbulbs because we haven't found anybody who'll go to Walgreen's for free and buy those 99-cent lightbulbs. We have to pay somebody almost $20.00 an hour to go to Walgreen's to buy a lightbulb and it costs more than $6.00 for a bulb to do this. So, please don't take one lightbulb. Take them all."

Most landlords who treat their real estate as a hobby dread the move out process and tenant turnover. They assume if the tenant challenges their move out charges by going to court, they must gather all of their receipts and still expect they're gonna lose in court. They have no system. PLUS, the hobbyist does his own repairs and cleanup. They don't get a receipt for their own labor. How insulting when standing in front of a judge and they order you to return all the security deposit back to the tenant, and worse yet, accept only the receipts documenting cash out of your pocket expenses with absolute ZERO worth to your time, effort, and labor.

Here's a partial list of items used in Tenant Tracking to assist you in getting 110% or more of your rents. You can change prices, too.

- Keys—one for $10 or two for $15 (believe it or not, most buy two keys).
- Deadbolts keyed the same as their knob set lock, allowing one key to fit all of the doors on their home. Only $45 each—yes, they buy these too during the move-in process. We simply play musical locks.
- Filling Out Forms Fee ($15.00)—banks do it to you.
- Missed Work Order Appointments ($85).
- Late Fee—10% of monthly rent.
- Daily Late Fee—$5 per day.
- Payment plans for tenant chargeable repairs.
- Dirty Air Filter in SFH—$25.
- Missing Air Filter in SFH—$35.
- Any Code Enforcement or Fines—charge Tenant 125% of each fine that is their fault.
- Elite Lawn Care Service.
- One Hit Wonder Lawn Care Cut.
- Cleaning Gutters—just cipher up at $35 hour.

Here are fees associated with the Move-Out Process:

- Re-Rental Charge, Breaking Lease (1.5% of a month's rent).
- Electric off ($75.00).
- Water Off ($75.00).
- Floor Tile ($5.00 each).
- Cracked window glass ($80.00).
- Storm Door Chain ($15.00).
- Storm Door pneumatic closure ($35.00).
- Electric Cover Plate ($2.00).
- Car in Yard ($200).
- Trash piled ($200 pickup truckload).
- Smoke Alarm ($25.00).
- Air filter ($30.00).
- Cleaning windows ($10.00 each).
- Deadbolt locks ($45.00).
- Payment Plans and more payments plans.

A good proven system is your foundation to implementing an efficient business operation for your real estate. It will allow you to have a "business owner" perspective. Used properly you'll increase cash flow because you'll stay focused on the performance of your "forest" instead of one tree or bush.

Plus, dozens and dozens that are legal and allowed in your state and town.

Payment Plans and Payment Plan Form

You can use this in several ways.

1. Work Orders/Repairs/Maintenance Request: Tenant Chargeable Repairs while living in your rental. If the repair cost more than your great resident can pay in one lump sum, set them up on a Win-Win situation with a very affordable monthly payment.
2. After They Move Out and Still Owe You Money: Many will have a balance owed to you that is impossible for them to write a check for. When this happens, set them up on a Payment Plan and you can "finance" the balance for them.

Let me tell you about this powerful little tip. Tenants tear up stuff. Things get broken and these should be tenant chargeable repairs. What about those charges accrued during the move out process. If a tenant owes you money, most landlords play ostrich.

The Payment Plan is pretty easy. It can be as simple as having your tenant scribble, "I promise to pay your company $25.00 monthly for the next 15 months" and have them sign it and date it. It's my understanding this little simple scribbled message becomes a Promissory Note to You or your company.

Suppose a Tenant owes you $600. You could set up one of several payment plans:

Plan A—pay $100 per month for the next 8 months

Plan B—pay $50 per month for the next 16 months

Plan C—pay $25 per month for the next 35 months.

You are financing the debt they owe you. There's nothing wrong with charging interest. Pawn Shops do it every day, so don't beat yourself up over this. Wouldn't you really rather get $25.00 a month for a long time versus trying to jump up and down screaming to get $600 now from a tenant who doesn't have it and never will.

True story. I'm still getting $44.53 every month from a tenant who moved out of the property over 4 years ago. Talk about helping me get over 100% of my rents. I still send a monthly bill to this former tenant for his $44.53 he owes every month.

Tip

With everything I was juggling back when I got started, I discovered the hard way my quality of life improved a bunch when I hired a woman to be my part-time resident manager. She or he, can even work from their home.

You do NOT have to think about the added expense of hiring a part-time person. What You will discover is your part-time person will do this job 10 times better than you and they will produce MORE INCOME for your business. A good person driving your rentals for you, the late charges alone will pay you a lot more than what you are paying your part-time help.

Years ago, I pushed a button to see how much Late Charge income was received for the previous year. Amazingly, my report showed we received over $70,000 in late charges and daily late charges! This covered not only the cost of my full-time office manager, but it also covered the cost of my full-time maintenance supervisor! WOW!

I promise you, I could have NEVER achieved this with me trying to do everything myself.

Resources Needed

To go paperless and run everything from your smart phone, tablet, or laptop, you will need:

- TeamViewer.com allows you to access your desktop from any device, anywhere.
- Investor Books Pro System with Tenant Tracking www.InvestorBooksPro.com.
- Email and text your residents a monthly bill for next month's rent.
- Effective, interactive free website that allows for:
  - Online Resident Only Page.
  - Online Rent Payments that are direct-deposited into your bank account.
  - Contact Office form can be used for anything.
  - Repair or Maintenance Request form.

CHAPTER 13

You Really CAN Teach Pigs to Sing

Back in the day, my wife Tammy frequently reminded me of one of her favorite phrases she claims she discovered in a Beatles song years ago. This phrase was:

> *NEVER Teach a Pig to Sing,*
> *It Wastes Your Time and Annoys the Pig.*

Most of the time, she's right. But on occasion I'd hear one begin to hum a tune.

CASE STUDY 1: INHERITED TENANTS YOU INTEND TO KEEP

As an aggressive investor, I was buying, and buying, and buying property. I had the opportunity to purchase four single-family "shotgun style" houses from a slumlord. This guy never did anything properly. He replaced broken furnaces with used furnaces and it reflected in the quality of his tenants. Joe was his name.

Joe used to tell me one of his favorite investor truths was the property you were most embarrassed to admit you own, were usually the properties producing the most cash flow and profit. Perhaps for Joe, but his program is not for me.

I negotiated a pretty good deal with Joe on these four houses. These houses were all in a row on the same street and had HIS tenants in them. Horrible. We put the deal together and scheduled the closing.

In the meantime, we moved forward discussing the arrangements with his existing tenants. Joe informed me he had to stop by every Saturday morning knocking on their doors to collect rent. I boldly told Joe, "I'll NEVER knock on their doors to collect rent. These tenants will MAIL their rent payments

(*continued*)

monthly." He then gave me a thigh-slapping huge gut-wrenching belly laugh. And then another one, saying, "They will NEVER mail their rent. They don't know how."

Joe told me he'd had these properties for 20 years and not once, never, ever, has any of his tenants in these four houses mailed their rent. He PROMISED me this could not be done, but he still wished me good luck grinning his butt off.

Step 1

Before the closing, and before purchasing the properties, I made four copies of my "Inherited Tenant Information Sheet" and NEW TENANT PACKAGES, which include Move In Inspection Form, Rental Agreement, Lead Based paint pamphlets, and so on. The purpose of this meeting is to have a thorough "cleansing" from the previous landlord and transition these folks 100% into **my** system.

BUT, BUT, what if they have a signed rental agreement or lease with the previous owner? Use your great people and communication skills. It simply takes the agreement of both parties involved... the landlord, owner (YOU) and the tenant... both can agree to terminate and kill the existing agreement effective on a specific date. You can both enter into your rental agreement with a new effective date. The exception would be any kind of government program such as Section 8. You would be forced to step into the owner's shoes.

I would have their folder(s) and clipboard and visit each tenant. These tenants did not have telephones or cell phones, so I had to stop by unannounced. The purpose of this meeting was to gather information from each tenant about the property, their past financial relationship with their landlord Joe, to verify such things as rent, security deposits, and so forth. You must do this before the closing, allowing you the opportunity to take it up with your seller, (my Joe) before buying the property. So much easier to work these bugs out on the front end than after your closing.

For example, suppose a tenant says they have a $600 deposit paid to the landlord and your seller says they've got a $300 security deposit. Wouldn't it be best to discover this before buying this property and tenant?

I stop by and visit each tenant to identify myself as the probable new "Property Manager". Here's their opportunity to vent and blow off steam about anything they choose, including the soon-to-be previous owner.

Remember, these folks don't need an application to rent from you. They're already in the property.

Letting these tenants vent will give them the opportunity to feel important and valued. They probably haven't been treated this way in a while. While you have them eating out of your hand, you complete all of the paperwork to transition them completely into your system, including your new rental agreement.

At this time, I school them on our great new program for them. I let them know they'll get a bill from our property management company mailed to them on the 20th of each month. Inside will be a monthly statement detailing charges on their account, an envelope already addressed to mail their payment, and a monthly newsletter just for them with all kinds of tips and coupons.

Here comes their static. They might start bucking. They've NEVER mailed their rent before. Joe always came back and collected weekly or several times a month. I tell them this will never happen again. You MUST mail your rent payment.

Hold their hand mentally. Let them calm down and show them how easy this is for them. Nobody will knock on your door early on Saturday morning. You can sleep in now. All you have to do is get some stamps. You can get them at the grocery store. Put your money order or check into the envelope and take a clothes pin and clip it to your mailbox. Your mailman will pick it up! You don't even have to go to a mailbox.

Some of these tenants balked, stating they have no bank account, or they don't get their check till the 3rd of the month.

RENT is due on the 1st. PERIOD

Guess when it's late? It's late on the 2nd. PERIOD.

Late Charge: 10% of the monthly rent.

Daily Late Charge: $5.00 a day.

Here's how I handle those wannabe problem children. Suppose you acknowledge their checks come in their mailbox on the 3rd. You offer a simple solution. Remind them they will get a monthly bill again. It's mailed to them on the 20th. Tell your tenant to put their payment in the envelope and mail it before the 1st.

We Use the Postmark Date on their envelope as the PAYMENT RECEIVED DATE.

This does happen. I do receive payments in the mail on the 3rd and sometimes the 4th with a postmark date of the 1st. This means no late charge for the tenant.

(continued)

No competent judge in any court will not use the postmark date as a payment received date. This totally eliminates those stupid tactics on the part of tenants trying to mail in a check on October 5th and they've handwritten September 30th on their rent check, thinking it will prevent a late charge.

Back to the tenant who gets their check on the 3rd of the month. I tell them to put their payment in the envelope and mail it in before the 1st with a note "PLEASE HOLD TILL THE 3RD." If we receive their payment with this note BEFORE the 1st, they will not be hit with a late charge. This works great.

Joe saw me a few months after I bought his houses and asked how things were going. He also asked me how I liked knocking on their doors weekly to get the rent. I told him I've never knocked on their doors and they're mailing their monthly rent payments in like instructed. He was shocked and didn't believe it. He went over to see his old tenants to verify my story and they told him the same.

Joe thinks I'm the best landlord on the planet because he sure would've bet $1,000 I could never get these tenants to mail their rent payments monthly.

So, Yes, You Really Can Teach Pigs to Sing.

INHERITED TENANT INFO FORM

Address: ________________ Date: ______________

Tenant Name: ________________ Phone: ____________

SSN: ________________ DOB: ______________

Monthly Rent: $ ________________ Security Deposit: $ ____________

Occupants: ________________ DOB: ______________

(Name and Number)

________________ DOB: ______________

________________ DOB: ______________

________________ DOB: ______________

Moved-In Date: ________________ Phone: ______________

Rental Agreement: ________________ Expire date: ____________

Emergency/Alternate Contact: ______________

Remarks: ________________________________

CASE STUDY 2: INHERITED TENANTS YOU WANT OUT NOW

No need to make this difficult. The current tenants and occupants have your Seller pulling their hair out. For whatever reason, you want these tenants GONE and GONE NOW. They don't fit into your program for whatever reason.

Here's what I've done many times. First, you must coordinate your activities legally and safely so you never throw out money BEFORE you have control and own the property. One of the worst mistakes you could make is to take your expertise and make their problem tenant leave quickly BEFORE you buy the property. You might have just fixed their problem for them and they may change their mind about selling you the property. You made it nice again. So, just be careful doing this before you actually buy the property.

You own the property and you want to get these idiots out of your property FAST. You have two avenues to get them out.

1. Figure out how to do it yourself.
2. Use the court system, with attorneys, and legally evict them.

I can tell you that Option 1 is the better one for you.

Option 2 can be very expensive, making money for the attorneys, dragging out your access to the property. You can't start working on it and your overhead meter is running. Taxes, insurance, and they're just making the property worse. PLUS, you can bet they're gonna leave you a huge mess when they finally get evicted.

How much money, time, and effort will you be out with Plan 2. In my town, I could easily be out $1,000 to get these idiots out using the court system.

Here's my solution: After you buy the property, stop by and visit these idiots. As hard as it may be, bite your lip, and try to be real friendly while maintaining your firm professional attitude. Here's how the conversation goes:

Hey, Billy, I have a deal for you. Can I talk to you a minute?

Billy, even if an idiot, will usually agree to this one.

"Here's the deal, Billy, my name is Mike. I know you and dumbass Tom, (your seller) aren't getting along at all right now, but I don't have any problem with you at all. Can you understand this?"

Billy may start to blab about Tom. Don't tell him to shut up. You'll piss him off too, just like Tom did. In fact, it would do you some good to agree with Billy by shaking your head in acknowledgement of his situation.

Let Billy vent a little, continue calling him by his name, and then tell him about your deal. "Here's your deal, Billy."

"First of all, I have no issue with you at all. You understand that, right?"

"But I've bought this property and I've got plans and unfortunately you're gonna have to move. We can do this as friendly folks and I can help you out OR you can choose to make it difficult and you and I will both lose and the attorneys will win. They just want to always make a mountain out of a mole hill and make us pay for it."

(continued)

"So here's your deal in a nutshell, Billy. I can give you money to help you with your move or I can let the attorneys have your money. Are you interested?"

He'll say, "Tell me more."

"Here's the deal, Billy. If you get all of your stuff, and I mean ALL of your stuff, out of here by 4 P.M. on Saturday, have it "broom clean" with all your trash hauled off and not stacked up anywhere, I'll give you $600 cash on the spot. All you've got to do is call me and let me know you got it done. I'll show up here to see you've really done it, and you'll get your money, no questions asked. This might help you get a truck or help you with getting a new place."

Most of the time, Billy will jump on this. He might say 4 P.M. on Saturday is impossible. Acknowledge it and ask what will work for him. You want this to be a WIN-WIN situation. Suppose he says 4 P.M. on Monday will work for him.

That's still good. And I'd remind him: "Remember, Billy, this means nothing in here, broom clean, no excuses about anything. All out, all gone. Not a chair left behind or even a fork. You got it and do I have your word on it?"

If Billy agrees to this, I've never had one not do as agreed. Pretty amazing, isn't it?

CORRESPONDENCE Is Now 100% Digital

Since you are using the Tenant Tracking system, billing your tenants monthly, this sets the stage for you to incorporate written correspondence into your program. It's amazingly simple to implement once you start billing your tenants. You're already emailing them a monthly statement, and many times when they mail their rent or pay online, they scribble some kind of note.

Don't get me wrong. I'm not saying this is normal. I'm guessing perhaps 1 or 2 out of 100 tenant payments will contain a written note of some kind. Anything from a complaint, a work order request, or information they deem important for you to know.

The important thing is you did not waste time on the phone and now you have it in writing. Use your RECEIVED date stamp on their written notes and attach it to their tenant record.

LATE NOTICES: most states require a specific PAY OR QUIT POSSESSION NOTICE of X number of days to be given to tenants who haven't paid their rent. Do it right and legally in your town. It will save you a lot of grief.

Tip

Most states include language stating if a landlord accepts any partial payments of rent after the landlord has started the eviction process, the accepted partial payment of rent will KILL and cancel the landlord's pending eviction action.

Therefore, we don't accept partial payments once the eviction process has started.

Also, as part of training your tenants, suppose a tenant has a monthly rent of $800 and your late charge is 10% ($80.00). Using my Tenant Tracking system of billing our tenants, a chronological order of events might occur like this:

			BALANCE
8-20-18	Rent for next month (Sept)	$800.00	$800.00
9-2-18	Late Charge	$80.00	$880.00
9-3-18	Payment Received	–$800.00	$80.00
9-20-18	Rent for next month	$800.00	$880.00

Now, if this tenant mails in a payment of $800, for example, and we receive it on the 1st or before, WE WILL REFUSE THEIR PAYMENT and return it with a late notice and a late charge.

YOU MUST stick to your guns and be firm, fair, and friendly. IF YOU ACCEPT the $800.00 payment when you mailed them a bill for $880, you are training your tenant this behavior is acceptable to you. DON'T DO THIS! It might be difficult to get started, but it works in the long run.

Touché, Tammy. As you can see, on occasion I can train a pig to sing.

Resources Needed

- Email
- Text messaging (Mighty Text is a good, free app to text from your desktop, laptop, tablet, and smart phone)

Tools Needed to Go Paperless:

- Online fill-in-the-blank forms on your free OnCarrot website
- Smartphone apps to take photos, videos, and scan items to PDFs
- Tenant Tracking allows you to attach items to each tenant record
- TeamViewer.com on your desktop, laptop, tablet, and smartphone to access EVERYTHING on your desktop – all you need is internet access.

Tip

Most states include language stating if a landlord accepts any partial payments of rent after the landlord has started the eviction process, the accepted partial payment of rent will KILL and cancel the landlord's pending eviction action.

Therefore, we do not accept partial payments once the eviction process has started.

Also, as part of training your tenants, suppose a tenant has a monthly rent of $800 and your late charge is 10% ($80.00). Using my Tenant Tracking system of billing our tenants, a chronological order of events might occur like this:

BALANCE			
8-20-18	Rent for next month (Sept)	$800.00	$800.00
9-2-18	Late Charge	$80.00	$880.00
9-5-18	Payment Received	−$800.00	$80.00
9-20-18	Rent for next month	$800.00	$880.00

Now, if this tenant mails in a payment of $800, for example, and we receive it on the 1st or before, WE WILL REFUSE THEIR PAYMENT and return it with a late notice and a late charge.

YOU MUST stick to your guns and be firm, fair, and friendly. IF YOU ACCEPT the $800.00 payment when you mailed them a bill for $880, you are training your tenant this behavior is acceptable to you. DON'T DO THIS! It might be difficult to get started, but it works in the long run.

Touché, Tammy. As you can see, on occasion I can train a pig to sing.

Resources Needed

- Email
- Text messaging (Mighty Text is a good, free app to text from your desktop, laptop, tablet, and smartphone)

Tools Needed to Go Paperless

- Online fill-in-the-blank forms on your free OnCentral website
- Smartphone apps to take photos, videos, and scan items to PDFs
- Tenant Tracking allows you to attach items to each tenant record
- TeamViewer.com on your desktop, laptop, tablet, and smartphone to access EVERYTHING on your desktop – all you need is internet access.

CHAPTER 14

Digital Work Orders and Repair Requests

Always instruct your tenants to go to the RESIDENTS page on your website. On your website they can fill in the blanks and attach photos of their repair request. When they hit the submit button, it is auto-emailed to you. Now you can attach everything in this email to their tenant record in your Tenant Tracking company file.

Work Orders are your golden opportunity to have your handyman, service technician, and all of your licensed trade vendors to be your eyes and ears. Groom them to be observant and look for things that don't look right. Here's what is required on all of my Work Orders. It does not matter if it is in-house or assigned to a vendor.

1. Clearly Spell out what is need of repair. If there are three tasks in the request submitted by your tenant, you must authorize or approve each of the three.
2. In Your Work Order—Do NOT write a month-long paragraph or story to give instruction to the person who will be doing the repairs. Here is what my work orders look like:

Tenant reports blah, blah, blah. (After this, you will enter each of the following tasks)

1. **KITCHEN:** sink does not drain—repair properly
2. **BATHROOM:** faucet constantly runs—repair properly
3. **BEDROOM, Second Floor:** electric outlet does not work—repair properly

Now this is very easy on the eyes and whoever is doing this Work Order has a very clear understanding of what needs to be fixed.

On top of this, whoever does this Work Order must take photos of:

- Front of house
- Rear of house
- Working Smoke Alarm
- Furnace Filter—if dirty replace, if missing, replace—both are Tenant Chargeable
- BEFORE Photos of items in need of repair
- AFTER photos of items repaired
- Photos of anything that will support Tenant Chargeable items such as pulling out grease, or toothbrush, fork, knives, out of clogged-up drains
- PHOTOS of anything else that is out of order—3 pit bulls chained up in the basement, dope growing in the attic, piles of garbage and trash in back yard, grass too tall, and more.

As you already know by now, all of this gets attached to the tenant's record in your Tenant Tracking company file. Remember, you can attach photos, pdf, audio recordings, videos, scanned anything etc.

Your Tenants may freak out when photos are taken. Don't worry; this is normal. Your service person can simply tell them this is required by the insurance company now. This is new to your tenant and they will get in the groove in short order.

Every Work Order should also be treated as an inspection of your rental property. If your service person has properly documented rental agreement violations, you can email them your legal form giving them notice of lease violations. In my town, they have 14 days to fix the violations or we can start the eviction process.

TRUE STORY:

I had a great tenant who called us three days in a row that her toilet was not flushing. For the first two days, I created a work order and Dan did the work order. When she called the third day with the same request, she said "liquids" (peeing) the toilet worked fine, but, when she "took a dump" it would not flush properly. I told Dan to remove the toilet from the floor and see what was clogging it up. Dan found a ham hock bone wedged in the toilet. When he tried to remove the ham hock bone, the toilet cracked and broke due to the ham hock bone wedged in the porcelain toilet fixture.

The tenant then told Dan she had dumped her bean soup in the toilet. Holy Cow, Batman! Absolutely tenant chargeable—all three work orders, labor, and a new toilet and parts. Total to charge this tenant was $475. She did not have $475 to pay right now. You must understand this, too. It is up to you to create a Win-Win situation for you and your tenant.

Here is how I made this tenant caused repair a Win-Win situation. We put the tenant on a payment plan and financed the $475 owed by the tenant. I set up monthly payments of $100 for SIX months because we were financing it for her. Or you could set her up on $50 monthly payments for... let's say 12 months.

She was happy and thrilled with her very affordable payment plan program.

Work Orders, Repair and Maintenance Requests are a golden opportunity for your service people to be your eyes and ears because they are basically doing an inspection for you on the exterior of your rental and the interior as well if the item in need of repair is inside their home.

Always follow up with a simple survey, an online fill-in-the-blank form asking:

- Was the work done in a professional, timely manner?
- Have your repairs been completed properly?
- Add any other comments.

Of course, this gets auto-emailed to you. This is also a great, powerful tool giving feedback to you and your service staff. Implement this properly, and it quietly causes your service people to do a good job because they know you are sending a follow-up survey. Share these follow-up surveys with your service technicians.

In my business, I encourage all of my staff to get good, high-energy, exciting videos of folks telling the world why folks must rent a Vista Home. In fact, all of my staff get a $25 bonus if their video is good enough to put on our website. Tell your staff this is a promotion you are offering to them. When you get enough good videos, you can turn off this program for a while. Good Stuff.

While on this subject, think about social media stuff. Encourage all of your residents and prospects to share their 5 Star Experience with your company on Google Reviews, Yelp, Facebook, and anything else that your kids or grandkids would use to check out a business to see if it is good or bad.

Resources Needed

- Smartphone
- "Open Camera" free cell phone application

  NOTE: this camera cell phone app allows you to put a name, date, and time stamp on every photo and video if you choose.
- PDF cell phone app to add text and signatures to the PDFs

CHAPTER 15

Removing Bad Apples

Just like computers crashing, a tenant or their occupants dealing dope is simply a matter of WHEN IT WILL HAPPEN TO YOU and not if it happens. There are no boundaries in the arena of drug abuse. Although the media tries to portray it occurring primarily in low-income neighborhoods, dope is everywhere and dope dealers are part of our society at all levels. Your rental properties are not immune. I don't care if the rent is $100 a month or $15,000 a month, dope dealers are active in all areas.

This dope-dealing animal IS something that can sneak up on you. You can have the best tenant-screening program in the world; however, tenants are people. People have relationships. Some work out and some don't. Jerry Springer, Maury Povich, and many other talk shows have made fortunes capitalizing on the hidden aspects involved in relationships. Why are your tenants any different? They are not. A tenant can start off down the right path with you, have a falling out with their significant other and get swept off their feet with their new found significant other of the month.

Because your tenant has a good track record with you, you may or may not be aware that the old significant other has moved out and another has moved in. Your good tenant is responsible, has a job, handles responsibilities properly, and shows no signs of any pending or brewing problems.

The point I am trying to make here is no landlord is immune from having dirtbag dope dealers as tenants. Therefore, this is for all landlords of A, B, and C quality rental units.

Next, you get the dreaded phone call or a note from the good neighbor of your tenant in Apartment 3, who "confidentially" reports the tenant in Apartment 2 is dealing dope. If the landlord doesn't fix this problem yesterday, they will be moving out. This is contagious. If this information has made its way to you, you better believe it has saturated the entire building. You should thank this good tenant for letting you know.

This tenant lives close to the dope dealer. I am shocked at how landlords ask this good tenant for their help. Landlords repeatedly and unwittingly "drop in" on the good tenant who gave them the helpful but bad news.

NEVER ask your tenant who gives you this information to help you by putting them out front as the source of reporting the suspected illegal activity. It took a great amount of courage and loyalty to you for this good neighbor to inform you of the problem. The easier path for your tenant is to simply move away from your building.

If one tenant is reporting this to you, you better be aware that many more good tenants are fed up, scared, and ready to move at a moment's notice without any visible action on your part to correct the suspected dope dealing problem.

The Challenge

Finding something to evict a tenant suspected of permitting dope dealing is a monumental task. Dope dealers usually have cash. In most states, it takes two months or more to forcibly remove tenants from a unit WITHOUT a legal challenge. This is way too long to satisfy your good tenants... they will be gone before the bad apple gets evicted.

Let's run the numbers with a standard eviction process. First, if the bad apple is paying rent on time, you must find another reason to evict them. Assume they are on a month-to-month lease. Isn't it fair to assume two months might be average before they are 100% gone and you have possession. This means a minimum of a month of ugly and they will not pay rent if you are pursuing legal action to make them move. (There is month's rent in the balance.)

How many good apples may take action and move because they see no visible action on your part to get the bad apple out quickly. (Now, there is month number two of rent, along with two vacancies and tenant turnovers... yuk.)

The entire eviction process costs are usually in the neighborhood of a month's rent with attorney fees, court costs, sheriff department fees, and the labor costs involved with the physical "set out" or removal of their personal property from your unit.

All combined, it is fair to assume at minimum, with this traditional process, you can expect to lose three up to three months' rent along with two vacant units and a reputation in the neighborhood of "the building that has dope dealers."

Barney Fife: "Nip It in the Bud"

Take Action, the right way. After evaluating and verifying the information received from your good tenant is true, it is time for you to take action BEFORE the bad apple ruins the whole bunch.

Remember, the three months' rent. Do not forget it.

Listed here are some tips you may put in place. Each depends on your comfort zone. I have used all of these in certain situations with good results. These tips are presented in a smorgasbord fashion and you may select the best approach for each situation as you see fit. The objective is to get the bad apple out FAST while preserving the good apples.

Stuff to Do

ALWAYS RECORD ALL Communications with Problem Tenant

HIT 'EM IN THE FACE with a 2 × 4. Confront them face to face and ask them to move. This takes some skill and tact. My background is definitely helpful using this tactic. There are some do's and don'ts.

- NEVER accuse them of dope dealing, in fact, don't even mention it.
- NEVER drop in your good apples (your tenants who told you what is going on).
- Present yourself as a Problem Solver, helper, and solution for their problem.
- What is their problem, you might ask?
    - "Well, it's just not working out."
    - They may respond "How or What?"
    - Your answer again is, "It's just not working out and I want us to settle up on good terms."
- Avoid setting the stage of getting into a debate or "he said, she said" story. If you know for a fact, 100% sure, that traffic in and out of their unit has increased, then you may choose to say, "I have noticed a lot of people in and out causing disturbance to your neighbors." This is a delicate statement because it can open a can of worms and they may ask you, "When did you see this?" If you know your stuff, you can recite it back to them; but be careful using this one.
- OFFER A WIN-WIN SOLUTION for the bad apple with a comment like, "Look, it is not working out and I have an opportunity to help you allowing us to settle up on good terms. If we are both stubborn and attorneys and the courts get involved, we both lose, and the attorneys win. They try to make a mountain out of a mole hill. You find a place to move into and be out of here by next Saturday (select reasonable time) and have this place broom clean and I will pay you X dollars. (I usually gear it toward a dollar amount close to a month's rent).
- BITE YOUR LIP. Do not allow your principles to confuse you about good business sense.
- If you can pull this off successfully, YOU WIN BIG TIME across the board.
    - You have removed the problem.
    - Good tenants label you a hero.

- You SAVED two months' rent or more!
- No eviction headache or attitudes.
- Preserved the integrity of your building.

It takes special people skills and tact to use this action properly. If you have a quick temper, are hot-headed, and have no patience, you may want to avoid this face-to-face procedure. You MUST appear firm, fair, friendly, and HELPFUL to the bad apple regardless of the level of your blood boiling.

Effective Results with Police

Yes, still do the traditional "call your local police department" and in larger communities phone the narcotics unit; but let's put a different twist on getting effective assistance from law enforcement.

Many large apartment communities offer free rent or discounted rent to a police officer to live in their apartment community. This is nothing new and happens all the time. The real problem with this scenario comes from the police officer. These types are generally hungry for money, fairly new, and are not "homebodies." They work as much overtime and off-duty jobs as they can find, resulting in very little visibility in your building.

After determining "prime time" for the suspected dope dealing activity, make it a point to inconvenience yourself for a little time to contact the officer who rides the beat of your problem tenant during the hours of peak activity. For example, if you learn peak activity is Friday and Saturday night between 10 P.M. and 2 A.M. (which, by the way, is a very busy time for uniformed police) you should make arrangements to meet the officer who rides your beat DURING HIS SCHEDULED SHIFT. Ask to meet him somewhere other than your rental property. This does cause you an inconvenience, but sure demonstrates to this officer the seriousness of your concern.

NEVER tell the officer he or she has a problem at your property. Police are people, too. Many taxpayers talk down to police officers with comments such as, "You work for me; I pay your salary." This sure flips on the US AND THEM mindset and you have already lost. Believe it or not, most police officers really do want to help. If this is a motivating factor to be in this occupation, use it to get results for you.

Start your conversation with an attitude of "I need your help. I have a problem." Do more listening than talking. The more you let the police officer talk, the more they will like you and want to help. If you do all of the talking, you will feel better and they may be tuning you out. They hear this stuff all the time. Be PATIENT.

As a rule of thumb, the longer you let them talk and demonstrate their knowledge to you, the more apt they are to offer out-of-the-ordinary assistance to your problem while working their shift. Your property will get extra attention and patrol.

Do not ask them to ride by, stop by, or sit on your property. The challenge here is to get the officer to OFFER this to you as a way for him or her to help. Let it be their Big Idea to help you and you say WOW, Thank You!

Offer the police officer a way to contact you if needed. Ninety percent of the time they will not call, but offering your 24/7 availability means a boatload to the officer working the late shift and shows your level of concern about the problem. Offer your cell phone or home number confidentially.

These are some ways to get your tax dollars at work to help you solve the problem of the bad apple.

Signs

If you have a C or C minus Apartments and you are taking action to improve it to a B or B+ property, an effective and cheap tool it make some NO LOITERING, NO TRESPASSING signs and position the signs in visible locations on your building and premises. Before doing this, MAKE SURE to contact your good apples and ask for their assistance. Explain to the good apples, once the signs are in place, they, too, cannot hang out in the parking lot or porches. A short-term sacrifice on their part now can help run off the bad apples now. When peace and tranquility return to your property, no one will complain if peaceful people are loitering on their porches. David Alexander with BanditSigns.com is a great resource for all of your signs of any kind.

Hiring Off-Duty Police

Many landlords have been encouraged to hire off-duty police. Many communities have take-home cars for their officers.

Be Careful. This off-duty income opportunity for officers is greatly abused. Many schedule several off-duty jobs at the same time. For example, construction site A, Shopping Center B, and apartment community C, are all paying for an officer to patrol their property between 9 P.M. and 2 A.M. and the officer schedules all three jobs during the same hours because they are within three minutes of each other.

I am not anti-police. I am pro-police, retired myself, and I have two little brothers who are police officers. I have seen all of this first hand.

Empty Car: A Different Twist

If your town has take-home cars for officers, and if your peak activity of bad apple activity occurs after the sun goes down, contact an officer who works the day shift. Tell them you have a unique opportunity for them. Work out a deal to simply park their marked patrol car overnight right square in front of the bad apple's unit.

This can be done a whole lot more cheaply than having an officer SIT in the car. The results are usually spectacular. Who wants to go buy dope from somebody with a marked car parked at the front door? You might get an officer to sit in the car for $25–$50 an hour and you might get the car for a whole night for $50 or $100, depending on your negotiation skills.

The hidden benefit here is your good apples see immediate action on your part. The bad apple's business should immediately begin to suffer and they should get the message to move on down the road.

Technology

In addition to assistance from on-duty and off-duty law enforcement and No Loitering signs strategically placed on your buildings, technology can be a great and inexpensive tool as well.

LIGHTING I put lighting in the technology department because of big drop in pricing of LED light bulbs. They claim these bulbs will last a lifetime and are super cheap on using electricity vs. standard bulbs and flood lights.

Thugs, dopers, and bad people are like roaches. Remember walking into a dark house, turning on the lights and watch the roaches sprinting to go hide from you? Well, the same is true for these kind of people who hang out around your apartments.

LIGHT UP Your Apartment Building, Porches, Parking Lot is one of your cheapest and most effective ways to battle the hood rats. Combined with the signs and most of the time, this is enough to eliminate your bad news people.

BOTH Lighting and Signs will also give you another benefit. Your great residents will love their "property manager" for making them feel valued and important.

Next up, Video Cameras are CHEAP. Not the camcorders you see in the retail stores, I am talking about CCTV cameras. Check them out on the Internet or simply use any search engine. Entire video systems with recorders sell for less than $300. Put them up high on corners of buildings; protective weatherproof and bulletproof casings are available for them.

In addition to the No Loitering Sign, add "Premises Video Recorded 24 hours."

Yes, this takes some effort to start up, but today you can get cameras that are 100% wireless and self-powered for a year or more with long-lasting batteries.

Figure 15.1 shows the sign I put up on my buildings.

Let your local law enforcement know about your effort and action of installing cameras. Your good apples will see your action. It will hurt the bad apple business but it will also be your powerful tool to prevent new bad apples from landing in your units.

Here in Louisville, a creative take-charge investor has a number of units in a high-crime area. After learning of a similar situation in a visit to Chicago, he became involved with the local cable TV company, receiving not only permission to use their cable to be the conduit for transmitting the video images to the recorders placed in

FIGURE 15.1 Trespassing Notice

the office, but the cable company also installed the video cameras on the utility poles. With the new technology I do not understand, police officers can use their laptops in their car to dial up specific cameras to view. The point learned here is you may not have to burden all of the expense yourself. Maybe your cable TV company, phone company or other utility may agree to contribute resources to "help the community."

Resources Needed

- LED Light Bulbs
- Smartphone app "ACR" All Call Recordings
- Smartphone "Voice Recorder" app for face-to-face conversations
- Email
- Text
- BanditSigns.com for signs to mount to building

CHAPTER 16

Mike's Move-Out System Makes You Money

Imagine this.... Your resident has given you notice they will be moving. First, find out why they are moving. Job relocation, divorce, downsizing, upsizing, etc. If these are great tenants, do your darned-est to move them into one of your rentals to keep your great tenant in your rental portfolio. If you can not accommodate them, your next step is pull the trigger on using your Move Out Package and System. You send them the Move-Out Package by email and text. It includes four pages in PDF format.

Page 1: Notice of Receipt to Vacate. This page acknowledges your company has received their notice of their intent to vacate the premises AND it gives them a short synopsis of what to expect. They are very concerned about getting their Security Deposit refunded to them and this is addressed in page 1.

Also, you give them the opportunity to earn some huge bucks (referral fee) for cooperating with you in finding your next great resident.

Page 2: Move Out Instructions

Page 3: Price List for the most frequently charged items resulting from the Move Out Inspection.

Page 4: A simple four-question survey.

Use this system properly, your moving out resident will make your rental "rent ready" while they are paying you rent! Sounds crazy, doesn't it? But it works. This is amazing and will slash your turnover costs. I can't tell you how many times our residents who are moving out have the place immaculate and a lot more than just "broom clean." In fact, many times, all we have to do is change the door locks. We don't even have to cut or trim the grass.

Here are some Move-Out Inspection Photos from a nine-year resident:

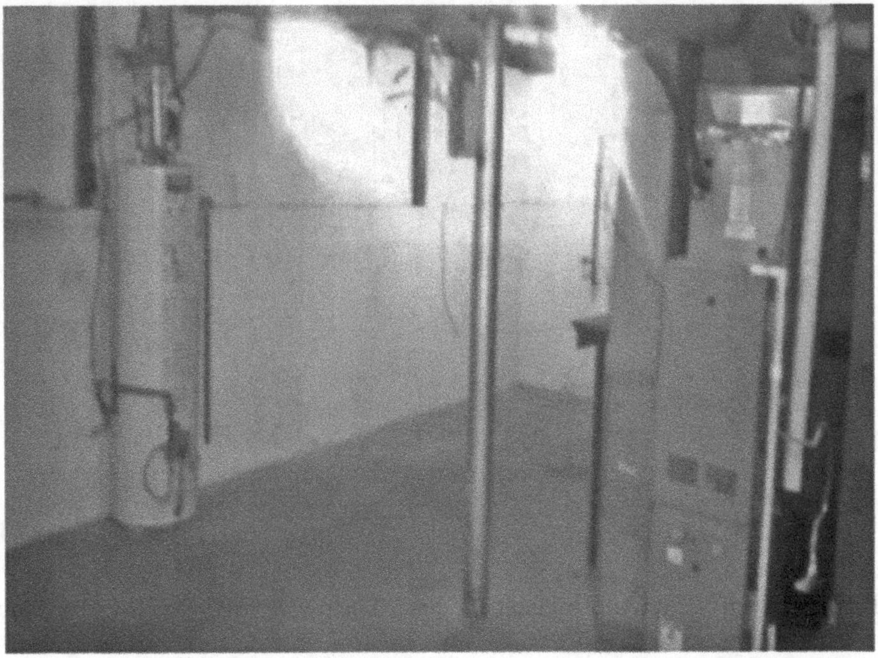

Turnovers are by far, your biggest expense. The fewer you have, the more money you will make.

Once I figured out how to use this system properly, it is working like a champ. Even folks getting evicted are sent Mike's Move-Out Package and almost all of our evictions end up being "broom clean" with very little to do to make it Rent Ready again.

As an aggressive investor, landlord, and property manager, I watched my real estate very intensely like a sharp business owner.

I began studying the BIG PICTURE. Where was I making money? Where was I losing money? How could I increase cash flow and profits? How could I reduce expenses?

It didn't take me long to discover Tenant Turnovers and the Move-Out Process was cleaning my clock. In fact, just like you, I'd been shocked at how some of my great tenants crapped on me when returning possession back to us. It was mind boggling. Why and how was this happening?

Well, it causes me to remember when I, too, was a tenant. My first apartment was just a few blocks north of Churchill Downs. This is not a good neighborhood, but I didn't know this when I was 18. This first apartment was originally a three-bedroom shotgun style house. The landlord chopped it up into 1 bedroom junky apartments and he would pay the utility bills. He owned the house next door and did the same thing. He was so tight, he used one 30-gallon hot water heater for both houses. That's right—one water heater for all six apartments! My first exposure to tightwad, slumlord landlording.

I rented this junky trap for $30 per week, including utilities, while I worked part-time at Winn-Dixie stocking shelves at night. My furniture consisted of milk crates, bricks, and boards, along with the little black-and-white TV. When I became full-time, I got my butt out of there fast. I was moving on up to a nice apartment with curtains on the windows.

I can remember being so excited to get out of that apartment, that my energy and focus was to get out of there as quick as I can and GIVE HIM THE KEY so he could get it ready to rent again. This is what our tenants do to us. They simply don't know any better. We are the investor and we assume they should know what to do. Have you ever given them instructions?

Because I was getting my clock cleaned with tenant turnovers, I created and developed a system to nip this nightmare in the bud, too. The result is my Move Out Package. It's a four-page package mailed to your tenant upon receiving notice that they wish to move. You should also use it on your tenants getting evicted because they're moving, too!

Do Not Balk at the Idea of a Referral Fee

Do you want to get the property rented quickly and have your Tenant contribute their efforts to accomplishing your objective? A referral fee is an easy price to pay.

After you complete the move out inspection using YOUR Move Out Inspection Form, use the included **Summary Report** and **Office Checklist** to cover bases properly. These are simple and they work great!

As a last resort, included is a **Return Possession without Inspection Form** to use when a Tenant wishes to return possession on the spot. If you have an office, use this form if they stop by the office unexpectedly to turn in or drop off their keys. Without an office, simply put this form on your website (keep it as a hidden page) and simply text the link to them when this happens.

Although you have good planning and organizational skills, there are always exceptions to every rule. You will still receive a phone call from a tenant informing you they have already moved out or the Tenant with an eviction pending with no hope. The eviction pending Tenant may contact you to report they are out or you may encourage them to move out a little sooner. When these situations arise, use this last form to properly document that they have returned possession to you.

Tip

- SEND MOVE-OUT PACKAGES upon receiving notice **and again seven days prior to the Move out date**
- SEND TO YOUR TENANTS WITH AN EVICTION PENDING—they are going to move, too!!

Tenants with evictions have followed the move out instructions!
Good Luck, Mike Butler

This Is Page 1
From: ____

RECEIPT OF NOTICE TO VACATE

TO: ________________ **DATE:** ________________
____
____
____
____
____

RE: Tenancy at: ______________________________

This letter is confirmation that we received notice of your intent to vacate the home you are now renting at: ______________________ **before** ______________, **20**______________.

SECURITY DEPOSIT: In order to prevent any misunderstanding regarding your refund, move out instructions and procedures are enclosed.

MOVE OUT INSPECTION: Please go online to our website to contact our office at least ***three to five days in advance*** of the exact date and time you will be completely moved out in order to schedule your Move Out Inspection.

UTILITIES: Please make arrangements to transfer the billing of utilities to the first business day *after* your Move Out Inspection has occurred.

You Can Earn Cash to Help with Your Moving Expenses! It is very important to keep your home looking its best as prospective Tenants may be riding by your home. There will be NO Open House showings. If someone knocks on your door, Do NOT allow them in your home. Only a Preapproved Applicant, with your permission and coordinated appointment may be invited to see the inside of your home before you move out. If this pre-approved applicant decides to rent your home, you will EARN some big bucks for your help. Help us find a great resident like yourself to earn your referral fee. Be sure to tell friends at work, church, and any clubs or associations. We may also place a Yard Sign to help you earn the referral fee.

IMPORTANT: *We will NOT send people by to see the inside of your home*. We will inform prospective Tenants that your home is scheduled to be available by the date you have listed above. We inform people of the address to allow them to ride by. Again, we will NOT send people over to knock on your door and see the inside of your home without your permission.

THANKS & GOOD LUCK WITH YOUR MOVE!

Property Manager

I know things are getting ready to get busy; but, if you get a chance, could you please fill out the enclosed survey and return it promptly, as we value your comments and suggestions. Attached you will find your Move Out Instructions, Price List, and your Survey.

Resources Needed

Now you can do all of this 100% paperless:

- Print to PDF all of the forms of Mike's Move-Out System
- Email and text the four-page Move-Out Package to the resident who is moving

SECTION IV

MASTER THESE TO MAXIMIZE YOUR INCOME AND PROFITS

CHAPTER 17

MARKETING Makes It Happen, Not Advertising

Operating a successful rental property business requires effective Marketing. You can do this very cheap, even close to a zero-dollar budget for advertising.

Here's my TOP four marketing must-haves for your rental business:

1. **REFERRALS**—These are by far, your number 1 source of effective marketing. Let your tenants, your sellers, your buyers, your real estate agents, your attorneys know you rent homes (and buy houses). Offer to pay them a referral fee, if legal in your state, if a referral becomes a tenant or a deal.
2. **BUSINESS CARDS**—get 1,000 thick, double-sided color, glossy finished for $25 with free shipping at ZooPrinting.com.
3. **WEBSITE**—get one like mine + all kinds of free investor training—$49 month
4. **YARD SIGNS**—corrugated plastic 24″ × 18″, $10 each (buy 100 approximately $3 each, one-zee two-zee are about $10 each)

Marketing is your BIG, powerful word here. Simply put, it is everything you do to promote your business and generate leads. This does not mean you have to spend money.

Advertising on the other hand usually involves paying for a product or service.

Referrals

Use your cell phone and capture videos and photos of super-excited and satisfied customers, residents, sellers, buyers, and so forth. You can put them on your FREE YouTube.com channel within your Google Gmail Account.

Referrals are old school and new school and work in any town and in any market.

Before we jump into the marketing with today's market and technology, let me give some proven, simple, and almost free things you can do to promote your business.

OLD SCHOOL Proven and simple, homemade yard signs, even the generic ones from Home Depot and Lowe's. Second is your tried and true homemade, created by you scribbling with a big Sharpie or flyers or brochures you make on your home computer. Use the flyers to promote your vacancies and just flood your neighborhood grocery, laundry, car washes, and more.

SOCIAL MEDIA I am NOT an expert on this stuff. I still frequently call Facebook Book-Face and YouTube Tube-You, Twitter, Instagram, LinkedIn, and Snapchat. But this much I do know. SOCIAL MEDIA is HUGE and it is FREE!

When you see on every TV channel, radio station, newspaper ads, restaurants, retail stores, EVERYWHERE You Turn, we are bombarded with all of the social media icons to "follow us" on this social media or that social media. My daughters are experts on this stuff, but I truly have a long way to go before I really get it and that's fine with me. (I will probably end up hiring a person to do only social media stuff for me sometime down the road.)

Many investors have a Facebook thing for their real estate business and treat it like a website. Yes, it is free, but I have not figured out how it will replace a truly effective, interactive website for your business. As far as I know, you cannot put fill-in-the-blank forms on your Facebook page.

In the arena of Social Media, ask your kids, grandkids, or great-grandkids to do it for you or teach you. I am not your go-to guy on this one. The one thing I can tell you is that works to get as much of your good company stuff on the Internet as you can, and keep doing it on a regular basis.

Business Cards

Almost always, your first marketing piece you will buy. You can get 1,000 of these high-quality, thick, glossy, two-sided color, with free shipping for only $25 at ZooPrinting.com. Many folks also use VistaPrint.com.

What is the purpose of your business card? No, it's not about letting them know how to contact you. The Purpose of business cards is to be a "Lead Generator" for your business.

You have about 2.5 seconds to grab the attention of anyone who sees your business card.

Here's what they say when they see your business card: "What's In It For Me?" If your business card does not loudly SCREAM a benefit to the person looking at your card, you lose.

You MUST be unique, creative, and craft a simple, short slogan explaining the benefits for your target audience—motivated sellers if you are buying, prospective tenants, and more.

You must have a "call to action." Tell them what to do—simple and straightforward. This could be a free report, free video, audio, and so forth.

Shown next are some examples of my business cards that I tried to make them SCREAM the benefits for the person reading them. The older ones are far from perfect. I really like my business card for my education and mentoring business.

In today's world, here's what to include on your business cards.

1. First and Foremost is Your Company Slogan
   a. Put some serious thought into this. Don't just do a quick, knee-jerk slogan. Run it by your family members, friends, and folks you trust. Does it Loudly SCREAM Exactly What Your Business Does?
      i. Mike's Real Estate Business Slogan
         "We Buy Houses, We Rent Homes!"
      ii. "Buy, Sell, Rent, Trade!"
      iii. "Best Realtor in Mayberry!"
2. Use simple, easy-to-read fonts, like
   a. Arial
   b. Trebuchet
   c. even Comic Sans
   d. Do Not Use artsy fartsy fonts; these are very hard to read.
      Blackadder
      Brush Scripts
      Edwardian
   e. Do Not try to have a funeral home wallpaper background with very light-colored fonts as shown below.

(Created by Mike Butler as an example)

3. Check these out and ask yourself, "What's In It For Me?"

Notice the QR code, open the QR Code Reader app on your Smartphone and scan the QR code with your phone (it's the small, postage-stamp size image of weird lines). Now imagine a prospective tenant holding your business card. They will know exactly how to scan this QR code. Do a little test right now and check it out for yourself.

The preceding cards are effective and they work. Jiru is my in-house leasing agent.

Then there is the business card I use today for my education and consulting business.

After this book is published, you'll see the second-edition book photo on the back side of my business card.

PEEL 'N STICK Business Card Magnets You can buy these in packs of 10 or 25 at Office Depot, Staples, and Amazon. It's 10 times cheaper and a more effective than buying custom made magnets.

You can put one in your "New Tenant Welcome Package" and slap one on every fridge you come across in your day-to-day activities, especially of those folks who want you to buy their house.

Website

You MUST have an effective, INTERACTIVE website in today's market. NO EXCEPTIONS, NO EXCUSES. There's no need to have 25 separate websites, as many experts try to persuade you to have—one for buyers, one for sellers, one for tenants, one for private lenders and so on. You can do it all on one good, properly structured website *(You can get America's Best Website for real estate investors—Trevor Mauch's Investor Carrot website—for free when you join our Gold Membership at* www.MikeButler.com/join*)*

Interactive means folks who visit your website can do stuff versus just looking at your business card or billboard in the cloud somewhere. Things to have on your website to make your life easier:

- Make them pay your application fee BEFORE they get to your online, fill-in-the-blank rental application—(when they hit the SUBMIT button, it is auto-emailed to You)
- A clean, simple, home page that is easy for your website visitors to navigate. Take a look at the home page of Google.com and you will exactly what I am talking about.
- On my home page is a summarized list of available homes for rent. You can check it out at VistaKY.com. Here's a snapshot of my home page.
- Check out the navigation bar showing a page for Residents and Buy My House.

Do You Print Flyers for Your Available Homes List? Simply print this home page and it is already set up as a flyer for you. It lists all of your available homes and if they want more details and photos, they simply scan the QR code already contained in your home page.

Take Good Quality Photos This is one the hardest challenges for many real estate investors, property managers, and Realtors. Most have a very hard time taking good photos. The biggest blunder happens on taking photos of the front of the house. They stand in front of the house and take a photo of the "front wall" of the house. This is wrong. Here's a page from my "How to Take Photos Guide." Using a typical house in a subdivision, you should stand at each corner of the property line and take a photo. In my police world, we called this "4 Corners" and this phrase is also used involving documents when trying to use them as ammo or proof when you step into the world of legal stuff and the courthouse. This is an excerpt from my simple 18-page guide on how to take photos/videos.

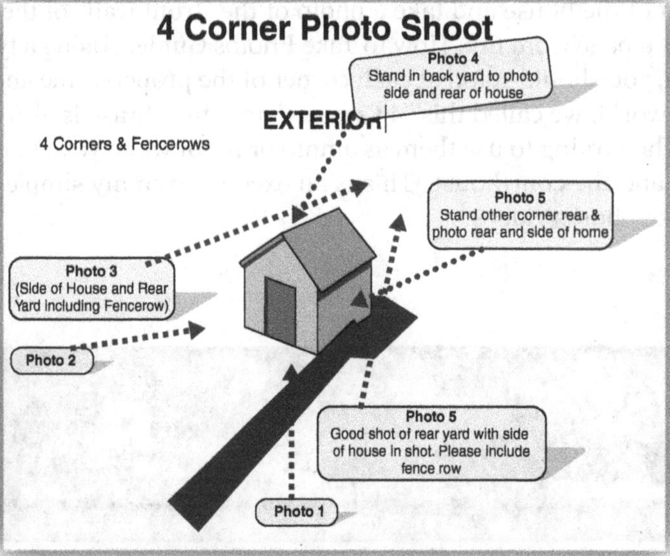

Shown here is part of the one-page, 159-point Rent-Ready Checklist showing the simple, short cheat sheet on how to take photos and videos.

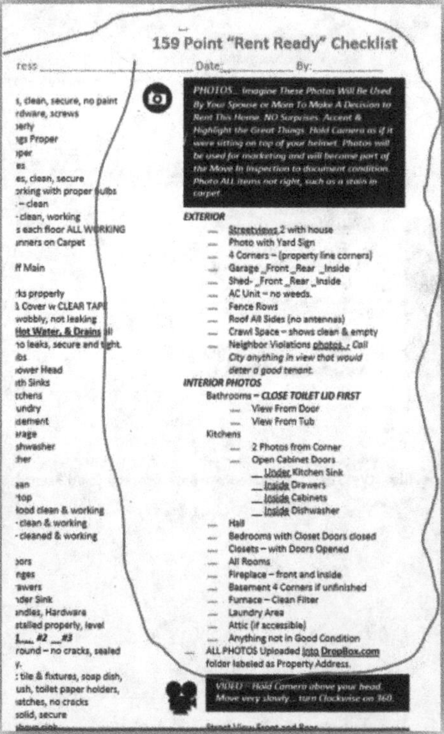

159 Point "Rent Ready" Checklist

Date:__________ By:__________

PHOTOS... Imagine These Photos Will Be Used By Your Spouse or Mom To Make A Decision to Rent This Home. NO Surprises. Accent & Highlight the Great Things. Hold Camera as if it were sitting on top of your helmet. Photos will be used for marketing and will become part of the Move In Inspection to document condition. Photo ALL items not right, such as a stain in carpet.

EXTERIOR

- Streetviews 2 with house
- Photo with Yard Sign
- 4 Corners – (property line corners)
- Garage _Front _Rear _Inside
- Shed- _Front _Rear _Inside
- AC Unit – no weeds.
- Fence Rows
- Roof All Sides (no antennas)
- Crawl Space – shows clean & empty
- Neighbor Violations photos.; *Call City anything in view that would deter a good tenant.*

INTERIOR PHOTOS

Bathrooms – *CLOSE TOILET LID FIRST*

- View From Door
- View From Tub

Kitchens

- 2 Photos from Corner
- Open Cabinet Doors
  - __ Under Kitchen Sink
  - __ Inside Drawers
  - __ Inside Cabinets
  - __ Inside Dishwasher
- Hall
- Bedrooms with Closet Doors closed
- Closets – with Doors Opened
- All Rooms
- Fireplace – front and inside
- Basement 4 Corners if unfinished
- Furnace – Clean Filter
- Laundry Area
- Attic (if accessible)
- Anything not in Good Condition
- ALL PHOTOS Uploaded into DropBox.com folder labeled as Property Address.

VIDEO – Hold Camera above your head. Move very slowly... turn Clockwise on 360.

Take a look at these two photos to drive this point home.

Next up is making your photos "web ready," which basically means the resolution setting on your cell phone photo app for pixels/resolution should be 640 × 480. Most cell phones do not have a resolution setting this low. "Open Camera" is the smartphone app that allows you to use this "low res" setting.

This works great for putting your photos on websites, emails, flyers, and your move in inspection photos. Do NOT allow your phone to use the default resolution settings of gazillion billion pixels. This causes the file size of your photo to be humongous and it takes up a lot of space on your phone and website. Most of the time, you can't upload large photos like this because of its size. To make this simple and easy for you, everyone in my company uses a cell phone app called "Open Camera." You can find it on Google Play and the icon looks like this. Remember to TURN ON the Date and Time Stamp feature inside this cell phone app.

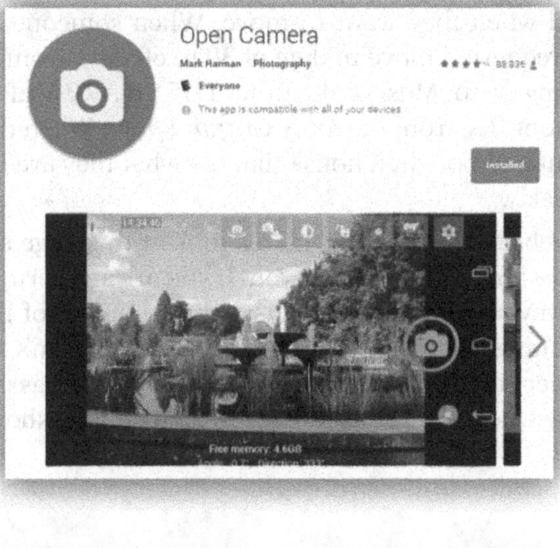

Always use the "159-point Rent-Ready checklist" (a simple one-page checklist), which contains a short cheat sheet on what to take photos of and how to take photos and videos. Make sure your unit is clean and bright. No tools, ladders, or other stuff in background. Make sure the toilet lid is closed. Turn on all the lights you can before taking photos. Try this on for size. Also open the kitchen cabinet doors, especially the ones under the kitchen sink and take photos under the sink, showing it is pretty bright and clean. The same applies to bathroom vanities. (You will be killing three birds with one rock. Photos for your website, photos for Move In Inspection, and accurately documents condition of your property)

Let's pretend your Mom lives in Mongolia and she wants to move back home to be closer to you. She has asked for your help in finding her a home to rent and your Mom will be making her decision based on your photos. Now take your photos with this mindset—you will take several photos from several angles of the kitchen and bathroom. Plenty of photos of bedrooms, hallways, laundry area, basement, garage, and several photos of the exterior of the home from many different angles. If you do it the right way, when you carefully take these photos, you can use them on your website and you can use them to document the condition of your rental when attached to your move in inspection form.

Include a Google Interactive Map Doing this allows your website visitors to zoom in and out on the map, enlarge the view, add satellite imagery allowing a view from a bird's eye in the sky, and now you can even drive down the street! Incredible, and it's all free.

List of Available Homes Include a summary list of available homes on your home page, including links to get all of the details, amenities, and more detailed photos and videos. Always include several links and images with links to Apply Online Now.

Can't Find What You're Looking For? Has been set up as a property on my website and, believe it or not, we get more paid applications for this than probably all of the others combined. It is unbelievable. There is also a "Call Back Form" where the prospective tenant(s) complete a short, simple, fill-in-the-blank form telling us what they want and when they want to move. When someone submits this "Call Back Form" with a requested move in date of 30 to 60 days from now, these are the ones you want to hang on to. Most of the time, THESE ARE VERY RESPONSIBLE PEOPLE, just like Aunt Bee from the *Andy Griffith Show*. When this happens, many times I have gone out and bought a house that fits what they are looking for. Stay in touch with them weekly.

FAQ Page Most websites have them. Take a look at this page on my website and you will see how it is a huge timesaver for you. If you are answering your phone from all folks interested in your vacant rental, just think about all of the same questions they ask and your almost-canned, "sound like Charlie Brown's teacher" response. This is brutal. Put every question you can imagine they might ask on this page. Your Benefit is huge. Now when and if they ever call, it's a simple, short question or they want to make arrangements to see the inside of your rental. You can also add audio clips and photos to this webpage. AudioPal.com is a great free tool to add audio.

Showing Vacant Units We do NOT show homes in my business and you should do the same. First up, let me show you how we do it; then I will share how to do it if you do not have an office.

I do it this way. The prospective applicant has to travel to our office and fills out a one-page Key Sign Out Form. Then we make a copy of their valid photo ID and they give us a $20 key deposit. This is POWERFUL, Folks! Why? Because this is the first step in prescreening and prequalifying a prospective tenant.

Here's how you can do it if you do not have an office, even if you are out of town. Your prospect sees your yard sign or visits your free Investor OnCarrot website. Odds are they will call you while in front of your vacant rental. Tell them to go to your website and click the button "To View a Home," which takes them to the very short and simple fill-in-the-blank form, which is basically the same thing as my Key Sign Out Form. Your prospect completes the form and uploads a clear, crisp, readable photo of their valid photo ID or Driver's License and a "selfie photo" standing in front of your rental unit. This photo must match their valid photo ID and you must be able to see your vacant rental in the background. This completed form is auto-emailed to you. If everything appears legit, you can give them the access code to view the inside of your rental unit. There are several ways you can make this happen.

Here's how this is so powerful for you. For starters, even if this home is on the other side of town, these folks are so serious, they will travel to your office by car, bus, or even uber. This is not some bozo calling you while sitting in front of your rental demanding you to drop everything right now and come down and let us in to see the inside of your house. Please don't beat yourself up if this sounds familiar. I did it too and as we both know, many times they folks have disappeared when you arrive. This is not fun. We'll talk about this more in processing rental applications.

Other Things to Include in Your Website

Google Translate Although not perfect, it will get you, your residents, your prospects over the hump if they have a hard time speaking English. Google allows you to put this in a lot of places and it is free. For your website, it will be a WordPress PlugIn.

Forms Already built into your free Investor OnCarrot is a tool allowing you to create your own forms that are auto-mailed to folks you choose. Here's some of the forms already built in to your free website.

- Online Rental Application Form
- Contact Us Form

- Resident Only Page with Repair Request Form
- Buy My House Form
- Build Your Buyers' List Form

Other Forms you can add, or have my office set up for you.

- Job Opportunities Form—great free tool to find good handymen and skilled tradesmen.
- Independent Contractor Agreement Form
- Animal Application Form
- And any other form you can imagine or want to put on your website

Text Messaging This form of communication is all over the place today. I have incorporated this into many pages in our website. It reduces phone calls and is great documentation.

Google Voice This is a MUST for your business. You must be a Google User to make this free tool work for you. You must have Gmail to make this work best. Go online to www.Google.com/voice to get your very own free 2nd phone number. Here's what it can do for you.

- You get to select your phone number. Try to get one in your area code so it looks like a local number.
- Use your Google Voice phone number as your Office phone number.
- Set up your Google Voice number to autoforward all calls to your cell phone.
- Set it up so you use Google's Voice Mail feature and not the one from your paid cell phone provider.
- When you can't answer your phone, the caller will be able to leave you a voice message just like any other voice mail services.
- Google Voice can transcribe their voice mail message into text and their voice mail can be transcribed into text be autoforwarded to your Gmail account. It can also be text messaged to your cell phone with a link to listen to the voice mail as well!
- Get this—just like when you open your Gmail account and see a list of all of your emails, Google Voice does the same thing. Log in to your Google Voice account and you will see a list of all of your voice messages, just like your Gmail account. You will see date/time stamps, the transcribed message and a link to play the voice mail. On top of that, you can text a replay, add notes, or call them on their phone. POWERFUL.
- Think about this: NEVER again will scribble your chicken scratch on a piece of paper, nor will you listen to all of your voice mails. PLUS, now you have a

date/time stamp and the original voice mail mp3 audio file. If this is from one of your residents, simply download the mp3 audio file and attach it to your tenant's account in your Tenant Tracking company file!

- As an added secret tool, create a few new Gmail accounts that are automatically forwarded to your real Gmail account. When I discovered Google Voice a number of years ago, I immediately created 30 new Gmail accounts and I set up a unique Google Voice number for each of these new Gmail accounts.
- Imagine this:
    - A number used for personal stuff with a greeting you set up
    - A number for a particular vacant rental property—you get to record your greeting with all of the details you want your caller to know about.
    - Perhaps another number for anything else you are involved in.

I have not listened to any voice mails for over 10 years now. Here's a snapshot of my Google Voice account.

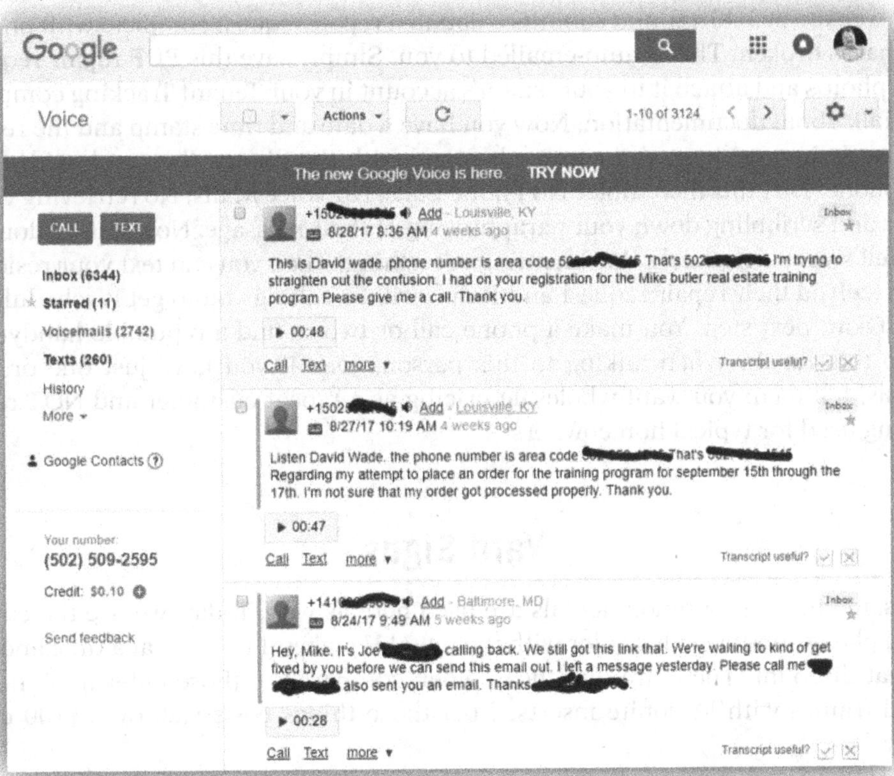

I try to incorporate absolutely everything I can imagine into our website in my continuing efforts to be paperless and to make everything in my business a lot more efficient. All of my staff, Maintenance Supervisor and all of his service technicians do everything on their smartphones or tablets. This includes Work Orders, Repairs, Move-In Inspection photos, Move-Out Inspections and photos, recording videos of happy and excited residents, taking photos of invoices, receipts, quotes, and more. I require every vendor, contractor, and small business that wants to do any work with our company to complete an Independent Contractor Agreement before they are awarded a job or get a check when completed. This is after you have done your homework checking references and more. This online form is hidden within our website. The vendor completes this form using their smartphone and allows them to take a photo of their valid photo ID and upload it with this form. Absolutely awesome, isn't it? No more paper forms and all of these completed online forms are auto-emailed to you. You simply attach the PDF to their vendor file in your Investor Books Pro company file. The goal is 100% paperless and we are well on our way and almost there! You can do this too!

Let me give you an example of how this can help you and your business. Okay, so let's say you don't have a bricks and mortar office, nor do you have any staff.

Suppose you have two rental houses and one of your residents goes online to your website at 3:40 A.M. and submits a detailed repair request complete with photos of what is broken. This is auto-emailed to you. Simply save this PDF repair request with photos and attach it to your tenant's account in your Tenant Tracking company file. Talk about documentation! Now you have a date and time stamp and the repair request is in your tenant's own words along with the photos they took with their cell phone. Isn't this incredible? No Phone Calls; No Voice Mails; No retrieving voice mails and scribbling down your paraphrasing of their message. Now it is all done in one fell swoop accurately, documenting everything! Then you can text your resident you received their repair request and Ralph will be calling you to get it scheduled.

Okay, next step. You make a phone call or two to find a reputable handyman to do this repair. When talking to this person, even if you have just one or two rentals, tell them you want wholesale pricing as a repeat customer and NOT retail pricing used for typical homeowners.

Yard Signs

The same marketing fundamentals are used here as well. Today, we use the corrugated plastic, double-sided color with the metal H stakes. I buy 100 at a time and get a great discount. These are dirt-cheap when compared to those old-school, heavy metal frames with Masonite inserts. I bet those things costs well over $100 each today.

If the sign disappears because a prospective tenant wants to keep others from knowing about it, they will take it, trash it or destroy it. That's okay and it really happens. Best of all, most of the time, I get to use these signs many times over and over. Perhaps three, four, five, or more times.

I view these 24″ × 18″ plastic signs as disposable. You can place more than one sign in the front yard to catch more attention. Maybe even three signs in a row. You have seen large apartment communities place multiple yard signs in a row next to the roadway. Some of these signs I have seen are "Two- and Three-Bedroom Available Now," "FREE Cable TV," "Swimming Pool," "FREE Clubhouse," "Fitness Gym!" and more. If they are in a tight market or have too many vacancies, you can expect to see "First Month FREE!" as well.

Here's the yard sign I use today:

In keeping with the marketing fundamentals, this Yard Sign loudly screams FOR RENT, and it also lets folks know we have homes for sale, option to buy and rent to own, and We Buy Houses!

Just as important is to give folks several ways to get more information on this home. They can get more information this way:

- Go to website www.VistaKY.com
- Scan the QR Code. Try it yourself and see it work.
- And finally, our office phone number.

KEY TAGS Another great, cheap way to market your real estate business. I use they key tags any way imaginable. New tenants get their two keys on these key tags and folks signing out keys get the key on these key tags. ALWAYS include your slogan and website on these key tags. Hopefully, as you can see, these are very nice, bright yellow plastic with blue reflective foil embedded into the plastic. Avoid key tags with the text printed on the plastic because the text will wear off. You'll end up with a blank bright yellow key tag.

INK PENS Everybody and their brother seem to be doing these. I have never been able to figure out how to track the ROI (return on investment) for investing in custom ink pens. Yes, you can get them dirt cheap, but not free.

BALL CAPS These work great in my business if you use them the right way. Here's what I learned the hard way. You want these ball caps to be seen, right? Here's your secret to make these work to get the biggest bang for your buck. You MUST only give out ball caps to people who wear ball caps every day! People send me ball caps all the time and I just have them stacked up in a corner in my closet. I never wear ball caps and these folks are wasting their money on me.

SHIRTS These are awesome and work if you have the right message and contact info on them. My maintenance guys get ash-colored T-shirts in the summer and black T-shirts in the winter. My office staff and supervisors get Golf shirts or Polo Shirts with a collar to look more professional. This will help big time in branding your business in your town. John Byron does a great job and many investors have told me about QueensBoro.com, although I have not used them yet.

CALENDARS, Peel 'n Stick These cheap peel 'n stick calendars were placed in almost every Louisville Police cars and almost every Yellow Cab in my town. It is also included in our "New Resident Welcome Package" inside of their coffee cup, along with a Zip-It Tool to clean out drains, and a good, old-fashioned plunger. Attorneys and real estate agents got them too. These are super cheap and effective ads to keep under their nose all year long.

DOOR HANGERS Create your own and use these in addition to your business cards.

Keep these in your car, truck, and pass out to bird dogs and your maintenance crew. Use them in your property management business too. Missed Work Order Appointments, nastygram notes to tenants to do this or that, or EVEN a positive mention for a good job on their flower boxes, and so forth.

Door Hanger cards are precut with a loop at the top to fasten to the door. They are cheap and sure work more efficiently than trying to tape or slide a business card into a storm door.

I buy a thousand at a time and they cost a few pennies apiece.

If you don't want to buy that many at a time, contact our good, ole friend John Byron. Boy, old John is getting a ton of recommendations and attaboys!

Please remember, I do not get a plugged nickel for recommending John. Simply put, he offers good service and great products at great prices.

COFFEE CUPS and MUGS These are great to put in welcome packages and more, and they definitely help with establishing and promoting the "branding" of your company in your town. Order a few at time. No need to go hog wild and buy hundreds. As expected, get the cheapest, white, ceramic coffee cups. Don't get sold on the bronze turbo-charged, glow-in-the-dark cups. The cheapest white coffee cups with black text on BOTH sides are most effective.

Plus, in today's world, I am thrilled to see young adults and teenagers Drinking Coffee instead of booze. Only if you are in a position to spend a few extra bucks, you might want to give this one a shot.

I have a good relationship with my closing attorney, Harry Borders, and I consistently refer folks to do their closings at his law firm. He has them on every closing table in their office to have a dozen or so of their Law Firm ink pens in each coffee cup. Awesome. Imagine your Seller's perception of your real estate business when your coffee mug is sitting on the closing table at your city's number 1 closing attorney. Also give them to your vendors at the holiday party, to new tenants, renewing tenants, and more. It seems coffee cups last a long time. In fact, I still use the same coffee cup my bank gave me back in 1988. That bank was called Cumberland and today you might know it as Fifth Third Bank. Here's an example of my mugs.

BUS BENCHES Do it the cheapest way. On Your Own! Use the concrete ends where you slide 2 × 4s or 2 × 6s and using a weather-proven material (marine plywood, for example) have simple, professional signs created that you can attach to the back wooden boards. Where you place these bus bench signs is critical. Remember, there are companies out there that sell bus bench sign space. Make sure you place your bus benches with your sign at a location that will be appreciated by bus riders. They can last for a decade. This greatly reduces the risk of someone reporting your bench to the bus bench police in your town. This is a great marketing tool when used properly because all of the traffic driving down the road will see your bus bench sign "We Buy Houses!" AND the folks who are riding the bus will see "We Rent Homes!" To get the best results, position your bus bench so your sign is angled to face oncoming traffic. Do Not place it parallel to the roadway because the only folks who can see it at that angle will be folks who happen to stop their car right in front of your sign. Look at highway billboards. Are they parallel to the roadway so you cannot see them until you stop in front of them? NO, they are placed perpendicular to the roadway so you can see the billboard from far away as you are approaching the sign.

BILLBOARDS Yes, the huge, old billboards you see along the highways. Only for the high-dollar budget investors. My experience is these cost almost $10,000 a month per sign. Needless to say, this guy has never used billboards. Why Not? Because everything else I was doing was giving more leads than I could handle.

TV COMMERCIALS I have tried TV commercials, cheap TV commercials that did not run on the major networks, but those placed on the "B" and "C" TV channels. Channels like MeTV, TV Land, and the same channels where you see your local pawnshops buying time. This helps big time, but I never committed to more than one month at a time. Interestingly enough, I ran our TV commercial just a couple of times. As far as "branding" goes, it gave me results for years because many of our leads that came in were asked, "How did you find us?" They replied, "From your TV commercial. My TV commercial was a short 30-second blurb, where a good, happy, excited speaking voice simple read this page out loud. There was NO Video. This kept it super cheap. You MUST use OUTRAGEOUS Background color to grab the viewers' attention and light up their room if it is dark.

HOLIDAY RENT COUPON What is your worst month as far as getting all of your rents paid on time? Think about it again. It's not November or December. Your answer is January. Christmas happens for the month of December. Most tenants overspend and then January 1st sneaks up on them. It's hard to understand how it sneaks up on them when it happens every year. But it does. It's one of those things in their "Bubble."

Our challenge is to figure out a way to get your rent payment not put into their "A" stack of bills to get paid, but also to make sure it is the first bill to get paid in their "A" stack of bills. I discovered this years ago.

Using my Tenant Tracking system, every month we prepare a bill for next month's rent and snail mail and email it to every tenant on the 20th of each month. This serves as a 10-day reminder that rent is due in the next few days. It works great.

Now, let's jump to December. Therefore, on December 20th, you fire out your regular monthly statement. Hmm, this is five days before Christmas and it gives you a great opportunity to spread some of your holiday cheer. You get to "Cherry Pick" who gets one of your very precious and valuable "Holiday $10 Rent Coupons." These are already made up with three to a page. All we do is change the year on the coupon and print them again for this year.

Simply place on of your Holiday Rent Coupons in each statement you mail to your tenants and attach it to their email statement when sending emails.

The front side loudly announces this is their $10 Holiday Rent Coupon. To redeem it, January's rent must be paid on or before January 1st and it is void with a late payment. On the back side are fill-in-the-blanks to update their contact information Enjoy!

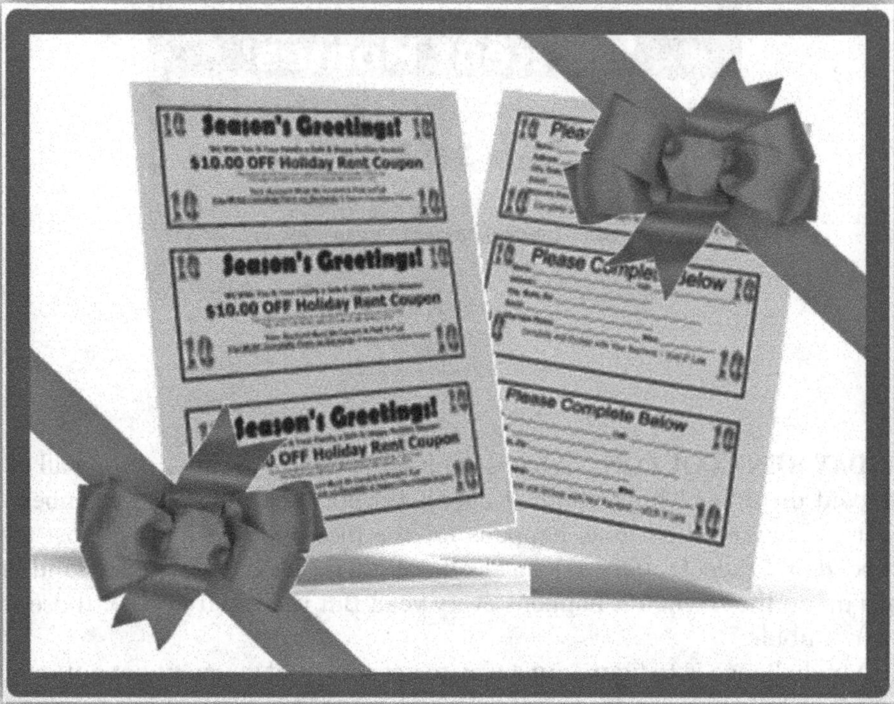

YOUR BIG PICTURE for Marketing

Carefully chew on and measure the strategies you implement to generate leads. Figure out how to laser focus your marketing to where your niche target market hangs out. Years ago, I learned that a very high percentage of my motivated sellers and tenants attended the local stock car races. Yup, you guessed it. I sponsored the best driver at that track and I am still getting "Wows!" from folks who come in our office. (That track closed about 15 years or more ago.)

Here are some ideas on where to target your marketing. Retail stores that rent toasters by the week, pawnshops, cash advance shops, coin laundry, local grocery stores, mom and pop restaurants, church bulletins and newsletters, any place that has a corkboard of some sort allowing folks to pin their business cards or announcements on this community bulletin board, hospitals, colleges and universities, and large employers in your town. Now it's your turn. Be creative. Where do

the folks you want to target hang out? Where will you find a higher concentration of prospective leads?

Congratulations and remember to always track where your leads are coming from.

Resources Needed

Go to Recommended Resources in the back of this book.

CHAPTER 18

PERSONAL SAFETY Is a MUST in Today's World

This goes for anyone and everyone involved in any business, especially your family members and loved ones.

Real-World Tragedies

1. Beverly Carter, only 27 years old! Beverly was Mom to her kids, a wife to her husband, a daughter of her mom and dad, a sister to her siblings, a coworker and friend to many.

   Little Rock, Arkansas Twenty-seven-year-old real estate agent/broker gets killed showing a house in Arkansas. The suspect in the killing of Arkansas real estate agent Beverly Carter was asked this week by reporters: "Why Beverly?" Aaron Lewis, 33, answered directly. "She was a rich broker," he said. "Because she was just a woman who worked alone; a rich broker."

2. Kenny Embry stabbed his ladyland. This year in my hometown, Louisville, Kentucky: Landlord stabbed by Tenant with butcher knife. I know this knucklehead because I went to grade school with him. He was bonkers back then.

3. Ashley Okland, only 27 years old! Ashley was Mom to her kids, a wife to her husband, a daughter of her mom and dad, a sister to her siblings, a coworker and friend to many.

   West Des Moines, Iowa Ashley Okland was a 27-year-old real estate agent from Iowa who was killed while working alone at an open house in a community of townhomes.

4. James Tolle, only 49 years young. James was a Dad to his kids, husband to his wife, the son of his Mom and Dad, a brother to his siblings, a co-worker and a friend to many.

   Louisville, Kentucky Tenant kills Landlord over $58 utility bill.

   Police said James Tolle, 49, was shot around 3:30 P.M. Monday, after an argument with Anthony Jecker in an apartment on Fegenbush Lane. The dispute was over an unpaid electric bill. "At that time, some point later, the suspect came back with a handgun. They got into another argument and that's the time he fired fatal shots," said Louisville Metro police Lt. Todd Kessinger. A bullet hit Tolle in the chest, killing him on the spot.

Folks, look at these locations where these tragic crimes occurred. You do not see Chicago, New York City, Miami, Dallas, or Los Angles, all of which are big cities.

These horrific crimes and murders occurred in Mayberry USA! Yes, my town and other towns just like Mayberry all across America!

PLEASE, PLEASE, TAKE NOTICE. We live in a very Violent World Today! No town, city, neighborhood, or zip code is exempt from violent crime. You see it on the news every day.

How Can You Protect Yourself, Your Family and Loved Ones, and your team and staff?

If you're like me, one of my biggest reasons that motivates me to be successful is my family. I want to be the best provider, the best dad, the best husband, and so on, just like the movie *Talladega Nights*—"If You Ain't First, You're Last!"

PERSONAL SAFETY IS a MUST in Today's World

Prevention is your simple solution. To drive this point home, you can almost guarantee you will never get hit by a big truck on the interstate highway as long as you never play tennis on the interstate. Yes, it's a little goofy, but it is true.

With my previous occupation and profession, a police officer in my hometown, I am going to get pretty passionate about this topic to protect all of your family, loved ones, and your team players.

I'm old school. I have two beautiful daughters and I want them to do whatever they want to do with their life. There is no ceiling, no limit; however, let's add a little common sense when it comes to the personal safety department.

NEVER Allow Women to go on any appointment alone. NO EXCEPTIONS. This includes the luxury neighborhoods and not just the normal and low-income neighborhoods.

As you grow your business, you may decide it's time to open a real office. There's a tendency among us entrepreneurs to get our kids involved in our business. Both of my daughters worked in our real estate office as an after-school part-time job. By far, the best part-time job for kids in high school. Weekdays from 3 P.M. to 6 P.M. and Saturdays 9 A.M. to 1:30 P.M. Keep in mind, most of their friends were waiting tables or flipping burgers on every Friday and Saturday night.

NEVER Accept Any Cash Payments of any kind or anywhere, especially at your office AND put up some simple, bright, effective signs announcing the same. If you accept cash payments at your office, it is not a matter of "If" you will get robbed, but it will be "When" you will get robbed. Real Estate offices and property management company offices have been the new target for folks looking to get fast cash the illegal way. No longer is it your local liquor store or the stop and rob food marts.

My good friends, Mark Lechner and Chris Dischinger, opened an office in downtown Louisville. As you might expect, their family members worked in their office. Knowing what you know about rental properties, guess what happens on the first of EVERY month? Yup, their tenants stop by and pay their rent. The criminal element studied this, did their homework, and then violently robbed their office of all of the cash. Not only did they just get their cash, but they pistol whipped their family members who worked in the office. One got his head split wide open from getting hit with the gun from one of the holdup guys.

Folks, I don't know about you, but if anything happened to my daughters while working in my office, I would be absolutely devastated. So what is a poor investor to do?

I vividly remember one day when my daughter came back into my office all upset and super-scared. She told me she just got off the phone with some crazy lady who said she was coming to our office right now to "Kick Your Ass!" referring to Rachel. Rachel was shaking, she was so upset. I listened to my daughter first, and then told her, "Dad will take care of this for you, Rachel."

I opened Microsoft Word on my computer and made a simple, bold sign like the one shown in Figure 18.1. I printed three of them on very bright yellow paper and placed all three of them in our front office area.

FIGURE 18.1 Homemade Security Sign

Sure enough, a lady did arrive in our office and Rachel believes it was the same lady who threatened her on the phone. But guess what? Not one peep. This woman never raised her voice or used any cuss words. She was as cool as a cucumber. Rachel is convinced these signs worked big-time and prevented an ugly situation.

If you have an office, this kind of sign is a MUST and I would also have two or three signs that loudly announce "No Cash Payments Accepted." Prevention is key.

What about video cameras in your office? Yes, we do have video cameras in our office. My staff initially went bonkers over it, the "Big Brother watching me" attitude; however, after explaining the purpose of it and how it can be a tool for them, they now love it. Should some idiot come in the door and start acting like a buffoon, they can simply point to the camera, and amazingly, it takes the wind out of their nasty sails and they start behaving in a much friendlier and almost professional manner.

The camera is also a great CYA tool to record everything in your office. From Key Sign Outs to Sign Lease papers and more.

PERSONAL SAFETY on the Go Years ago, my wife and daughters carried a clip on their keychain "Pepper Spray" device. The idea was to have your finger or thumb on the trigger as you were walk to or from your car, or anywhere else. You can find good ones for less than $10.

CARRYING CONCEALED FIREARMS This is a hot topic. As a retired police detective, I have my Concealed Carry License; however, seldom do I carry any of my pistols or revolvers with me. At best, I may have one stashed in the glove box or console or my car. All of my firearms, I can confidently take them apart, put them back together, and operate them blindfolded with one arm behind my back. In fact, for the most part, I refuse to purchase additional firearms because of all of the proper training, I must learn to be just as efficient with a new firearm as my already owned firearms.

The point is, if you want to get your own Concealed Carry License, You MUST get all of the training you can so you, too, can operate this weapon blindfolded with one arm behind your back. It frightens me to see so many folks who attend the training sessions because they have to, not because they want to learn how to be proficient. It does you absolutely no good if you cannot access your weapon fast and operate it very effectively.

Additionally, remember you can NOT push that bullet back into the barrel. When you pull the trigger, that bullet has been launched. You can no longer control the bullet. Did you look past your target to see what was behind your target? Bystanders, kids, other people? What if you miss your target? Did you know some bullets, depending on what part of the body is hit, will simply pass right through and exit the body, continuing on past your target? You don't see this stuff in those TV cop shows or movies.

Unless you are a properly trained law enforcement or retired law enforcement officer, I highly recommend some other, safer, alternatives for you and your family members.

TASERS Seem to work. (I have never used one.) Almost every law enforcement officer carries a taser today. This is a huge lifesaver when used properly, especially on the mentally ill. I'm just trying to give you some safe alternatives to firearms.

James Bond 007 Secret Spy Gadget This can get really lengthy, but here are some you may want to consider.

> **Video Recording Ink Pen** Simply turn it on, then place it in your shirt pocket. It is your secretly hidden personal body camera. Cheap and amazing quality.
>
> **Spy Glasses** Yup, you guessed it: glasses with an audio and video recorder built into them. Pretty snazzy.
>
> **Dash Cams** These are very, very affordable today. After pulling up to the front of your rental property or any property, for that matter, many investors simply rotate their DashCam and point it toward the front of their rental property. Remember, to hit the "record" button and it would also be a good idea to lower the window(s) just a tad on the side next to your rental. This allows for better audio recording on your video. With the windows 100% completely closed, most of any audio will end up being muffled or not heard at all. If all goes well and after you are back home, turn off the recording button and reset it for your next adventure.

Going back to undercover police detective days, there are all kinds of James Bond–like gadgets to record audio and video. Back then, some of them were pretty expensive. As with any technology, these prices have dropped considerably, even on the high-quality gadgets. Here are some of the already-made-for-you, plug and play gadgets.

- Ball Caps
- Clocks
- Exit Signs
- Pin Hole Cameras: Go to the room next door, and with a long, stiff needle, you simply poke a very fine, small hole in the drywall of the room you want to record. This hole is smaller than the lead in a pencil. You then insert the pinhole camera so it butts up against that hole, giving you a crystal-clear view of the entire room along with audio.
- Cell Phone Charger Plug-In with USB port
- Shirts
- Motion Sensors for Security Systems
- Smoke Detectors
- Ceiling Speakers
- Insulated Mugs/Drink Containers
- Thermostats for HVAC systems
- I love all of this stuff and many times, we simply built our own wireless recording devices inside birdhouses, cable TV boxes hanging on telephone poles, light fixtures, and a lot more. The sky is the limit.

What About Setting Rules to Remove as Many Opportunities for Bad Things to Happen? Here is a simple list of some:

NEVER Knock on Doors to Collect Rent NEVER! NEVER! NEVER! This means you are not in control of your business. It's the old tail wagging the dog business model. Don't try to say none of my tenants are like that. BALONEY! They might have friends who are whacko.

NEVER Accept Any Cash Payments Except rental application fees, but you can do this online today, too.

NEVER Allow Females to Go to any Property Alone

Implement the School Bus Rule on properties in low-income neighborhoods As a rule of thumb, even my maintenance and service technicians must be out of those neighborhoods before the school bus drops kids off from school. Think about it for a moment. Most of the dirtbags who commit crimes and more, stay up all night and go to bed when the birds start chirping in the morning. Taxpayers are getting up in the morning when the birds start chirping and kids get on school buses to start their day as well. Those tax-eater dirtbags, sleep all day and get up about the same time the school bus is dropping off the kids. So, to keep your folks safer, make sure they get in and out of those neighborhoods BEFORE the school bus drops off the kids.

TRAINING, TRAINING, TRAINING You must force yourself to do "continuing education in personal safety." It's just too darned easy to get complacent and take things for granted. There are several reputable companies that provide personal safety training for you and your team. I have a personal safety training program for your team as well. You can do it one-zee two-zee or in a group, all online. Short and to the point to save your precious hard-earned money. Train your maintenance and service technicians to LOCK UP all of their tools. NEVER leave them lying in the bed of a truck or an unlocked van. The same goes for tools used when working on your rentals. KEEP Both the front and back doors LOCKED while working inside. Educate your team on using personal safety devices that fit their comfort zone and train them in their use. Please discourage them from carrying firearms unless they are law enforcement or retired law enforcement. FYI, yard signs are a Big RED FLAG for thieves. When they see a yard sign, they immediately think, "Hey, here's a house I can steal stuff from." What can they steal? You Name It, they can steal it. Furnaces, materials, cabinets, water heaters, siding, piping, and on and on. Here's a biggie that will draw negative feedback on me: Instruct your team and staff to NEVER confront criminals and thieves. Yeah, I know this will ruffle a lot of feathers, including mine. But here is the ultimate question to ask yourself—"Would you instruct your son, daughter, brother, or sister to challenge a criminal or thief?" Now you see why.

CARJACKING This can happen anywhere. ALWAYS check your back seats and be observant looking all around your vehicle before entering. ALWAYS lock the doors!

CONFRONTATIONS In your office, in a tenant's home, with any member of your team, staff, or vendors. If it happens in your office, save the video recording. If it happens onsite on a turnover or an occupied rental, instruct your team to document properly with notes, photos, or even videos and leave. Tell them they have to call the office first before they can return any do any of the work requested.

LIFE IS TOO SHORT!

Make Personal Safety for your Team Number 1 on your Business Model Blueprint. If you are like me, my family is what feeds me and drives me to be successful. I trust it is probably the same for you, too.

Be Safe, my friends.

Resources Needed

- Smartphone video camera and/or audio recorder

- Free cell phone app that lets your family, friends, and so on to see where your phone is located
- Key Chain Pepper Spray

BOTTOM LINE When it comes to protecting your family and staff, please take advantage of all of the free technology to use on all of your portable devices.

> **GPS Phone Tracker** Smartphone and tablet App found on Google Play—over 10 million people are using this app. Although many folks, family members, and staff may get their panties in a wad because you are "Big Brother" violating their privacy. Remind them this is about their personal safety and not their privacy. Install this app on their smartphones and everyone can see where everyone else is located. Almost every commercial vehicles and trucks have GPS tracking devices on them these days, running 24/7. Plus, you can manually turn this app off when you are not working.

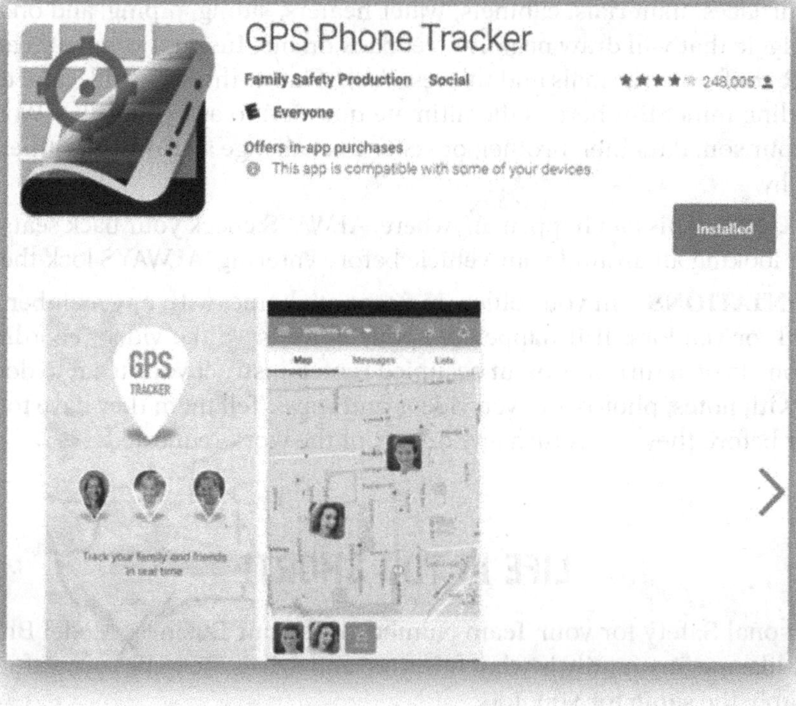

CHAPTER 19

Laws, Laws, and More Laws—*Oh My!*

You MUST understand each column in the figure below. Do NOT mix them up!

Take a close look at the image. It's a simple and powerful tool to help you wrap your head around the big picture.

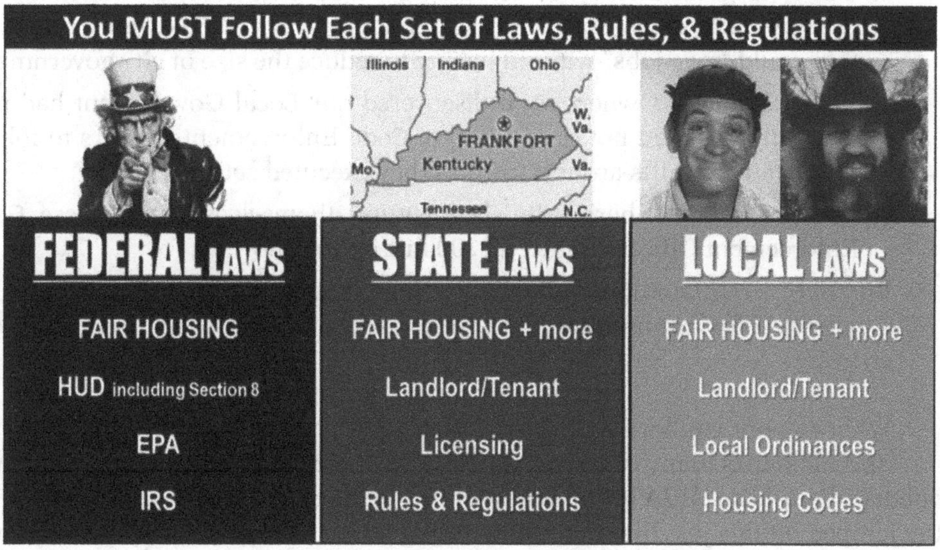

Now, before digging in here, please remember one of the big three fatal mistakes of investors is getting "Bad Advice." The guy on the far right is my old police detective partner, Eddie Stewart.

Be very careful when hiring tax advisors, accountants, CPAs, and attorneys.

As shown here, you hopefully get see each level of government has its own set of laws, rules, regulations, and more. Your challenge is to remain in compliance in all three. Unfortunately for you and me, these different levels of government don't give a flyin' rat's ka-hoonah about the other two. More times than you might imagine, this leads to big-time, major conflicts between them.

Let me give you an example in my town involving evictions and set-outs with the sheriff.

1. *Our State Landlord-Tenant Law* says the Landlord shall set out everything from the house and stack it curbside or at the street. The Landlord MUST wait 48 hours from the time of the set-out to allow the evicted tenant the opportunity to return and retrieve their personal property.
2. *Our Local Government*, after the city and county merged into one local government, enacted an ordinance in an effort to hold property owners accountable for keeping their properties clean and free of trash, debris, and junk. Code Enforcement Officers patrol neighborhoods in their city vehicles in search of violations. When a violation is found, they issue a $200 fine per day, on the spot, without any kind of warning, for improper set-outs of trash, debris, and junk.
   a. Our local government was screaming about their revenue shortfall. City Council leaders were frantically searching for ways to make more money so they could "save jobs" without having to reduce the size of city government.
   b. Rental Property Owners soon discovered our Local Government had permanently assigned not one, but two, Code Enforcement Officers to follow the Deputy Sheriffs around town as they executed set-outs.
   c. As soon as the Sheriffs finished getting themselves ready, these Code Enforcement Officers issued a $200 fine on the spot.
3. But, but . . . our Landlord-Tenant Laws state that we have to let tenants' "stuff" sit curbside for a minimum of 48 hours before we can touch it and make it go away.

What's a poor landlord to do?

Special thanks to my good friend, fellow investor, and mentor Rue McFarland, founder of our local REIA group and past president of our local board of Realtors. Rue jumped on this just like General George Patton, battled our City Council, and forced them to make some adjustments that factor in compliance with our State's Landlord Tenant Law. Thanks again, Rue!

Your town, and every town, needs to have your very own Rue McFarland.

NEXT Up is a simple, but great example of so-called experts mixing up these three different sets of laws and rules. I can promise you this: some of your experts are going to challenge me on this, but I am sticking to my guns and with my real estate investing expert CPAs' recommendations and advice.

Security Deposits

This is your tenant's money you hold until after they have moved out of your rental unit. Their Security Deposit is used to pay for any property damage caused by your tenant. Fair enough, you get the idea.

Keep in mind, most of the time, if your good tenant does not follow your move out instructions properly, a good chunk, if not all of their security deposit will be used to pay for any or some of the property damages caused by your tenant.

I am not trying to scare you. Most of my tenants do get a check for the remainder balance of their security deposit after deducting the fees for the damages they caused.

The battle involves your bookkeeping and accounting.

Here's the BIG ISSUE: Your State's Landlord Tenant Law versus The IRS. These are two separate, independent sets of laws and rules.

Do you think the IRS gives a hoot about your State's Landlord Tenant Laws? Nope.

So why do so many accountants and even CPAs try to force feed your Landlord-Tenant Laws into your IRS laws. Let me explain. It is your State's Landlord-Tenant Law that you must comply with regarding your tenant's security deposit, if you choose to collect a security deposit.

Please find me where it says in the IRS tax code detailed instructions on how to report your tenant's security deposit.

Here's my frustration. I have learned the expensive and hard way to listen to my CPA. In the big picture, remember the majority of the funds held by you for your tenant end up as reported income anyway to help cover the cost of property damage and similar expenses.

For IRS purposes, many accountants want to use your State's Landlord Tenant Law as the guide on how you handle Security Deposits. They want you to enter them as a Liability Account. This just creates a monster expensive headache at tax time and here comes the INSANITY . . . when your tenant moves out, you then change it from a liability account into INCOME. Double and Triple work that is waste of time and money.

Yes, in order to be in compliance with my state's Landlord-Tenant Law, I am required to keep those funds in a separate bank account used "exclusively for security deposits." As long I follow this rule, I am in compliance with my local Landlord-Tenant law.

My local Landlord-Tenant Law Does NOT Tell Me How to Report Security Deposits on an IRS Tax Return.

Therefore, to keep things brain-dead simple for me, I deposit their security deposit money into that exclusive bank account.

AND . . . I report this security deposit as "Rental Income." This is an IRS thing, NOT s landlord Tenant law thing. You will never get in any trouble for reporting too much income.

But Mike, what if they move out and you have to refund their Security Deposit? That's a wonderful thing because my tenant turnover costs will be next to nothing.

It is very simple. Using a check from that separate bank account used exclusively for Security Deposits, simply create a check made payable to your Tenant. Now for the bookkeeping part, if you reported it as Rental Income when you made the bank deposit, you will simply pull this money from the Rental Income account as well. This will reduce the dollar amount of rental income for the year for this property. Simple. Easy. Done.

Please remember to not allow yourself to get bent out of shape when listening and gathering bad advice.

The easiest way to stay up to date on current federal, state, and local laws is to join a REIA group or two in your town. They do a good job of keeping members updated.

What's the METHOD TO THIS MADNESS?

Here's the point I'm trying to get across. There are many, many different forms, rules, regulations, and laws. You cannot become an expert on one particular set and assume you've got all of the bases covered.

MANY LAWS contradict one another! You will find local, state, and federal laws that have different rules and regulations on the exact same topic or situation. This is our wonderful legal system. Get used to it. It will not change. The long and short of the frustration about the tenant's property being placed at curbside from an eviction:

- My Landlord/Tenant Law says it must sit there for 48 hours.
- My Local City Ordinance issues a $100 per Day fine for debris not set out properly.

What's the answer? As an investor, I'm in a Catch-22 position. I'm backed into a corner and sunk either way. But I know one thing for sure. . . . I am NOT touching their personal property for 48 hours! I can appeal to some boss about the $100 daily fine, but if I violate the Landlord/Tenant Law, the tenant might be in a position to take me to court to replace all of their valuable personal property ("junk" to you and me).

HATS We Wear

In one position, you're wearing the hat of a property owner. The other hat labels you as a Landlord. Then you see all of the other hats involving your job, family, investor, coach, and more.

This is not information about the eviction process. This information is intended to show you how frustrating it can be to operate legally and successfully in our world of real estate investing.

Here's another goofy example. Odds are you've probably heard of HUD's Section 8 program and FHA. Both are federal government agencies involving residential housing across America.

This made me pull my hair out when I discovered this the first time. Let's look at house inspections. The Section 8 program requires the housing unit to pass their HQS (Housing Qualification Standards) of the Section 8 program before a family can be placed in your unit and receive subsidized rent payments from HUD. Being a good and responsible investor, I got my own copy of the HQS Housing Qualification Standards for Section 8. Here are a couple of things I recall. To qualify as a "Bedroom," the room must have a minimum of 70 square feet, a ceiling height of no less than 84 inches (7 feet) and a window with a minimum of 5 square feet for an exit in case of a fire. Sounds pretty reasonable, doesn't it? I thought it was pretty reasonable except for the 7 feet on the ceilings. (As a kid, I stayed in an upstairs room with a ceiling height of about 5.5 feet.)

During part of my early investing career, I also bought broken houses, rehabbed them, and sold them at retail prices, usually to a first-time homebuyer. Almost always, the first-time homebuyer would use some kind of FHA guaranteed loan, resulting in a home inspection to meet FHA housing guidelines. They have a totally different set of requirements for FHA-approved loans.

I dropped my teeth again. I took an ugly house, made it real pretty and nice. A Super renovation! New cabinets, wiring, roof, kitchen, bathroom, and all of the bells and whistles. This beautiful renovated home failed the FHA inspection because there was not a closet in a bedroom. This house happened to be a "shotgun"-style house and never had closets in any bedroom to begin with.

I made a huge mistake assuming the HUD Section 8 housing program guidelines were used by all federally funded agencies. WRONG!

FHA has its own housing qualifications and many items are completely different from other federal agencies.

The Ultimate ICING on the Cake!

In the late 1990s, Dick and Sandy Vreeland, along with Rob Massey, encouraged me, along with several other investor/brokers in our town, to create a local chapter of NARPM (National Association of Residential Property Managers). I signed on as one of the local charter members.

We met once a month at a nice country club and the leadership of our group would have a speaker at our luncheon to keep us up to date in our field of investing and managing property. One of the very first meetings featured an "Enforcement Officer" from the Federal Fair Housing Agency office. This was a very eye-opening experience for me as both an investor and a landlord.

This well-educated lady represented her agency very professionally and offered a question and answer session following her presentation. This was the same era about the ADA (American Disabilities Act) rules and regulations were coming out of Washington.

Here's the eye-opener: There were many questions about Rental Applications, especially since this new ADA law was out in our world. This Enforcement Officer, after being asked a question, rattled off a small list of things you can ask and not ask on a rental application.

I can't tell you how many real estate investor seminars and conferences I've attended where I was blasted for having certain questions on my rental application, one specifically being an applicant's date of birth. We were all told you can not ask for their date of birth because it violates something in HUD's Fair Housing. This was learned a few years before this meeting and all of us had already removed DOB from our rental applications.

Me and about a dozen other very sharp veteran investors about fell out of our chairs when the Enforcement Officer told us . . .

"It's okay to ask for a DATE OF BIRTH for identification purposes on your Rental Application. . . . You can NOT ask how old they are!"

Talk about our tax dollars at waste! We could not believe what she just said. Here's what is amazing: This lady was dead serious. She was not laughing!

What Can You Do?

Here are some TIPS to minimize your forced placement into the School of Hard Knocks.

- Get your own real copy of your state's and your town's Landlord-Tenant Laws and become familiar with the basic do's and don'ts.
- Find a **competent local real estate attorney** who's knowledgeable about real estate investing in your town. Avoid family members and friends at work or church. Remember, Veterinarians and Brain Surgeons are both called "Doctors."
- Join a group in your town allowing you to network and stay abreast of local laws involving investors.

Be super-cautious with FORMS. Run it by your competent real estate attorney or take the ideas and concepts from my forms and work them into your forms by adding another paragraph or section. As an active sworn police officer in my town, I thought I had a pretty good grip on the legal system and our court system. Although I was greener than Shrek when it came to real estate investing and landlording, I honestly believed I had the upper hand, or "trump card," because I was a police officer. . . . WRONG! Let's go through just a few of the "School of Hard Knocks" real-life seminars I attended and graduated from with flying colors.

School of Hard Knocks

LESSON 1—FORMS—Rental Agreement or Lease

Now remember folks, back when I got started, I had access to no one, absolutely no one, to act as a mentor or go-to person for simple, basic advice about landlording and investing. As a cop, I expected to know all of this stuff following the good, old-fashioned "common sense rule." I resorted to asking the good criminal defense attorneys or our prosecutors. They don't have a clue about landlording laws other than what they recall in law school.

Make it part of your investing program to have an EXCELLENT, knowledgeable real estate attorney on your team. Have them review your rental agreement for several reasons.

- Fair Housing.
- Lead-Based Paint laws.
- Mold, mildew, environmental hazards, like asbestos.
- Compliance with your Landlord Tenant Laws.
- Make sure it's legal in your town. *(Some states, such as Pennsylvania, almost require lease agreements to be approved by the State's Attorney General with a consumer protection concern of making it easy to understand for the tenant. They also require a certain font and font size!)*
- Get as much stuff in there to protect you.
- FORMS, such as late notices, "Pay or Quit Possession Notices"
    - Make sure they're legal and proper.
    - Learn how to do it properly.
    - Ask about the most common mistakes made by Landlords so you won't fall victim to it, too.
- Do the same process for all of your important legal forms, such as:
    - Rental Application.

- Rental Agreement, Lease Agreement.
- Lease/Options.
- Option to Buy Agreement.
- Move In Inspection Form.
- Late Notices for nonpayment of rent.
- Rental Agreement Violation Notice for things other than nonpayment of rent—grass too tall, music too loud, and so forth.
- Maintenance/Repair Requests.
- Property Inspection Notices, 48 hours, 72 hours, and so forth.
- Proper Handling of Tenant's Security or Damage Deposit.
- Fair Housing Laws, both Federal and local.
- Collections—do's and don'ts.
- Tenant Chargeable Repairs during Tenancy and after they move out.
- Unauthorized Occupants.
- Animals are HUGE issue today.
- Locks; some states do not allow deadbolts.
- Smoke Alarms.
- Multiunit Buildings have a whole set of additional issues:
  - If there is central heat and air, what are the seasonal change dates?
  - Common area housekeeping responsibilities.
  - Utilities.
- Renter's Insurance.
- Catch-up payment plans—are they allowed? Do they kill your eviction process? Most states say if a landlord accepts any kind of partial payment of rent after the eviction process has been started by the landlord, the eviction action will be dismissed.
- FEES and Forms associated with Tenant Chargeable Fees.

Lesson 2—SAVE ALL Correspondence—It's Your EVIDENCE or Proof

Just like Judge Judy on *The People's Court,* she begins the case allowing each party to tell a short story. After that, she wants proof. It doesn't really matter what it is, as long as it is not noise coming out of their head. It could a phone log, a note with a date stamp on it, a chronological record or a notepad, in addition to receipts and other things. The point is to have SOMETHING other than "He said, she said" to make your case.

Although this may sound overkill to some, document messages you receive from your tenants. You can save every message and upload it to your tenant contact file. You can save any kind of computer file. This includes PDFs, mp3 audio files, mp4 videos, photos, and more. If you get a:

LETTER in the mail Scan it and save it to PDF. Then upload to your tenant record file. If you do not have a scanner, use the smartphone app called "Office Lens," which turns your smartphone into a scanner.

TEXT message Save the screenshot of your smartphone and email it to yourself. Then upload to your tenant record file.

VOICE MAIL First, use Google Voice, which will translate it to text for you. Now you can download the transcribed message as a jpeg image and you can download the actual audio recording of their message. Both will have a date/time stamp on them. Upload both and attach to your tenant record file.

PHOTOS emailed to you This would include not only photos from your tenant, but also photos from Move In Inspection, Work Orders and Repairs, and Move Out Inspection Photos. Upload and attach all to your tenant's record file.

VIDEOS Same as photos. Remember to always try to get great, positive, upbeat 30-second videos from your great residents to use on your website.

Lesson 3—Learn the Difference in All of the Rules, Laws, Regulations, and Ordinances in Your Town

You will be totally amazed at how many laws conflict. In my town, we have a local ordinance requiring property owners to be given a 10-day notice to cut their grass if an inspector sees grass 10 inches or higher or the property owner will get a $100 per day fine for each day in violation of the local code.

Get ready to pull your hair out! My town's Landlord-Tenant Law says I must give the tenant a 14-Day Notice to correct the rental agreement violation of the grass being too tall and unkept. How can this be? This happens in many towns across America, not just mine.

Your challenge is to become aware of these conflicting laws and figure out how to operate the best you can in this challenging arena of being a real estate investor and landlord. You are not the first landlord to discover this. Many have gone before you and survived and many are doing it today and survive.

Once again, many of these challenging issues are totally preventable by doing your homework on the front end and selecting only quality tenants.

Resources Needed

Today, you can do everything in digital format. Here's how you can document everything in your business, including all correspondence.

ACR All Call Recording cell phone app—in settings, select "Ask Me to Save Each Call."

DOWNLOAD Your Own State's Landlord Tenant Law http://askmikebutler.com/free-training/landlord-tenant-laws-by-state/

Gmail Google Voice: Carefully go through settings and it will transcribe and save all of your voice mails.

TEXTs Save them, screen capture them if you need to.

Emails Save them.

Cute PDF Free software allows you to print anything to PDF.

Website Make sure it is interactive. This allows your residents to contact your office. This is beautiful because when this form is completed, it is auto-emailed to you with a date/time stamp, and the message is in their own words, plus any photos they may include.

CHAPTER 20

Your New "Pain-in-the-Butt" Business Partner

You have always had Uncle Sam as your business partner. The Internal Revenue Service, aka the IRS.

If you got married and had a business, your spouse probably ended up as your business partner.

Both of these partners can be hairy at times. FYI, I recommend to avoid getting "partners" in a business venture. Many times, I have seen great friends for more than 20 years go in together as partners in a business only to see it fall apart, ruin their friendship, and they never talk to each other again. This sucks big time.

I can give you permission to have a partner on very short-term deals. Such as a buying a fixer-upper and selling it within a month or two.

Long-term partnerships are always fine when they get started. But life happens and people will change their priorities in life, especially when it involves their immediate family members—Mom, Dad, kids, grandkids, brothers, and sisters. These kinds of long-term partnerships usually crash and burn because one partner believes they are carrying most of the weight, doing the work and having to split the profits with a partner who is not holding up their end of their partnership.

Coming to a town near you, if not already. Drum roll please...

Your new "Pain in the Butt Partners" are your state and local governments! This includes HUD's Section 8 Program.

Here's what has been going on and will continue to happen. Bottom Line, they are on a mission to find money, to generate revenue for the government. Just stop and think about all of the hidden taxes you pay every day without realizing you are paying extra taxes over and above income taxes.

- In many states, all sales are taxed except for food, including:
    - Tires
    - Gasoline and Diesel Fuel
    - Telephone Bills

    - Cable TV Bills
    - Utility Bills
    - Inspection Fees
    - Libraries
    - Luxury
    - Sports Stadiums
    - Cigarettes and Tobacco
    - Airports and Airlines
    - Tourism Districts, Hotels
    - Business Registration
    - Toll Roads
    - Insurance Premium Taxes
    - Public Schools
    - Parking Meters
    - Recycling Fees
    - Disposal, Oil Changes
    - Dog Licenses
    - Permits
    - Driver's License Fees
    - Entertainment Tickets
    - Real Estate Transfers
    - Booze and Liquor
    - Passports
    - And many more!
- My state has a 6% sales tax.
- Our neighbor to the south, Tennessee, has a whopping 9.75% sales tax on everything except food.

Our state and local governments are desperately searching for ways to increase their revenue. Call it whatever you want, it still boils down to more tax burdens on the existing taxpayers. Government leaders claim they want to "save jobs" and God forbid, the thought of downsizing government like the rest of the world had to do to survive back in the day. These knuckleheads honestly believe they are doing good. So warped!

I have said for decades that America is made up of two kinds of folks—there are Tax Payers, and there are Tax Eaters. Never mind about partisan politics. This is what it boils down to.

Since America's last financial tsunami our economy has had a hard time recovering for the good old American Taxpayer. Many taxpayers are not better off than they were 10 years ago.

Just take a look at what state and local governments have done in recent years to increase their income. I think it is in the State of Minnesota's local government, they required an Occupancy Certification Inspection (for a fee, of course) BEFORE you could list a house for sale. Here's the headache: They also mandated that no residential property could put be up FOR SALE until AFTER it passed this inspection. This meant all of the houses that needed any kind of repairs, minor or major, could not be listed for sale.

I found this out years ago from the inner workings of the back office of the Fifth Third Bank. This bank had a large number of mortgages on homes in that town. When Fifth Third Bank foreclosed on these properties, they simply deeded them to the city because they were not allowed to offer them for sale "as-is." I don't know if this crazy law is still in effect today, but it was back then.

Next up on the bandwagon of local governments generating revenue is a Rental Property Registry. In short, another tax on rental property owners. It requires all owners and property managers of rental properties to register each and every rental property. Failure to do so in my town results in a $100 per day fine on each property not registered. Many other cities and towns in America already have some kind of landlord tax already in place, and if not, it will be soon.

Another local tax, not in my town, involves a percentage of your total rents received for the year as tax.

The new and trending local tax hitting towns now is the tax on Airbnb rentals, including VRBO and HomeAway. Talk about highway robbery. And our goofball city leaders deny it is another tax on property owners and managers. They try to convince everyone that this "fee" is paid by the person who rents the Airbnb rental. The annual registration fee is several hundred dollars, requires a public hearing involving your neighbors, and some kind of B.S. tourism tax to be levied on your customer. INSANE!

I try to keep my finger on the pulse of what is going on in government in my state and city. You can find me tuned in to our local cable TV show called *Gavel to Gavel,* where you can watch city council meetings, committee meetings, hearings, budget hearings and a lot more. Check this out on what I heard myself one day on this show.

Several years ago, our city council was smack dab in the middle of their annual budget meeting and hearings. At the time, they were facing a $20 million shortfall. The Director of Code Enforcement Department stated during his presentation that each of his 41 Code Enforcement Officers generates over $2 million in fines and fees. He invited the City Council to increase his department's budget to allow for 10 additional code enforcement officers, he could take care of the $20 million revenue shortfall.

I was shocked because we recently had a meeting with this same director concerning the aggressive targeting and fining of rental property owners. As with any typical politician, he promised nothing and told us he would get back to us. All he did was provide lip service and kick the can down the road.

Look at Illinois and California. These states have raised their property taxes, along with other taxes so much, business owners and investors have fled their states to land in more business owner and investor friendly states and towns. Texas has seen a huge BOOM from folks leaving California. Indiana's economy was catapulted to another level from everyone bailing from Illinois.

For real estate investors in states like the two just mentioned, owning rental property is ugly when compared to owning the same property in my town. I have investors from Illinois and California who buy turnkey rentals from my business. My property management company manages their properties no differently from how they manage the properties I own.

A 3 bedroom, 1 bath, 1,000 square foot ranch in Illinois might produce $50 per month positive cash flow. Put that little puppy on a truck, move it to my town, and this same investor can generate $400 to $500 or more in positive cash flow simply from the difference in property taxes.

So, stay tuned, get involved with your local investor groups, and associations, and take action BEFORE the damage is done. It is so much harder and more expensive to go back and try to unravel laws, rules, and ordinances already in effect.

Now you should be better prepared to meet your new Pain in the Butt Partners....

Your State and Local Governments...oh yeah, don't forget about your Homeowner Associations, too.

HUD's Section 8 Program: BEWARE!

I have participated in HUD's Section 8 Program since 1991 or so. Our local government agency, LMHA, Louisville Metro Housing Agency, has gradually become impossible to work with over the past three years. Our local agency was one of the agencies nationwide selected for an OIG (Office of Inspector General) the Federal Government Police Department who investigates and audits government agencies to ensure your federal tax dollars are spent and used properly. They make sure these agencies are following all of the rules and regulations required with receiving federal funds. They also have the power to arrest people who have committed crimes from improper use of these federal dollars.

In my town, it seems like over the past three years, our Section 8 Program flipped a switch and began a very aggressive Anti-Landlord campaign.

In years past, Section 8 inspectors had common sense and treated the good and responsible landlords and property managers like people. Today, Section 8 inspectors are worse than the Gestapo. It is not the inspectors' fault, but it is because their supervisors are beating them up every day to find violations on every inspection.

For many years, my company ALWAYS passed the initial inspection. My good friends, Jay Long and Chris McCarty, ALWAYS passed their initial inspections. All of us run a tight ship in our property management business. All of us are Professional Property Managers and not slumlords. For the first nine months of last year, <u>not one initial inspection passed.</u> All three of us had every initial inspection fail. Keep in mind, the tenant on Section 8 cannot move in nor can you receive any rent payments until your unit passes their HQS, (Housing Quality Standards).

As you might expect, I got involved with other great investors to find out what the heck was going on. We learned that our local agency was required by HUD to use the 2012 International Housing Code. Unbelievable! What happened to our local and state housing codes?

Rental units were failing inspections for such things as:

- Dirty Bathtub—believe it or not, this is now an Owner Responsibility.
- One burner not working on a tenant-owned stove.
- Tire tracks, not ruts, in the yard from the previous tenant moving out.
- If you want to see some of the war stories, check out my FaceBook group page called "Louisville Landlords Love Section 8."
    - We failed an annual inspection this week. The deadbolt was hard to operate. It worked. It was just tight. The tenant had added weather stripping and you need to push the door in to get the deadbolt to lock. That is worthy of a failure? Really? These inspectors are nuts!
    - A tenant broke a closet door. We removed the broken door. When we did not replace the door, the tenant filed a complaint against us. The city's Inspections, Permits, and Licensing department (IPL) did an inspection and found (a) weeds over 10 inches, (b) an unregistered vehicle, (c) bedroom windows obstructed by furniture, (d) trash in the yard, (e) a missing light fixture globe, and (f) the back door obstructed by her kitchen table. And, of course, under Louisville Metro's new and improved procedures, all of these are the owner's responsibility. Louisville no longer holds the tenant responsible. All of the violations listed, even though caused by the tenant, are listed as the owner's responsibility. This creates an interesting problem under KRS 383.705. The statute does not allow a landlord

to bring an action for possession after a tenant files a complaint unless the violation was caused by the tenant. By IPL reporting these to be the owner's responsibility, there could be complications if the wrong attorney got involved. Oh, by the way, the inspector had no problem with there not being a closet door. Removing the broken door was the correct thing to do. No need to replace it, as closet doors are not required.

- Landlord Failed Inspection: Apparently, I've just been demoted by IPL to housekeeper. I am responsible, "House needs general cleanup. Trash, clothes everywhere, and so forth. OWNER Responsibility. Such lunacy!
- House flunked annual Section 8 inspection. Fixed it. Called inspector for re-inspection. Inspector refused. Said I have to call the Section 8 re-inspection number at 569-6468. Called that number several times. Recording says landlords will be ignored. ONLY THE TENANT can call for a re-inspection. Tenant refuses to call. Tenant doesn't have to play their part. Tenant has no motivation.
- I had an annual inspection fail today. A skinny window adjacent to the picture window in the living room is painted shut. The window in question is 24 inches from the front door. Really? Someone may need to exit through a 15-inch-wide window when there is a 3-foot-wide door on the same wall just two feet away? How stupid is that?
- I'm also quitting Section 8. I'm not renewing the leases for two tenants in October and no new tenants will be Section 8. One of the items I failed for was a 2-inch hole in the wall behind the water heater that no human could access. They wanted me to pull the water heater and fix it. My tenants are very pissed at Section 8.

As you can see, our local agency running HUD's Section 8 program are very anti-landlord. In fact, just a few weeks ago, I helped arrange a couple of meetings with our local HUD leadership, involving Federal, State, and local representatives and leadership.

The Federal HUD director told us there are no more Tenant Responsible violations. All violations are now Owner Responsible. This includes a dirty house, dirty bathtubs, and junk or debris piled up outside. Insane.

Here is what was happening. You receive an application from a person on the Section 8 program. We process their application the same as any other. Once approved, our office has to complete the forms in their package. The approved applicant then takes their package to their assigned caseworker at the agency.

Get this, the agency is open only Monday through Thursday. They are closed every Friday for paperwork. Baloney!

Once the paperwork package is submitted, you will receive a notice of your date and time for your Initial Inspection. Now it is taking four weeks for an initial inspection. A full month of lost rent.

The inspectors are encouraged by their supervisors to fail every initial inspection. When this happens, the owner repairs the goofy violations. One was failed because of a light bulb not working. Then you pester the heck out of them, calling and calling and calling to get a "Re-Inspection Scheduled." This is another four weeks out. Now you are out two months of rent.

That is headache enough for us, but just imagine what it is doing to the poor tenant. Telling their current landlord they will be moving on the initial inspection date and time. Plus, making arrangements to take time off from their job for their move, lining up help, truck rental, boxes, packing, utility deposits, kids in school, and so on. Because of Section 8, look how much grief and expense they are causing to the very people the program is intended to help.

On top of all this, my resident manager was spending about 75% of her workday dealing with Section 8 issues and problems.

After participating the Section 8 program since 1991, as of January 2017, our company was no longer participating in the Section 8 program. This is sad for the good families on the program.

Should You Participate in HUD's Section 8 Program?

It depends. If you live in a large city, check with your fellow members in your local REIA groups. They will tell you the good and bad of your local Section 8 program. I hope our local Section 8 government agency could go back to using common sense. Until then, my company will not participate in our Section 8 program.

If you live in Mayberry, USA, a small town, the odds are, everybody knows everybody. This means you probably know the folks who work at your local Section 8 office. From what I hear from investors across America, they report their Section 8 program is no problem.

Do your homework.

Warning

Check your local Fair Housing Laws. In California, Section 8 participants are a protected class. This means you cannot refuse to rent to anyone on the Section 8 program.

Resources Needed

You must remain plugged in to what is happening in the town where you have rental properties.

- Join a reputable local REIA group or two where you can get newsletters with updates emailed to you.
- Section 8: Do your homework first. If you live in Mayberry, you might be okay. If you live in a larger city, it could be the kiss of death.
- Education, Training—stay current on updates to anything any government agency can ram down our throats. These include EPA things and environmental concerns and issues, crazy updates to Fair Housing, and so on and more.

CHAPTER 21

Insurance and Environmental Concerns

Rule 1: Always Make Your Resident(s) Buy Renter's Insurance BEFORE You Give Them Keys!

Your tenant's Renter's Insurance policy is your first line of defense and protection and it will help keep your insurance premiums as low as possible.

If your new tenant needs help in getting Renter's Insurance, please do yourself and your insurance agent a favor by referring your new tenant(s) to your insurance agent.

This creates a WIN-WIN-WIN BENEFIT for everyone involved. Here's how:

1. **Your Tenant:** You know ~~that~~ they will be getting good coverage at a good price.
2. **Your Insurance Agent:** Your agent will love you for the referral(s).
3. **You:** You will get a double or triple dose of benefits. Let me show you how.

Suppose one of your residents decides to cook bacon naked on a Sunday morning.

For whatever reason, your resident gets sidetracked and forgets about the bacon. The next thing you know, your resident has your kitchen engulfed in flames with a big grease fire.

Neighbors see the smoke and call the fire department. Your local fire department rushes to your house on fire, they quickly climb on the roof and saw or chop holes in your roof, they use their master key (axe) to chop in the front and back doors, and they drown your house with tons of water.

If you are lucky, you might even see it on your local evening news if it's a slow news day.

Okay, now let's get back to your BENEFIT. Quick review. Your resident started this fire and they have renters' insurance with Your Insurance Agent! Yes!...now you can contact your insurance agent, and let them know what happened.

You should also congratulate your resident on having renter's' insurance, otherwise they could have lost everything! Ask them if they want you to help them by calling your insurance agent for them. They will almost always thank you for helping.

Imagine this . . . your insurance agent is handling the whole kit and caboodle regarding this fire caused by your resident. Your agent will submit a claim on your resident's renter's insurance and NOT on *your* insurance policy. Your resident's policy should cover all of the property damages to your rental house, including new cabinets, perhaps an electric update, roof, and more. Good Stuff for you!

Warning

Regarding your insurance, please be very careful about accepting your family's "been using them forever insurance agent," or worse yet, your 23rd distant cousin twice removed or an in-law or out-law insurance agent. My good friend and real estate investor, Ed, The Cuban Guy, hired me to attend a meeting with his Dad's longtime insurance agent to review his insurance policies, coverages, and premiums on the approximately 30 rental houses he owned.

Thank goodness, Ed has enough sense to ask me to attend his meeting. I was shocked! Ed was paying anywhere from $1,300 to $1,700 annually on each policy. Ed was clueless he was getting ripped off. He trusted this guy because this agent was part of his family's insurance tradition. Now keep in mind, we are NOT talking about luxury rental houses, just plain, good, simple 1,000-square-foot, three-bedroom, one-bath, one-story ranches.

I informed Ed and confronted his insurance agent about his company's outrageous premiums with piss-poor coverages. After making arrangements with my insurance agent, Ed was able to lower his annual premiums to about $350 per policy along with raising his liability coverage to $1 million per incident and $2 million aggregate. (I think his old policies may have had only $100K liability coverage.) Ed was able to SAVE Over $1,000 per policy every year and he had better coverage!

This does not mean to go out and get the "cheapest" insurance policies. Insurance companies are no different from any other business. Some insurance companies have a reputation of trying to wiggle out of paying claims, while others are rated as A+++. Do your homework; ask your seasoned veteran investors in your town if they could share their insurance agent's name and company with you.

YOUR INSURANCE is something "you got to have but never use." Years ago insurance was viewed as your tool for asset protection. I cannot tell you how many veteran season Real Estate Investors who own tons of rental properties would tell me they're not worried about getting sued because that's what their insurance is for.

A few decades ago, there was no *Jerry Springer Show* with attorneys advertising to "help me find somebody to sue!" Most of the first round of commercials were probably of the personal injury kind.

Now in today's world, the sky is the limit. These attorneys want you to call them to sue BIG TRUCK companies, nursing homes, personal injury, asbestos class action lawsuits, wrongful deaths and serious injury from prescribed drugs, medical procedures, and now, yes, even landlords!

Recently something happened in a lawsuit in the city of Baltimore, which opened the floodgates for attorneys to sue landlords who owned rental properties built before 1978. They are targeting lead-based paint poisoning of your tenant(s) and the occupants in their household, especially children.

While in Baltimore recently, I got to meet a landlady who has been in the business for over 30 years. She shared with me her company was getting sued for lead-based paint poisoning in one of her rentals. She told me her jaw about hit the floor when her insurance company told her that her insurance policy does not cover lead-based paint nor any other environmental hazards. They let her know she was on her own in this lawsuit and wished her good luck.

I felt like this landlady still had the "deer in the headlights" look while I was talking to her. She wrapped up our conversation stating, "Well, I guess I am going to have to write a check for $30,000 to make this lawsuit go away." Although I did not want to ruffle her feathers, my thoughts wanted to ask her, "What about your next lawsuit?" It's not "if" anymore; it is "when."

Although this is an extreme case, this has already become the norm in the city of Baltimore. If you own rental property in Baltimore, brush up and dig in to learn what the heck is going on. If you do not have rental property in Baltimore, you'd better brush up on it as well, because it will probably be coming to my town and your town in the near future.

Big lesson learned. You must understand what your insurance policies cover and do not cover. Do yourself and your business a huge favor and schedule a must have, sit-down Pow-wow with your insurance agent to review in detail all of your questions you need answered.

Tip

Prepare your list of questions before your meeting.

Here are some of the questions you might want to ask your insurance agent at your Powwow.

- Does my policy cover me on lead-based paint, asbestos, mold, radon, and any other environmental issues?
- Does my policy cover me if someone gets bit by a tenant's dog?

- Do you still buy real estate if you come across a good deal? If yes, what if you have a property under contract and you want to wholesale it to another investor for some fast cash. You tell your investor to go check out the property. If they fall or get injured while checking out this property you do not own yet, does your insurance have you covered?
- How much liability coverage do I have with my policy? (I highly recommend $1 million per incident, and $2 million aggregate.)
- I have heard about negligence. Can you give me some examples of negligence that my policy will not cover?
    - One example could be several neighbors and your tenants calling you about a dead tree that needs to be removed. You simply ignore it and then that dead tree falls and injure someone. If your insurance company finds out that you were given notice before the tree fell and you did nothing, the insurance company may not cover you because you were negligent.
    - Another example could be a resident reporting to you the steps on the front of the house are broken, weak, or in need of repair and you do nothing. The next thing you know, somebody falls because of the steps, gets injured, and files a lawsuit against you. Odds are, your insurance company will not cover you on this because you were negligent.
- Assuming you are satisfied with your insurance agent, also ask how you can refer your tenants to buy their renter's insurance from your agent. In my office, for example, when it's time to sign the lease and all the other docs, we require proof of paid renter's insurance policy. If this new tenant can't produce a paid-up policy and needs help getting insurance, there is a fill-in-the-blank form on our website to make it brain-dead simple. Just fill in the blanks and then it is auto-emailed to my insurance agent and my resident manager. This is saved as a PDF file and placed in the tenant's file.
- Did you know if you call your insurance agent's office and ask a question to see if you are covered for this or that item, your phone call with a question may get flagged on your insurance record as an inquiry, which can hurt your insurance score? This is very similar to getting a speeding ticket or drunk driving charge that would hurt your driving record. That one little question may cause you to be labeled high-risk on your insurance record. If you have several questions, through a phone call, email, or text, can this result in higher premiums or cancellation of your policies? Ask your agent if this is true with their company.
- True Story: An investor has 10 rental properties. He has an insurance policy on each rental property. Not too long ago when scrap metal prices were high, he had three outside air conditioner compressor units stolen within two months. This investor filed a claim for each stolen air conditioner. Because of his three claims, his insurance company canceled all of his policies. To make

matters worse, while searching for another reputable and affordable insurance company, he discovered the hard way that he has already been labeled "High Risk" on his insurance record. Behind the scenes, insurance companies share your insurance record just like your driving record. All of his insurance quotes were super-expensive because he was labeled "high risk." This ain't good either.

So the bottom line for insurance is " You Gotta Have It, But NEVER Use It."

I view my insurance policies to be used only for big-time tragedies.

Years ago, one of my rental houses caught on fire, killing both of the tenants. Long story short, our male tenant, after killing our female tenant, started fires in three places in the house. We can only assume he was thinking this would cover up his murder. Because this home was so energy efficient, the smoke and toxic fumes knocked him out before he could exit the house, and he, too, perished in the fire.

Yes, I did call my insurance agent on this one and filed a claim. The estates of our tenants were trying to figure out a way to sue the owner to get money from my insurance company. My insurance company took care of everything and did not bother me with any headaches. (My liability coverage allowed me to rest peacefully.) My insurance policy did cover and paid for the replacement cost to make this rental house "rent ready" again. Of course, all of this was done after their deductible.

NEVER file an insurance claim for a stolen air conditioner, stolen tools, stolen supplies, stolen carpet, stolen pipes, stolen furnaces, vandalism, or stolen anything. Pay for this out of your pocket. You do not want to jeopardize your insurance record from these puny claims.

Therefore, if you never file an insurance claim for things mentioned here, you can protect your wonderful insurance record. You can also reduce your premiums by increasing your deductibles. When I got started eons ago, I had a $1,000 deductible. Today, most of my policies have a $5,000 deductible and some have a $10,000 deductible.

What kind of insurance policies should I get?

As you know, a huge part, and the first step in my Asset Protection Program is PRIVACY. This is your first line of defense. Imagine one of your tenants slips and falls on the step out front and calls an attorney to sue you. This attorney, while sitting in their chair, will ask your tenant where they live (your rental house). The attorney will let his fingers do the walking on his keyboard to visit the internet and look up public records to see who owns this property. Their next step is to see what other properties have the same owner. Do you really want some attorney to push two buttons and see everything you own? So what if you have them in LLCs? They will get to see all of them as well.

Now you can get ready to blow a gasket. You won't believe this.

True Story: I had a tenant with a pending eviction contact an attorney stating she had slipped and fell in our rental house and she injured her buttocks or something similar. This attorney called me and explained he was representing our tenant regarding this slip-and-fall case. Next he wanted to know what insurance company had insurance on this property. This infuriated me because he should not be given this information to make his job easier. This is private information for my eyes only or so I thought. Being professional and friendly, I told this attorney I was going to contact my insurance agent and I would get back to him. I jotted down his name, phone number, and email and then contacted my insurance agent.

Unbelievable! SHOCKING! My insurance agent informs me our state law requires we furnish a copy of my policy or "deck page," which summarizes all of the coverages and limits on my insurance policy. This is the law in Kentucky and in many other states. Ugggh!

Now, here is where it really gets ugly for you behind the scenes.

Once Upon a Time, way back when I was getting started, my insurance agent would simply add a rental house to my existing homeowner's policy. This happened for the first three to five properties.

At approximately the fifth rental house I purchased, my insurance agent told me I could no longer put these rental houses on my regular homeowner's policy. He said I had to get a "commercial policy." I was super excited, proud of myself and my achievements! This grew-up-poor kid from the south end of Louisville had built a real estate business so successful that it required a "commercial insurance policy." That made me so happy! (I was clueless and wrong.)

With a commercial policy, as you buy more properties, the insurance company simply adds those new properties you buy onto your existing commercial policy. Therefore, you have one policy with all of your properties listed on the "deck page."

Now keep in mind, your "deck page" lists every property on this policy along with the coverages and limits for each one.

So, let's chew on this one for a minute.

Suppose you have 25 rental houses on your one commercial policy.

- You have a $1,000 deductible for this commercial policy.
- Your liability coverage is $1 million per incident and $2 million aggregate.
- Suppose you have a double fatal fire like I did and somehow it was determined the owner of the property, which is you, has some liability. Your insurance company decides to settle this for $1 million to make it go away.
    - Now remember these attorneys get a copy of your "deck page" detailing all of the rental houses you own. This ain't good for you.
- Because you have only $2 million coverage for the life of the policy, you are now left with only $1 million in liability coverage because your insurance company just paid out $1 million on the lawsuit just mentioned.
- I am NOT trying to be a "Debbie Downer" or a "Negative Nancy" by saying the sky is falling. This is real-world stuff I'm trying to share with you to help you protect everything you have worked your butt off for and earned. Now suppose

before the end of this policy, you have another tragedy of some sort. It really doesn't matter what the tragedy is or what the lawsuit involves, but let's say the plaintiff, the person suing you, is awarded $1.75 million. Now what? You only have $1 million of coverage remaining on this policy. This means you get to shell out $750,000 hard-earned cash, out of your pocket or the plaintiff can go after your assets, all of the other good stuff you own.

- I'm also a hard-money-lender to help investors purchase and renovate investment properties. One of my requirements before their deal is funded, is proof of a paid, full-year insurance policy on the property. I recall when a good friend and fellow investor wanted to borrow some money to do a deal. This guy is absolute BONKERS about his PRIVACY. He spent a fortune with so-called experts and gurus to hide everything he owns... but he forgot one HUGE important part that exposed everything he owns!
  - Take a wild guess on what his privacy experts overlooked? Yup, you got it. They never considered taking a look at or tweaking his insurance policies. Here's how I know.
  - He must provide proof of a paid insurance policy before his deal is funded.
  - Well, guess what gets faxed over to my office? His commercial policy "deck page." His "deck page" listed ALL of the properties he owned along with the coverages and limits on each property. I quickly saw that he had well over 100 properties he thought were blocked from the public record. I hope you can see how his commercial policy being overlooked became a huge nightmare and just destroyed all of his privacy strategies!

Now it's time for Your Big Picture.

Hopefully, you can now see all of the huge benefits for your real estate business by getting a separate insurance policy for each property. But what if it costs a little more? Is it worth it? I think so.

But wait, there's more... *(just like the late-night infomercials tell you)*. If insurance is something you gotta have, but never use it... you can drastically reduce your annual premiums by having a sit-down powwow with your insurance agent again. Review your policy in detail, line by line, coverage by coverage, and see what you can WHACK out of your policies.

If you have two dozen or more single-family rentals, take a very close look at "Loss of Rents." If you see this on your policies, odds are, the cost of this coverage far exceeds any benefit you may get with a claim. As a rule of thumb, loss of rents will pay you up to six months of lost rent should a tragedy happen to this single-family house.

Now take the annual cost for your "Loss of Rents" coverage and multiply it by the number of single-family houses you have, and you will probably see you are better off removing this coverage from all of your policies.

When it comes to the cost of your insurance, I have never seen any years when my cost of insurance has gone down. I can almost guarantee the cost of your insurance will increase every year, especially with the rash of natural disasters and the frequency at which they occur.

- Hurricane Katrina
- Earthquakes
- Tornadoes
- Hail damage
- Floods and more floods
- Hurricane Ike
- Hurricane Harvey
- Hurricane Irma, along with who knows what is going to happen around the corner

All of the claims paid out to policyholders involving these catastrophes will be passed on to me and you with higher costs for our insurance.

Additionally, FYI, my insurance agent told me all insurance companies are pulling their hair out over auto insurance claims. Why? How? In today's world, car wrecks have just skyrocketed because drivers are texting, emailing, and doing stuff on their smartphones while driving. Needless to say, look for your auto insurance rates to keep increasing.

Only you and I can understand how hard you have worked, all of your "burning the candle at both ends" in addition to working your full-time job. Sweat Equity, strategizing, education, and your precious and valuable time invested to build your nest eggs. What really sucks in today's world is how many folks want to legally steal your golden eggs from you.

Now is the time, before it is too late, to carefully craft your Investor's Ultimate Privacy and Asset Protection Program. I help investors all over the United States by creating your very own custom plan for privacy and asset protection. Just ask yourself now, after learning about all of the exposures you still have, even with insurance... shouldn't you take one more step and invest in yourself to protect everything you've worked your butt off for? Just send me an email to News@MikeButler.com to get all of your details and more to get started.

Resources Needed

Insurance Agent A competent Insurance Agent who own investment property just like you. Ask several successful investors at your next local REIA group meeting whom they use for insurance. Try to keep one insurance agent for everything. It will make your life easier.

Renter's Insurance This is a must for every tenant. NO EXCEPTIONS in today's world. Try to get them to buy from your insurance agent and have your real estate company listed as additional insured, just like lenders do on your insurance policies now.

Lead-Based Paint If your rental was built before 1978, you must use the one-page Federal HUD form regarding lead-based paint. It is a simple fill-in-the-blank form.

Website Create a page with a fill-in-the-blank form of basic information as a lead for your insurance agent to write up a Renter's Insurance policy for your new or renewing tenant. You do NOT sell insurance unless you are licensed to do so.

CHAPTER 22

Biggest Mistakes of Investors

Before we categorize the biggest mistakes of investors, let's start off with the Big Three Fatal Mistakes:

1. CASH FLOW: No system to keep their finger on the pulse of their business.
2. PROPERTY MANAGEMENT: No system, at most using spreadsheets.
3. BAD ADVICE: Especially from poor people and wannabe experts.

Now, let's see if we can categorize these mistakes. Here is some general stuff:

Bullwinkle Syndrome A person with a know-it-all attitude. When my daughters were young, my sister called our home, my daughter answered and screamed to my wife, "Mom, It's Aunt Bullwinkle!" (oops, the cat flew out of the bag at that point). Why is she a "Bullwinkle"? Because she is THE Expert on anything. Just ask her.

Super Extremist TIGHTWAD Too cheap to invest in yourself. There is no free lunch with super-successful investors. Of course, you must live below your means, but if you are busting your butt, working your gazongas off, I hope you will reward yourself and your family with the good things you always dream about. Some investors are so damn tight, they don't pinch pennies with their hind end; all you barely see are sparks from those pennies they won't let go of. You must invest in yourself, in education, training, coaching, mentoring, health, and systems and tools, allowing you to Work Smarter, Not Harder. Most the super-extremist hardcore tightwads who I know seem to never be satisfied or happy. They just want more for free.

If You Pay Peanuts, You Get Monkeys! It NEVER fails and it just keeps happening over and over. Sometime within the next two weeks, an investor will schedule a one-on-one coaching session for help on the mess they created by trying to get off super-cheap. So cheap it sounds too good to be true. If it sounds too good to be true . . . it probably is. These messes happen on a regular basis because the investor tried to get something done for peanuts. It amazes me how these "pray and keep their fingers crossed" people hope they will get high-quality results. Quality people have value. Pay them and treat them as quality people for their quality work. But don't overpay; that's not good, either. But if you want good results, do your homework, check and verify their references and pay them accordingly.

Refusing to Build Your TEAM of Experts This goes hand in hand with both being a super-tightwad and paying peanuts. Some investors have a hard time acknowledging and accepting this. When you build a quality team in your business, even if they are just part-time, you will end up getting 2 + 2 = 8 results. Here's one of my examples. How many rental houses must I own to have a regular part-time or full-time handyman to take care of all of my maintenance requests, repairs, and so on? I did view this question as reducing my income. This was viewed as a way to work smarter, not harder. It allowed me to focus and concentrate on the things I should be doing in my business.

Independent Contractor Agreement This is a MUST before you allow or authorize any work to be done on any of your properties. This is a CYA contract for you and it keeps your nose clean at tax time. It spells out in detail the relationship between you and this contractor. It requires their contact info, SSN or TAX ID number, and a valid photo ID. In my business, this fill-in-the-blank form is a hidden webpage within my website... no paper.

Before hiring a contractor, always get a copy of their insurance declaration page and You MUST contact their insurance agent to make sure their policy is valid and current. I have caught many wannabe contractors who have used the equivalent of old-school "White Out" to change the dates on their declaration page. This happens most frequently with roofers and tree services. Here's the reason I am telling you about this. Did you know, in most states, even with your properly signed Independent Contract Agreement, if one of the contractor's helpers get injured on your property, they can come after the owner of the property. I am not speaking for all 50 states, but a good number are, like my state (Kentucky).

Education One of the most frequent questions I get is, "Mike, should I get my real estate license?" My reply every time is "Has someone told you not to get your license because of all of the laws and headaches?" Most of the time they said yes. Then I ask them if they admire the head that noise came out of, and they with a sad face... nope, "I do not admire that person." Okay, great, now we are making progress and let them know that every single one of my mentors and investors who I admire, had one common denominator... they all had their broker's license. It might be escrowed, but when they were churning and burning, they had their broker's license. Many investors believe because they own their home, they are knowledgeable about real estate investing. This is no different from playing a game of checkers. Good old homeowners know how to play checkers. But now this investor attends an investor meeting in her town and happen upon a couple of investors talking about a pending deal or a deal they recently made. This new investor listens intently, trying to be a sponge and soak up every tidbit of knowledge she can. As the two investors were wrapping up their conversation about their deal, this new investor asks them, "What's a FSBO?" As you could expect, those investors had a very disappointing facial expression. Investing in real estate is like playing "CHESS." You must learn the pieces and moves before you can play the game. Therefore, I will always recommend you go get your real estate license for the education, training, and access to all of the resources for your business. Do not get your license to chase commissions and listings.

NEVER Rent to Family, In Laws, Outlaws, Friends, or Vendors There's just too much at risk. Why are they asking you to rent? Something is ugly somewhere. Yes, you will become their guardian angel, their hero, in the beginning. When it goes wrong, you will be labeled worse than the devil. The only exceptions allowed are your own kids.

NEVER Swap Repairs for Rent Another huge can of worms. Once you allow this to happen, it will happen over and over again. It will. This behavior also destroys the value of your rental property.

ALWAYS Report ALL Income You will run into old-timers who will brag about putting cash received from tenants into their hip pocket. Here's three reasons why this is a huge mistake. Number 1—It's against the law (IRS thing). Number 2—It devalues your rental property. Somewhere in your future, you will probably sell one or more of your rentals. If you are selling to an investor, they will probably want to see some kind of operating statement or even tax returns, depending on type of real estate. Put yourself in your buyer's shoes and your seller tells you, "Hey, the rental income is really a lot higher because I put all of the cash payments into my pocket." Would you believe your seller? Number 3—This is probably the biggest reason. Your actions will get back to your resident manager or staff. When they see you pocketing cash, guess what they might start doing. Yup, you guessed it. It's the old "two for you and one for me" program. Not good at all. I could go on for a full day sharing with you all of the ways investors have lost money and income from providing opportunities for their resident managers and staff. The more income you report, the higher the market value of your rentals.

Not Requiring Renters' Insurance This is your first line of defense in protecting your rentals from something caused by your residents. I expand a lot on this in the chapter on insurance. This is very important.

NEVER Waive Late Charges Once you waive a late charge, you have just trained your resident that you do not enforce them. Stick to your guns. I use a daily late charge of $5.00 a day to protect our 10% late charge. My resident manager does have the authority to waive the daily late charge, but she cannot waive the 10% late charge. When done properly, your resident will thank you for your help in waiving the daily late charges.

NOT Raising Rent Every Year This will bite you in the butt and you will lose a great resident because you failed to raise the rent every year. Investors say, "I don't want to raise their rent because they might move. To make this brain-dead simple, in our lease right on the first page is shown the 2.9% annual cost of living rent increase for the next three years. That's only $29 on a $1,000 monthly rent.

POOR Record Keeping Whether we like it or not, we live in a society that refuses to accept good old-fashioned verbal or written statements from "eyewitnesses." Jump into a criminal court trial with me on a robbery of a business. The jury will listen to everyone who testifies on the stand about what they saw or heard. But what the jury really wants to see and hear are the videos and audio recordings of the robbery itself. This is what you must have in today's world. PROOF, not just your words or your scribbled-down, hard-to-read notes that paraphrase your perception of voice mails and phone calls. Most investors have absolutely no trouble documenting how much money each tenant owes you, but that's about it. Most investors fall short on properly documenting everything in their business.

Refusing to Accept Things That Comes with the Turf Many investors, especially new investors, have a very hard time separating their personal core values from good, sound, business sense. A great example to drive this point is a tenant who contacts an attorney and tries to file a B.S. lawsuit against you or your company.

You know all of the details of this B.S. claim inside and out and you have done absolutely nothing wrong. Your insurance company tells you they will take care of this for you and not to worry. Later on, you discover your insurance company paid several thousand dollars to your tenant who filed a bogus complaint. Immediately, your knee-jerk mental reaction is, "That's B.S." They should not have gotten one red cent, but yet your insurance company blindsided you on this one.

Here's the deal from your insurance company's perspective. Should this case or lawsuit ended up in court, your insurance company will have forked out tens of thousands of dollars in legal fees, even if they win. By settling the case now with a few thousand out-of-pocket for legal expenses, your insurance company comes out ahead because this is cheaper than running this whole thing through the court system with a full-blown jury trial. In case you did not know this, our governments, at all levels, do this on a regular basis, year after year.

Okay, here's an example of what and where you are 100% in control. Imagine you have a resident who has gone bad and has stopped paying rent for whatever reason you can imagine. You already know the eviction process in your town will end up costing you over $500 in legal fees and court costs, plus approximately two months of lost rent on an uncontested eviction process. So, let's do the math really quickly. $500 for legal stuff, and with $1,000 monthly rent times two months, this adds up to $2,500 really quickly AND this is if they do not show up in court. If they show up in court to challenge your eviction, it just adds more legal fees and more lost rents.

Knowing this beforehand, would you be better off contacting your tenant and offer a "Cash for Keys" program? An example of this could be:

> *"Hey Ralph, today is Monday and you and I can both see this is getting ugly pretty fast. You know you will ultimately have to move and with the eviction process, you will not get any help with your moving costs. Here's what I can do for you, Ralph. Get this place "broom clean" with all trash, garbage, and debris completely removed from the property by 4 P.M. on Friday and I will give you $500 to help with your move, and there will not be an eviction filed on your credit report and record. Plus, we can part ways in a friendly way."*

There is no magic formula for the dollar amount. Just use an amount that you believe will work and make it a dollar amount they will go for. That number in your town might be $750 instead of $500. Either way, it is a lot cheaper to do it this way instead of running it through the entire eviction process in court. Now, I can understand how this can really ruffle your feathers because they already owe you money, and now you are going to give them money to move? To the untrained investor, this does not make sense. But to the trained investor, this will save you a lot of money.

Resources Needed

To avoid the biggest mistakes of many investors:

- RENTERS' INSURANCE for all residents. PERIOD.
- Effective, efficient Office Operations including Tenant Tracking
- Investor Books allows you to push a button to see Cash Flow now by property and by rehab
- Online fill-in-the-blanks form hidden on your website.
- BUILD Your Team of Experts.
- EDUCATION, Education, Your Education Never Stops.

Imagine this bad tenant; would you be better off contacting your tenant and telling [illegible] An example of this could be:

> [illegible]

There is no magic formula for the dollar amount. Just use an amount that you believe will work and make it a dollar amount they will go for. That number in your town might be $750 instead of $500. Either way, it is a lot cheaper to do it this way instead of running it through the entire eviction process in court. Now, I can understand how this can really ruffle your feathers because they already owe you money, and now you are going to give them money to move? To the untrained investor, this does not make sense. But to the trained investor, this will save you a lot of money.

Resources Needed
To avoid the biggest mistakes of many investors:

- RENTERS INSURANCE for all residents PERIOD
- Effective, efficient Office Operations including Tenant Tracking
- Investor Books allow you to push a button to see Cash Flow now by property and by bank
- Online fill-in-the-blanks form added on your website
- BUILD Your Personal Support
- EDUCATION: Education/Your Education Never Stops

CHAPTER 23

The Hidden TAX BENEFITS

Especially If You've Got a Job

Always Check with Your Expert CPA or Tax Advisor. This section is my opinions based on my experiences involving this topic.

This one topic blindsided me. As a good cop raised in a good, old-fashioned, traditional family in a blue-collar neighborhood, I did not realize I did NOT have a clue about how my investment activity would affect me in the income tax arena. Big words like *depreciation, tax shelters, business expense,* and *"write offs"* might as well have been some foreign language. I was totally in the dark. Looking back today, what was really scary was not knowing any of this didn't bother me.

I honestly believed the good, old, simple math was how the whole investing thing worked. Buy an ugly, broken house at a bargain price, fix it up, and rent it. I thought as long as my rent was more than my house payment, I was doing pretty good, and this was called "cash flow." WRONG.

Here Comes My TSUNAMI! (A Good Thing)

If you will, jump into my shoes here for just a moment. Here's this guy, the long-haired, bearded, undercover cop who piddles part-time in real estate and NEVER works any overtime as far as police work goes. The other dozen or so detectives in your unit work all the overtime they can get, along with off-duty jobs, and look forward to tax time every year. They anxiously wait to get their TAX REFUND for their yearlong efforts. Many of these guys would get anywhere from $1,500 to as much as $4,000 or more back from Uncle Sam. What's kind of sad today is knowing they didn't realize the IRS was holding their money for them all year long for free.

Here's the frustrating part. Yes, I was buying rental property like it was going out of style. I watched my numbers, watched my cash flow, and tried to operate efficiently. What started happening to my surprise involved my Tax Refund checks from Uncle Sam. They didn't come in at $1,500 or even $4,000. I was getting HUGE refund checks. I'm talking $15,000 and more! How? Why? I didn't understand it. What do my fellow detectives who worked with me thought? Here I was, the guy who NEVER worked any overtime and I was getting 10 times more in refunds than they were.

They looked at me like I was doing something illegal. Honestly, I felt like I had done something wrong. I wondered how my CPA could've done this. This just didn't seem right. It didn't make a lick of sense to this kid who grew up by Churchill Downs.

DEPRECIATION "Dee-Pree-Shee-Ayy-Shun" the five-syllable word that works magic on your taxes.

Let me share with you what I didn't know. Let's pretend for a moment you're a self-employed painter. You buy your tools, equipment, and supplies. For example, as a painter, you purchase a 40-foot extension ladder for $1,000. You write a check from your bank account to pay for it and you use this ladder in your painting business.

Although you spent $1,000 of your hard-earned, after-tax dollars on a new ladder for your painting business, the IRS will not let you write off $1,000 as a business expense this year. The IRS has a schedule or report telling you the life of your ladder is 10 years and you can only write off $100 a year for the next 10 years in order to write off the cost of this ladder. They might use a term called a "capitalized expense," meaning the taxpayer writes off the cost over the life of the item.

So, if you were to spend $1,000 on a ladder, Uncle Sam says you can write off your $1,000 expense over the life of the ladder, for example, say 10 years. What's interesting about this, as a painter, is after 10 years, what is the value of your ladder? (If you can find it.) Odds are, the value of your ladder has dropped to next to nothing, if it's still intact. This same idea goes with plumbers, printers, and folks who have business expenses and investments associated with their making their earned taxable income.

Here's what so beautiful about real estate. Real estate is really dirt and those things attached to it...houses, buildings, and so forth. Uncle Sam will not allow us to "depreciate" dirt because dirt will always be here; however, Uncle Sam does allow us to say the improvements or buildings on the land has its own life. You might describe it as "How long will the building last or stand up?" Uncle Sam, for whatever reason, has come up with two schedules for real estate.

- Residential Improvements have a depreciation schedule (life) of 27.5 years.
- Commercial Improvements have a depreciation schedule (life) of 39 years.

So How Does DEPRECIATION Affect Me as an Investor?

Let's pretend you've purchased a single-family rental house for $100,000. Please understand you did not "spend" money here; you "invested" money here. At tax time, you'll ask yourself, "What's the value of the lot the house is sitting on?" Let's pretend the lot value is $15,000. Here's what should happen:

Purchase Price: $100,000.00

+ $1,200.00 (closing costs, title insurance, fees to buy)

$ 101,200.00 Total of your investment

Lot Value: ($15,000.00) (Subtract from your total investment)

$86,200.00 is depreciated over 27.5 years

$86,200 divided by 27.5 years = $ 3,134.54

This means you get a "phantom expense" of $3,134.54 for owning this investment property. The IRS sort of rationalizes this by saying the life of the improvements on this residential property is 27.5 years and theoretically, at the end of your 27.5-year period, the building(s) on the lot are worn out and worth ZERO, and all you have left is your vacant lot. There's still more.

Let's say you make $50,000 a year in "earned income," whether from your job or if you're self-employed. The simple version here gives you the following benefit NOW:

Your Income: $50,000.00

Minus Depreciation: ($3,134.54)

Your Taxable Income: $46,865.46

If you're in the 33% tax bracket, 1/3 of $3,000 is $1,000 savings right now in your income taxes. Let's bump it up a bit. Suppose you have 10 of these rental houses.

With 10 of the same Rental Houses

Your Income: $50,000.00

Minus Depreciation: $3,134.54 × 10 houses = ($31,345.40)

Your Taxable Income: $18,654.60

In this tax situation, the IRS allows you to pay income tax as if you only made $18,654.60 instead of the $50,000 you made during the tax year. WOW! This can be a huge tax savings. Let's try one simpler scenario:

With 20 of these same Rental Houses

Your Income: $50,000.00

Minus Depreciation: $3,134.54 × **20 houses** = ($62,690.80)

Your Taxable Income: ($12,690.80) YOU LOST MONEY!

If Uncle Sam and the IRS says you lost $12,690.80 for the year, this means **you pay no income tax!** In fact, if you have a job and have had money withheld from your paycheck for income taxes, odds are, you'll get all of your withholdings REFUNDED to You! This is exactly what happened to me. I didn't understand this depreciation thing. So all of my police officer wages and my wife's nurse salary was completely wiped out with this thing called depreciation. Some folks talk about a limit of 125K, getting tagged as a "Real Estate Professional," and getting tagged as a dealer. I am not the expert on these things, but I trust my CPA, Mike Grinnan, to handle all of this for me. He can cite all of the sections of the IRS tax code involved. He's the tax expert; I'm the investor and he is on my team.

Moving on, just to add some icing on your cake while we're here on this depreciation thing, my CPA, Mike Grinnan, also did additional things to benefit me and my family. I might be using the wrong official term here, but in investor language, let's call it a combination of "income averaging" both forward and in reverse. For example, because I began acquiring assets pretty darn fast and aggressively, my depreciation literally skyrocketed in a very short period of time. Perhaps in just two years' time, we were showing huge losses in the income department for tax purposes.

This is where my CPA applied his knowledge and expertise. This is what I pay him for! I'm not the tax expert; he is! On his own, without me asking, he then took our tax situation and tax returns for the last several years, applied his expertise, and somehow took today's losses and amended previous years' returns, PLUS did something else to carry some losses forward. I did not take detailed notes on the detailed steps of what he did. I just know he did more than I ever expected from him, resulting in MORE Tax Refunds from previous years.

In fact, this was so amazing to the guys I worked with, my boss began taking a serious interest in this real estate thing. He, too, then bought rental properties and retired and now my former boss, Sergeant Ron Cooper, worked for me at Vista Realtors. He passed away a couple of years ago.

What's the Catch with This Depreciation?

Here's the ugly part, but it, too, can have a happy ending. Let's go back to the $100,000 rental house you bought in the previous example. Suppose you operate it as a rental property for 10 years and you decide to sell this rental house for $200,000. Take a look at what might happen:

Selling your 100K Rental House after 10 years

Sale Price: $200,000

Minus Your Investment: ($101,200)

= Capital Gain (Your Profit) $98,800 (True for Real Cash Numbers)

(FALSE, for Tax Purposes)

Add Depreciation back in:

$3,134.54 × 10 years = + $31,345.40

Real TAXABLE Capital Gain (Your Profit) = $130,145.40

You'll be subject to Capital Gains tax or income tax on your profit from selling this rental house. Don't run yet. There are still several alternatives.

1. Remember Depreciation in the big picture. If you've enough depreciation annually already going on, it may very well totally wipe out all of your capital gains or profit from selling this rental property.
2. PLAN B: The IRS has another alternative for investors using IRS Section 1031 involving a "tax-deferred exchange." The simple, basic version of the 1031 tax-deferred exchange involves selling this rental property in order to upgrade into another investment property. Using this procedure properly allows an investor to "defer" the capital gain until the new property is sold.
3. PLAN C: as an "investor" and not as a "dealer," you'll have the additional alternative to use "installment sale" method of selling your rental property. This simply means Seller Financing or Owner Financing. You'll play the role of lender for your buyer. This sets the stage for investors to have the majority of the payment received monthly as "interest income" instead of capital gains income.

So, what really happens here is each year you own and operate this rental house, the IRS says the investment value of your asset drops by $3,134.54 each year. For tax purposes, what began as a $101,200.00 investment has decreased to $69,854.60.

There are many courses, books, and experts on Tax Strategies. Many investors are encouraged to accelerate their depreciation and "componentize" their investment, by chopping up parts of the property. For example, using the preceding example on a $100,000 rental house, one may elect to "componentize" their investment by breaking it down this way:

Purchase Price: $100,000.00

+ $1,200.00 (closing costs, title insurance, fees to buy)

$101,200.00 Total of your investment

Lot Value: ($15,000.00) (Subtract from your total investment)

$ 86,200.00 in improvements to be depreciated

Cabinets	$7000	depreciates on IRS schedule for cabinets
Carpet	$3000	depreciates on IRS schedule for carpet
Roof	$5000	depreciates on IRS schedule for Roofs

Plus, more stuff

The result using the "componentizing" method drastically increases your Depreciation Phantom Expense annually. Using the very first example earlier, an investor would get $3,134.54 annually to write off for depreciation by simple depreciating $86,200 over 27.5 years. Using this "componentizing" method may result in you being able to write off perhaps as much as $10,000 for a far fewer number of years. You're simply burning it up quicker.

Warning

Something to think about for the BIG PICTURE involving accelerating your depreciation using this "componentizing" strategy.

Scenario 1

- Suppose you have a high-income job or business. Perhaps as a successful attorney, doctor, or business owner, your taxable income is $500,000 or more annually.
- You don't have very much rental property.
- You're getting spanked in a huge way on paying income taxes.
- You'll benefit greatly NOW from "componentizing."

Scenario 2

- Suppose you're investing already.
- You've got a healthy chunk of depreciation annually, so it pretty much erases all of your earned income and passive income.
- You cannot benefit any more now from "componentizing."
- In fact, you're simply BURNING up your depreciation more quickly and you might really jackpot yourself down the road in just a few years.

Suppose you have $150,000 in depreciation annually and you make $100,000 the same year. The IRS views you as having lost $50,000 for the tax year. In short, you've literally wasted $50,000 in depreciation. So why in the world would you want to use the "componentizing" method in order to write off, say, perhaps as much as $250,000 right now, causing you to show a loss of $150,000 instead of $50,000.

Here's the method to this madness.

I've made it a point to pay attention to the old, veteran, super-successful investors in my town and across America. The old farts all have the same huge super pain in the butt. It is a common denominator found in all of the old timers.

THEY COMPLAIN ABOUT HOW MUCH THEY PAY IN INCOME TAXES! Huge dollar amounts. Obscene dollar amounts. WHY?

1. They're properties are usually paid off.
2. They're FRESH OUT of Depreciation! They have no depreciation left!

So, picture yourself a few years down the road, all or most of your properties are paid off and you have ZERO dollars' worth of phantom depreciation expense because you componentized your investments and wrote them off quicker. OUCH!

This taught me to keep piling on Capitalized Expenses because my goal was to NEVER run out of depreciation. If I can always have more depreciation than taxable income... is a good thing... no income tax.

Because I have so much depreciation today, my strategy is keep piling on capitalized expenses and improvements to d-r-a-g out my depreciation for years to come. I really don't want to end up like the old timers who are fresh out of depreciation and are crying with their huge income taxes. This idea is pretty much backward to what many investors are encouraged to do. Review your personal situation before taking action. Don't shoot yourself in the foot because somebody else says it's great for them.

My opinion on this DEPRECIATION thing. Today, I think of depreciation in pretty simple terms. In the big picture, I discovered I am very concerned about depreciation at two specific times or activities involving my real estate investing.

- When selling a property, I want to know my "cost basis" of the property I'm considering selling. ("Cost basis" is simply the dollar amount invested after writing off depreciation for X number of years operating it as a rental property)
- When preparing tax strategies for each year, I want to know how much depreciation I have for the year. My simple strategy to learn from my CPA, how much depreciation I have for the year. At this point, I know for the most part, I can make this amount of money before paying income taxes.

Let your CPA or accountant keep track and handle all of your depreciation and schedules associated with it. You're the investor. Become an expert at investing, not keeping track of depreciation.

EARNED INCOME versus PASSIVE INCOME

For investors involving taxes, these two words are very important. For the first few years, I didn't understand the difference nor was I really ever encouraged to know the difference. Many CPAs, accountants, tax attorneys and experts ASSUME that you and I know these terms and understand how these incomes affect us for tax purposes. My own CPA, Mike Grinnan, seemed a bit surprised years ago when I asked him if there was a difference. I'm gonna give my version of it from an investor's perspective.

Earned Income

This involves getting paid for something YOU DO. (Buy, Fix Up, and Sell is something you do and may be flagged as "Earned Income." Your job, my job as a cop, my wife's job as a nurse, real estate agent's commissions, and so forth, are all are "earned income."

The major difference involves your typical payroll withholding taxes.

As an investor, rental income, (income from assets . . . stuff you own) is considered "passive income" and not "earned income." This simply means you won't have to pay the huge 15.3% in additional income tax.

"INVESTOR" versus "DEALER" for Tax Purposes

Many investors have heard these terms. The worst thing for any investor is to be tattooed "dealer" by the IRS.

What's very frustrating to investors is Uncle Sam. the IRS doesn't spell out in black and white what *dealer* and *investor* actually mean. You won't find an answer anywhere that 12 of these or 15 of those means you're an investor or a dealer. Here's my understanding of it after years of absorbing all of this information.

Suppose you have 25 rental properties and you decide to buy, fix, up, and sell a property to enhance or to help your rental property program. My understanding is this one activity would be okay for an investor; however, if you've got two rental properties and your activity for this tax year consisted of 25 wholesale deals and 10 buy, fix up, and sell deals, I would be very concerned about being flagged as a "dealer" and not an "investor."

Passive Activity Loss Limitations

Check with your expert tax advisor or CPA on this one. The IRS is always changes rules and laws.

IRS Form 8582 publication details the specifics on this subject along with all of the exceptions and coordination with other limits. Here the website link for the instructions: http://www.irs.gov/pub/irs-pdf/i8582.pdf.

Some more benefits for investors: "Investors" use IRS Tax Form Schedule E. Here's a snapshot of the income and expenses contained on Schedule E.

All expenses deducted must be ordinary and necessary and not extravagant. Education would be ordinary and necessary, including seminars, boot camps, and conferences and yes, even this book is a business expense. Here's two links to IRS reports and information on this subject.

http://www.irs.gov/taxtopics/tc414.html "Rental Income and Expenses."

http://www.irs.gov/pub/irs-pdf/p527.pdf (22 page) IRS Form 527 on Rental Property.

My system of keeping everything organized allows me to "keep my finger on the pulse of my real estate business" while operating on a daily basis, PLUS it allows me to simply "PUSH A BUTTON" at tax time and email my books to my CPA. In May 2002, my CPA, Mike Grinnan, invited me to speak to a group of CPAs to show them how I keep all of my real estate stuff in a very simple system. I told him I preferred to show investors how to use my system allowing investors to save money from their tax preparers at tax-time while allowing them, too, to keep their finger on their investing business.

Today, investors in all 50 states, Canada, England, and New Zealand, and even Singapore are using my "Investor Books Pro System with Tenant Tracking." It is America's Only System for Real Estate using QuickBooks PRO. Get all of the powerful details online at www.InvestorBooksPro.com.

TAX FREE Profit and Income for Life! is absolutely true when you properly use your "Self-Directed Roth IRA." It is awesome. I'd love to expand on this, but there's not enough room in this book to do so.

In Summary, The Big Picture, The Simple "Cut to the Chase"

So much, so fast for investors. All of these items mentioned in this chapter are the tip of the iceberg for investors. They are very important and can affect your investing and tax situation in a huge way. Common Sense doesn't always apply. Good, old-fashioned horse tradin' math doesn't always apply.

Here are some simple guidelines. Tax Strategies also have to factor in a couple of other areas, namely Asset Protection and Estate Planning. When I got started, I really didn't have anything to lose, so I wasn't really concerned about Asset Protection and Estate Planning. As I grew our little empire, these two concerns became very important.

Once again, if you're just getting started and have ZERO properties, don't worry about having all of your entities laid out properly. Just do it. After you get several properties under your belt, perhaps a dozen or so, you may do some research into establishing an entity to operate as your property management company and to handle all of your DEALER activity. Keep in mind that this entity's profit will be flagged as EARNED income, and not passive income.

My objective and goal in this Hidden Tax Benefits chapter is to expose you to some of my experiences involving Income Tax. You can help yourself best by taking these few topics and discussing them with your CPA who is an expert in real estate investing.

I use two self-directed Roth IRA custodian companies. Equity Trust, formerly Mid-Ohio Securities in Elyria, Ohio, www.trustetc.com, and Carl Fischer's www.CamaPlan.com.

Just imagine having your 20 nice rental houses all paid for in your Self-Directed ROTH IRA account dumping Tax-Free Income and Profit for Life into your bank account.

Resources Needed

- A real estate investing expert CPA who owns rental properties just like you.
- A real estate investing expert Attorney who owns rental properties just like you.
- Investor Books Pro System with Tenant Tracking (the only complete system for real estate using QuickBooks PRO®.)

CHAPTER 24

What's Best: Houses, Duplexes, Trailers, Apartments, Commercial, or Dirt?

I'm asked this question frequently. The real answer depends on YOU. It should be determined by gathering as much information as possible on each option and pile all of this information on YOUR scales to see which one gives YOU the most benefits AND the least number of headaches. The number 1 answer for me and many investors getting started is a "no-brainer."

You'll get the good, bad, and the ugly on each. The ultimate decision is yours. Each will have a list of benefits, challenges, and problems.

Single-Family Houses

This by far, is the number one, simple, solid investment. From beginners to the old pro, it's a hard one to beat. Let's begin with the benefits for you.

- *Easiest to acquire*. Single-family houses, as a rule of thumb, are the easiest investment to grow your wealth with the least amount of risk. Houses can be bought at "wholesale" prices. You'll be dealing with owner-occupants or just good, plain, old consumers.
- Most house owners aren't investors; they're homeowners or "retail consumers." As a sharp investor, this puts you at a tremendous advantage. You can buy "wholesale" and sell "retail" and sometimes more than retail if you're really good.

Years ago, I asked my good friend, successful, experienced investor, and mentor from Sarasota, Florida, John Schaub, why he likes single-family houses. His answer was simple. Although not his exact words, here's my summary of his answer.

With single-family houses, I get to deal with everyday people—homeowners. I feel pretty knowledgeable, competent, and the odds are probably more in my favor of creating a good deal for me. I can use my knowledge and experience to create a win-win situation for both the seller and myself. In the commercial arena, you're usually not dealing with everyday homeowners. You're dealing with high-dollar specialized attorneys who are probably sharper and more ruthless than you are.

BUY WHOLESALE, SELL RETAIL is a sound business plan. You can do this pretty easily with houses. I'm NOT promoting buy-and-sell as investing. My point is, with single-family houses, you really can buy at wholesale prices, and if the opportunity arises as part of your big investment strategy or battle plan, you can sell these houses at retail prices and sometimes a little more! Done properly, you can avoid commissions, defer capital gains taxes, and most expenses involved with selling houses the traditional way.

You can buy wholesale, rent it for a while, and then sell it at full retail price with a tenant buyer. You may also choose to rent your house to a tenant with an option to buy. They can get their own financing somewhere down the road while renting from you and buy it. You may choose to help finance part or all of their purchase using the "installment sale" benefit for investors.

With the sale of ANY investment property, a 1031 tax-deferred exchange done properly allows you to transfer your profit/gain into another investment property. (You can use 1031 exchange on any investment property) This means you can "defer" the payment of capital gains tax while letting your deferred capital gain earn appreciation on the new property acquired.

Other benefits include each tenant lives in their own HOME. With single-family houses, most of the time, the tenant is responsible for all lawn care, trash removal, and utilities. Although not always required by your local Landlord Tenant Laws, many good tenants will actually do minor maintenance and repairs themselves and at their expense.

Another benefit for the single-family house investor involves spreading your risk. With several houses in the same town, if one were to burn, or get smashed by a tree from a storm, you wouldn't be shut down. With an apartment building and a tragedy strikes, you might lose all of your tenants until the property is livable again. For example, if you own an 18-unit building and a tenant can't cook. They burn up their bacon in a nasty grease fire on the stove. Wait until you see your local fire department in action. They ought to be in the crash demolition business. They'll chop holes in your roof, knock out windows and doors, even if they're unlocked, and will make the utility company disconnect service to your building.

Now what? What about your other 17 tenants? Looks like they, too, might be homeless for a while.

Flying below the radar is another benefit with houses. You can maintain a very low profile in your town. You can acquire a boatload of houses and wealth while maintaining a relatively low profile. Start acquiring a bunch of apartments and commercial property and you'll be flying very loud and proud on your local "who's who" radar screen.

Are you having a hard time trying to figure out which way to go with your real estate investing business? You are not alone. I struggled with this one for years as well. In this short chapter, you are going to get the Pros and Cons of each type of investment.

Let me assume you have no desire to compete with Donald Trump's success. My experience is part of my opinion on each of these, and let's assume it's just fine to be a big fish in a small pond.

To sum it up Fred Flintstone–style (three fingers)—would you like to make $15K per month and do what you want or make $50K or more every month and not have time to fart? Only you can answer this question. Let's take a look at each type of investment.

Single Family Houses: Pros

- Tenant pays all utilities (water, sewer, trash, electric, gas).
- Tenant maintains yard, lawn, fence rows.
- Tenant pays for their own cable TV, Internet, and so on.
- Tenant is responsible for all pest and critter control, including Bedbugs.
- Tenant keeps gutters cleaned.
- Tenant keeps tree limbs off roof.
- Tenant provides all appliances (range, fridge, washer, dryer) except for built-in appliances.
- Landlord decides monthly Rent (market conditions).
- Tenant pays annual cost-of-living rent increase (Mike does 2.9%).
- Assuming a decent neighborhood, great residents will stay six years or more.
- Reducing Tenant Turnovers increases your income and profit.
- You can always be the "expert" when buying SFH.
- You can always buy at wholesale and sell at retail-to-retail buyers. Not the case with apartments and commercial. You might get a great deal, but when you want to cash out, you can only sell to investors who want a killer deal, just like you.
- If you screw up and half-ass processing rental application resulting in an undesirable in your rental, you will obviously tick off your neighbors, but you can evict them and put a carefully screened, great resident in place.
- You buy at wholesale prices and sell at retail.

Single Family Houses: Cons

- I'm still thinking…

Duplexes and Houses Chopped into Units

This one gets my goat. I've heard these called FLATS and DOUBLES and TRIPLES. It doesn't matter; there are different names and terms for your region and town. It still boils down to a free-standing house with two or three units. These are "misery magnets." With single-family houses, most towns allow most regular maintenance, such as lawn care and pest control to be a tenant responsibility. With duplexes and triplexes, most communities make the landlord responsible for the "common area maintenance." You'll have the responsibility of lawn care, trash removal, water, perhaps utilities, and more.

Many bizarre situations involving utilities, heating, and trash may develop. Are your units separately metered for utilities? Will you have to pro-rate utilities between tenants or will you include utilities in the rent and cringe when you see tenants washing cars, or having windows open in the winter because it gets too hot inside? Some communities require separate meters for each unit if the landlord wants tenants to pay utilities. I've found some towns make it illegal for landlords to charge tenants for utilities without a meter on the unit. All of these things can be time-eating tasks or cash-eating monsters assigned to YOU. You should strive for an auto-pilot investment system. It's a whole lot easier.

If you want to argue, "But the cash flow blah, blah, blah . . ." take a moment to measure your time-eating tasks of babysitting these high "hands on" management units versus the same number of houses. You'll quickly see you'll have more free time. For example, I was doing an all-day Saturday workshop in Tampa and was challenged about the wonderful CASH FLOW on a huge two-story house in an older section of town. I allowed this person to ramble on about how they could "chop this house up" into seven efficiencies or studios and perhaps even restructure the rent period from monthly to twice a month or even weekly.

I cringed at this thought. This lady honestly believed her challenge was awesome and great and good and profitable. WRONG! I'll bet you I can operate 75 single-family rental houses or more with about the same or less level of "hands on" management. I know, because I operated 75 rental properties and a full-time job before I hired a 5-hour per week part-time office person.

The other eye-opening discovery for her involved my statement: "I'm not in the hotel business. How long do you want your tenants to stay in your rental property?" The whole class almost unanimously replied, "Forever." This is the correct attitude. Many of my rental properties still have had only one tenant. This is pretty darn good for the long term.

Tenants living in house call your house their HOME. Tenants living in an apartment usually call it their APARTMENT. I want my tenants to call their unit HOME and get real attached to it and stay a long time. Apartments, efficiencies, and studios are designed for short-term or temporary housing.

MultiFamily—Apartments

Let's say these involve 18 or more units.

There are basically three grades—A, B, C. Just like school grades.

"A" is high-quality and nice.

"B" is just a cut above average, but not much.

"C" although labeled "average" as far as school grades, a "C"-quality apartment community is not very desirable and is sort of viewed as "bottom of the barrel" by investors. Owners usually have trouble getting good insurance.

Apartment owners like the following benefits only because they're wearing blinders, preventing them from openly entertaining new ideas.

- Having everything in one place is efficient.
- Onsite help is easier to control and manage.
- No need for transportation for help.
- Many units in one location have less risk because the occupied units will cover the mortgage payment with several units vacant. They'll argue you can't do this with houses. (The very same thing can be achieved. So let's say you have a 60-unit complex and another investor has 60 single-family houses. I'll bet, with a good program, the investor with 60 single families is more profitable across the board, including time to manage them.)

MultiFamily: Pros

- One loan payment if you have borrowed money.
- One roof.
- One Property Tax Bill.
- On a per-unit cost, you can usually buy them more cheaply than a single-family house. Example, a two-bedroom house might cost you $60K in my town, but you can buy a building with two-bedroom apartments for as low as $40K per unit.
- One insurance policy.

MultiFamily: Cons

- Overhead Cost on Paid-For, FREE AND clear Apartment Communities = 50% of your gross rents.
- Multifamily (Apartments) fit somewhere in between a hotel and a rental house.
- More Tenant Turnovers in apartments.

- You can buy at a great price, but if you want to sell your apartments, you will be dealing with another investor who wants to beat you up and get a great deal just like you did. This results in buy at wholesale and sell at wholesale, not retail.
- Example: Building with 24 apartments. All are two-bedroom and Rent for $750.
    - You have five vacant units because it is harder to find great residents.
    - What can you do?
        - Reduce Rent to $699?
            - You might fill your five vacant units, but your other 19 tenants want their rent lowered too. Headache?
        - First Month Free! Same issues as the others.
    - Remember, me and you live in our "bubble" and your tenants live in their "bubble." Tenants do things we think are weird and not good. (Pawnshops, Aaron's Rent-A-Center where they rent a toaster for $24 every two weeks.)
    - Tenants in your apartments (building) talk and share information like a little village. If you do any improvement to an apartment, the others will start clucking like hens to each other about getting the same for their apartment.
    - You pay for Dumpster service.
    - You are responsible for pest control—roaches, critters, and so on.

In my town, the landlord is responsible to treat multifamily units every month for pest control. Such things as roaches, ants, mice, rats, and any and all kinds of critters, including BEDBUGS!

Bedbugs ain't cheap. Just imagine what is going to happen in your apartment building when a rumor gets out that the people in Apartment B31 have bedbugs! You may as well scream, "The sky is falling!" Once this rumor is launched, every resident in this same building will demand, not request, their unit be treated for bedbugs.

- You pay for lawn service, trash, house meter, electric, water, maybe cable TV, and more.
- If on a central heat and air system, you will pay for their heating and air conditioning.
- You pay for hot water for your building.
- You MUST be very careful when screening tenants. Should you screw up and end up with a terrible tenant in one of your apartments, you will cause all of your tenants to get super ticked off at you because of this one bad tenant. The unfortunate reality is your good tenants will move out faster than you can evict your bad tenant.

- If one of your tenants cook bacon naked on a Sunday morning and sets the kitchen on fire, the fire department will respond to put out the fire. They will saw and chop holes in your roof, bust out windows and doors, and drown your entire building in water. Then a BIG boom happens.
    - I've seen this happen over and over when I was a uniformed police officer.
    - The police are dispatched on every call reporting a fire to secure the area, allowing the fire department to do their work uninterrupted.
    - Usually within an hour, the power company shows up and cuts the electric wires to your building.
    - Now you have 24 tenants with no place to live.
    - Unfortunately, our society has groomed tenants to believe it is your responsibility to put them up in a hotel. Where does this come from? This is why you must make every tenant buy renter's insurance. Most policies will pay for their hotel bill should a tragedy like this happen.

Figure 24.1 shows an eye-opener: Experienced apartment community owners and investors will admit this STAGGERING rule of thumb with apartments.

So even the investor who pays a Property Manager 10% of their rent to manage their 50 Single-Family Houses will still make more money. It's plain to see how 50 houses SMOKES apartments, even with using a property manager.

Some more factors to consider: If you captured some apartments for a heck of price, who can you sell them to later? How long will it take? It will probably take longer to sell than a single-family house.

Who BUYS Apartments? Investors Buy Apartments

Investors are looking for a deal to steal; don't you? From a simple four plex to the several hundred-unit community, your buyer/investor, just like you, is looking to steal something. With a house, you can buy at wholesale and sell at retail.

FIGURE 24.1 OVERHEAD COST COMPARISON – SFH vs, Apts

OVERHEAD COST COMPARISON In Towns with Reasonable Property Taxes	
Single Family House PAID FOR	18 or more Apartments PAID FOR
30% of Your Rent To Cover Operating Cost	**50%** of Your Rents To Cover Operating Cost

If you ever needed to have a fire sale, you would have to take a huge hit on an apartment community versus single-family houses that you could sell off one or two at a time to meet your fire sale need.

How will you handle stigmas? Suppose a violent criminal act occurs at your apartments. I've seen this happen to a buddy of mine with his large apartment communities. He pretty much went into Panic Mode. They hired extra off-duty police to patrol the parking and were terrified their existing tenants may choose to move, along with new, prospective tenants avoiding their very dangerous, highly publicized, dangerous apartment complex you happen to own. You better have some cash reserves to weather these hurdles and storms like these.

What about tragedies? A storm, a tree crashing into a building, or worse yet, some kind of environmental concern from asbestos, lead, mold, and so on. Imagine the panic cancer spreading throughout your units. Tenants may jump on the bandwagon to get out of your dangerous and unhealthy units.

Lawsuits. The "help us find somebody to sue" attorneys will follow up if a tragedy strikes you. They already know where to find your tenants . . . in your apartments, they saw on TV. If you had houses scattered around town, it may take a little more effort.

Many apartment buildings have central heating and air systems. Simply put, this means "not IF it goes out, but WHEN it goes out," it's out for EVERYBODY. Then what? So, your boiler dies in the cold of winter. Are you going to put all your tenants up in a hotel? What will you pay for a temporary boiler while your cash evaporates paying the rental fee along with repairing or replacing the boiler? Houses have their own system easily serviced or replaced by any competent, licensed HVAC technician.

And finally, apartments for the most part fit the bill as "short-term temporary housing," just a notch above a hotel or motel. Yes, we can find folks who live in an apartment for years; but most tenants are short-termers and move more frequently than those who take up residence in a house.

Finally, apartments are very challenging to maintain their high-quality ranking. It takes some serious effort and money to keep everything in order. You absolutely MUST screen your rental applications very carefully. Many times as a cop, I saw investors simply get lazy and greedy, trying to cut expenses and plug vacancies and they'd put just about anybody into an empty unit. WRONG! This is one of the worst things you could do.

Picture this: you've got good tenants in your building. You screw up one time and without knowing it, you put a "dirtbag" tenant into your building. It will not take long for you to discover this. Your good, responsible tenants will let you know, making comments and demanding you fix this problem. Your good tenants will threaten to move if you don't take action NOW. Unfortunately, most states' Landlord Tenant Laws require the landlord to follow a specific process to evict a tenant. This isn't done overnight and may take anywhere from a month to three months to get the bad tenant out without any challenges from the tenant! What will your good tenants do before you get the bad tenant out? Yup, they'll move! Now you've started growing a cancer and your building will probably get labeled as the bad building.

One last important issue with apartments: Suppose you operate in a market where you have too many units and not enough tenants. In my town, this is happening now and it leaves us with the painful process of selecting "cream of the crap." How do you combat this kind of market condition?

I have no intention of lowering the quality of my tenants. However, I can lower my rent to drive good responsible tenants to my properties for a wonderful, below-market rent. (Keep in mind, with my Tenant Tracking system, I get more than 110% of my rents where most investor/landlords get only 85% of their rents.) For example, if market rent on a single-family house is $900, I might advertise the rent on this HOME at $799, coming it at least $100 cheaper than all of my competition. I'll get more applicants and will not have to resort to lowering our qualifying standards to fill the vacancy.

But, what about apartments? Can you take a building with, let's say, 24 two-bedroom units with a market rent of $700 and lower the rent to $599 for your next tenant to help fill your vacant unit(s)? No way! Regardless of what others tell you, TENANTS TALK! If you do something like this, you'd better be prepared to lower everybody's' rent to $599 across the board. With single-family houses, and the tenants not knowing each other, if the market conditions get brutal, I can lower rents on an individual house as needed to fill vacancies while maintaining the standards of a high-quality tenancy.

TRAILERS, Mobile Homes, Modular Homes, Trailers with wheels, Trailers without wheels; you got the idea.

Without a doubt, I'll admit, these can be CASH COWS. First of all, trailers should not be viewed as an investment. Investments are things you buy for long-term growth. Trailers are like cars and actually go DOWN in value with time. Many trailer owner-investors are very proud and protective of their trailers. These golden cash cows really crank in the cash flow department. The only problem involves the trailer itself. They should not be viewed as an investment. Perhaps you could look at them like vending machines (they probably cost about the same as well). You can purchase a vending machine and crank some pretty good cash flow if you place it in a good, high-traffic location.

Insurance can be a bear with trailers, especially those with fireplaces. Before my wife became an RN, she was involved in insurance. Going back to those days, trailer insurance was approximately three times the cost of a good homeowner's insurance policy on a house. If the trailer had a fireplace, they would really get spanked.

You must find a location to park your trailer(s). A trailer park will charge rent. You could buy your own trailer park and charge lot rent yourself. Keep in mind, that it's like owning a vending machine park or mall.

You could buy dirt, pour a concrete pad and park your trailer, or you could capture a "modular home" and set it on a foundation and tie it down.

Most of the time, a very taboo label is associated with trailers and modular homes. The modular homeowner will vehemently deny their home is a trailer; however, when their guests leave, it still seems everybody calls it a "trailer" or "mobile home."

There are always exceptions to the rules. In my town, I'll stick to my guns on my opinion about mobile homes and trailers pretty. I've made many trips into them as a cop. As I've traveled around the country, I've seen some pretty darn nice trailer parks. In Florida, for example, there are gated community retirement trailer parks. Super nice with all kinds of amenities including tennis courts, a clubhouse, swimming pools and golf course membership privileges. But, I'll still call them "trailer parks."

You could view trailers in the same arena or category as low-income neighborhood houses. I think of these houses as "disposable houses." Perhaps trailers should be viewed in the same manner. Buy them for cash flow and not necessarily for appreciation or tax benefits. I've seen some super sharp and lucky investors, buy beat up and ugly trailer parks full of Jerry Springer's guests and get rid of its use as a trailer park turning it into a very valuable commercial property. This takes some time, effort, and money, but many folks have done this too.

Mobile Home Parks

This is not buying one-zee-two-zee individual mobile homes.

Mobile homes are an interesting animal. In order to get a better understanding of the typical mobile home park, get on Netflix and binge-watch the series titled *Trailer Park Boys*. This series pretty much is a bull's-eye on the culture of "typical" mobile home parks, based on my experience from responding to all kinds of calls as a police officer.

Let me point out there are some luxury mobile home parks, especially in Florida, where many retirees end up. Funny how not many people want to retire and move north. These luxury parks are awesome. Do not include these in my definition of "typical."

Then you have the bottom of the barrel, low-end mobile home parks. Many of these mobile homes have patched-up plywood floors, furniture (if any) with springs popping up through the sofa, and mattresses thrown on the floor in the bedrooms. Rickety, old, nasty, and super-super cheap; but they fulfill a need in our society. Do not include these low-end mobile home parks in my definition of "typical."

Mobile Home Parks: Pros

- A fellow investor had 300 rental houses and 1031'd all of them into buying a few mobile home parks. Today his income and cash flow are through the roof with a lot less repairs. He LOVES IT!
- Mobile homes are cheaper than stick-built houses.
- You can buy, sell, buy-back, and resell over and over again.
- You control the "Lot Rent" (how much you charge a mobile home owner to park their home in your park)
- You get to rent the mobile homes you own.
- Mobile home owners in your park are responsible for all of their repairs.
- Many times, mobile home parks have a little extra, not used yet, land to expand your park if you want.
- Buy It Right, Run It Right and you will have a very huge cash cow!

Mobile Home Parks: Cons

- You pay for the water service.
- You are responsible for ensuring there is some kind of sewer service. You could be hooked up to city sewer system, which is best, or you could have your own, stand alone, large sewage system.
- You maintain roadways and parking pads in your park.
- You make arrangements for trash pickup—cans or Dumpsters.
- You keep up the maintenance of the park. Everything from picking up trash, to lawn service, fences, swimming pool, clubhouse, and so on.
- You pay for park electric service for streetlights.
- You are responsible for maintaining mailboxes.
- In a typical or low-end mobile home park, odds are you will experience a huge culture shock when you step into their world, or their "bubble," as I like to call it.
- Most of the time, what you and I call common sense is the farthest thing from their mind and you better get used to talking their language. Many choice words.
- Insurance is more expensive on wobbly boxes. If you own some of the mobile homes in your park, you may want to consider not purchasing insurance on some of these if you purchased them right.
- Do NOT pretend that each and every mobile home you rent out is an investment or has any real value. I view them no differently than low-income single-family houses and refer to them as "disposable properties." Why? Because they don't

really have any value, their value is the CASH COW and income it produces for you. Better quality single family homes do not have the high rate of return, but they have far less management, headaches, and so on.

Commercial Property

Just like a casino, commercial property might be viewed as a game for the big players. Many can say they have phenomenal returns on their investment; however, I've seen many, including me, almost cry like a baby when their commercial property is sitting vacant without a tenant. They don't sit empty for a day or two. They don't sit empty for a month or two. I've seen some commercial properties sit empty for YEARS. The big dilemma with commercial property is the value of your property. Your property's value is generally determined by the INCOME it produces. Therefore, if you discount the rent on your commercial property, you've just shot yourself in the foot big time because you've just lowered the value of your commercial property.

Suppose I had a fast-food building PAID FOR, with a national fast-food chain leasing the property for $5,000 per month. This would mean approximately $60,000 in annual rent and no mortgage payment. Investors like to consider the "CAP RATE" of the property when handicapping the property for investment. If there was the opportunity for this property to crank $60,000 to the investor annually, along with annual increases in rent, and there is a long-term, perhaps a 20-year, lease in place, the investor's desired "cap rate" would determine the value of this property to the investor when paying all cash having no loan on the property. Let's take a look—the cap rate is the annual return their cash investment is making for them:

- 12% cap rate: The property would be worth $500,000.
- 8% cap rate: The property would be worth $750,000.
- 6% cap rate: the property would be worth $1,000,000.

The great side and good stories with commercial property involve what's called "triple net NNN," meaning absolutely no expenses for the owner other than debt service or their mortgage payment. The tenant pays for all of the property repairs and maintenance, all of the property taxes, and all of the property insurance, including naming the owner as an additional insured on the tenant's insurance policy. This is beautiful when it works.

When this same property is vacant, things get ugly quick. You'll pay the commercial rate property taxes, insurance, debt service, utilities, ground maintenance, and advertising to capture a new tenant. When a commercial unit is vacant, it can sit and sit and sit and sit for a long, long, time. They just don't move as fast a house can.

Imagine putting a commercial lease together. Not as simple as your standard rental agreement with a house or an apartment. A competent commercial tenant will want to lock in as much as they can to control their expenses. They'll try to beat up on you the best they can. Large national anchor tenants have leasing departments with full-time attorneys assigned the specific task of negotiating lease agreements with owners.

John Schaub tells a story of an investor friend who owned a nice retail strip center. A national chain drugstore negotiated a detailed lease for the property. His buddy pursued leasing the other vacant units located behind the drugstore. Then his buddy had a huge bomb dropped on him. He had rented one of the units to a business that just so happened to sell the same competing item in their store as the chain drugstore.

There's a lesson here. His buddy did NOT rent to another drugstore behind the national tenant drugstore. It could've been something as simple as a hobby store. The national drugstore chain attorneys (or their reps) watched closely as new retail tenants began to set up shop in the strip center. They found one item sold by the new tenant that competed with products sold by them. This allowed the national anchor tenant to "pull the trigger" on a clause in their lease stating if the owner rented space to another tenant carrying anything of competition to the national anchor tenant, the national anchor tenant would not have to pay any rent during the tenancy of the competing tenant. Long story short, his buddy took a bath on this one and the national drugstore did not have to pay rent during the tenancy of the small retailer in the strip center. OUCH!

With commercial property, the stakes are much higher, but if done properly the payday can be phenomenal!

Dirt

Unimproved plain old dirt. No buildings, no structures, just dirt. For starters, I don't know many investors who actually get a check in the mail each month because they own dirt. Years ago, my uncle, who owned hundreds of acres, would rent X number of acres to a farmer who would grow crops and the owner would get a percentage of the monies received from the sale of the crop. He'd also lease ground to hunters on a yearly basis to hunt deer, squirrel, rabbits, and so on.

One of the best investment strategies involving dirt is purchasing an "option to buy" to gain control of the real estate. For example, in a desirable area, a dirt owner strapped for cash who is struggling to pay property taxes might be a good opportunity for you to step in with your Roth IRA and purchase an "option to buy" locking in your purchase price for X number of years in exchange for paying the property taxes every year.

Your Roth IRA gets to capture all of the appreciation of the property without the risk of ownership allowing you to shop at your leisure for a qualified buyer using the new appreciated value.

I've seen some sharp investors use this same idea to gain control of several parcels of dirt located next to each other and when all parcels are combined, their combined value has doubled or tripled in value over the individual smaller parcels. It's been used over and over in my town, especially in the high growth and expansion areas for shopping centers and apartment complexes.

Dirt is tough to have monthly cash flow now, but used properly it can have a place in your long-term strategic investment battle plan.

Self-Storage

I am not an expert on self-storage investments. Over the years, I have seen sharp investors with good management producing phenomenal income and profits. I have also seen some investors get taken to the cleaners and lose their butt.

One of the things that prevented me from jumping into self-storage was my furnace and air-conditioning guy. He bought a self-storage facility before the days of electronic kiosks, and his customers had a key to their rented storage area.

One company, later determined to be a phantom company, paid for 20+ storage units, and used them to stack and store dozens and dozens of 55-gallon barrels of toxic chemicals. Super-expensive mess and environmental hazard. The owner could not find any person or this company anywhere. They disappeared just like "Today, We Do Windows" people.

He also discovered many others dumping tires, appliances with Freon (fridges), and other pain-in-the-butt items with expensive removal costs.

Note

If you are going to do Self-Storage, Do It the Right Way: You must buy it right and you must manage it properly.

Marinas, RV Parks, and More

I am clueless. You are on your own.

Winner

Hands down in my book—single-family houses WIN by rar! (Although nice mobile home parks come in second.)

You can almost always be the expert when investing in single-family houses. You will have more knowledge and expertise than the typical homeowner/motivated seller in most situations.

Resources Needed

To help with doing your homework in your real estate business.

- Zillow.com website—chock-full of information, not always precise, but good fast info.
- RedFin.com's website is a little more accurate and is my preference.
- Cell phone/tablet app "Financial Calculator" is today's version of the old HP12c. It allows you to quickly cipher up any and all kinds of loan terms and results.
- Bookkeeping and Operations software—Investor Books PRO System.

APPENDIX A

Recommended Resources for Your Business

Congratulations and Welcome. The time is here to go 100% paperless in your business.

Here is my list of recommended resources for your real estate business. So much technology and most of them are free. Here are the tools I use in my real estate business plus additional tools many other investors are using.

FREE Investor Trainings for You

- FREE Fair Housing training video for you and your staff. Go online to http://askmikebutler.com/free-training/ (19 minutes).
- FREE Investor Training Webinars "POWER LUNCH Chalk Talks" happens every Tuesday at 12 noon Eastern at www.MikeButler.com/PowerLunch.

FREE Forms from Mike Butler

All the forms in this book are free for you to download 24/7. Go online to www.MikeButler.com/LLAPfreeForms

FREE Stuff from GooglePlay.com

1. *"ACR" (All Call Recording)* cell phone app. It asks me after every phone call if I want to save the recording of this phone call.

2. *Financial Calculator* does better than the old HP12c. This little freebie is powerful. Now you determine loan payments, interest rates, and much more, including how to buy discounted notes and mortgages with the return you choose.
3. *Open Camera* allows you to set your resolution settings to be website friendly. This simply means low resolution and it does not eat up a lot of storage on your device. This app also allows you to put a name and date/time stamp on every photo and video. Great for Move In Photos, Work Orders and Repairs, and Move Out photos.
4. *Office Lens*, made by Microsoft, allows you to use the camera on your smartphone as a Scanner to create PDFs.
5. *Square* turns your cell phone into a cash register! It allows you to take credit card payments on the spot. Make sure you sign up properly and they will send you a credit card scanner that plugs into the earphone jack on your smartphone. They will send you the scanner for FREE! (I carry it with me everywhere.)
6. *PayPal*—same as Square—you can also embed PayPal links into your website for things like your Application Fee.
7. *Voice Recorder* turns your smartphone into an audio recorder.
   Great for Personal Safety, too.
8. *Home Advisor* app allows you to search for prequalified contractors. Although I have never used their free service, I know many investors who use it on a regular basis.
9. Get *Google everything*—Gmail, Google Calendar, Google Docs, Google Drive, Google Voice, Google Translate for your phone, laptop, and website, Google Forms, Google Sheets, and anything else you might like. Google Drive gives you 15 gigs of storage for free in the cloud.
10. *GOOGLE CALENDAR and REMINDERS*—you can create additional calendars for different things.
    - My personal calendar
    - My business calendar
    - Lawn Service Guy Calendar
    - Maintenance Supervisor Calendar
    - My Resident Manager Calendar
    - My MikeButler.com LIVE Events Calendar
    - YOU CAN ATTACH things to Each Event in Your Calendar!

11. *PDF and Document Signing Apps*—there are many cell phone apps offering this service for free. You want to get the cell phone app that you are most comfortable with and test it. Email yourself a PDF document and open the email on your smartphone. Then try to sign your name on it somewhere.

12. *Home Depot*, *Lowe's*, and others

FREE Software for Your Desktop and Laptop

1. *Last Pass* is a powerful password tool. It is free to install on your desktop and laptop. I paid for the upgrade and it now syncs everything across all of my devices, including my smartphone and tablets. I think it is $24 year for this ultimate service.
2. *Mighty Text* for your desktop and laptop allows you to text message to one or more persons at the same time and it saves all of your texts. You can also add this to your smartphone and it all syncs across all of your devices for free!
3. *Team Viewer* free version allows you to access your desktop from anywhere in the world with internet access. This is your workhorse to allow you to run your business with your smartphone or tablet. You must keep your desktop turned on and you must have Team Viewer running on your desktop in order to access it. The neat thing about this program is you get to see your desktop monitor just like you are sitting in front it, and it is lightning fast!
4. *Google Forms* is a great FREE tool allowing you to create your own forms and embed them into pages on your website. Take almost any form you can think of and you can create it in your Google Forms app within your Google Drive account.

5. *Cute PDF* allows you to print anything to PDF. I use it every day in my business. You can download it at www.CutePDF.com.

6. *eFax.com* and *MyFax.com*. FREE Fax Service is a must today. Throw out your old Godzilla Fax Machine hooked up to your phone line. Imagine sitting in front of your computer and you want to fax something to someone. Just open the doc or PDF on your computer, click "print" and select your eFax or MyFax just like selecting your printer. Punch in their fax number and click "print" and away it goes to their fax machine.

7. Now it gets even better. Just imagine when someone sends you a fax, you get an email with the fax attached as a PDF and your free fax service saves it in your account online. NEVER again will you stand in your office waiting for a fax to come in. Both of these services allow you to do X number of faxes per month for free. If you exceed their number, you will get a charged a small fee.

Very Cheap and Awesome MUST-Have Tools

1. *SaneBox* is by far the best simple tool I have found to keep me from getting buried in all of the emails coming at me every day, especially all of the spambot emails. You can get this service, which syncs across all of your devices, for a measly $24 a year. It has saved me hundreds and hundreds of hours. Thank you, Cory Boatright, for telling me about this big timesaver.
2. *BlueRibbonBackUp.com* Automatic Set It and Forget BackUp System. Unlimited devices and unlimited storage for all of your devices. This is what I use in my business, and it works! It costs $5.00 a month. You must have an offsite automatic backup system for all of your data.

Recommended Products and Services (not free)

1. www.InvestorBooksPro.com Investor Books PRO System with Tenant Tracking. This is America's Only Complete System for Real Estate using QuickBooks Pro. This is a must for thousands of reasons, but simply put, it does your books as you pay bills and make bank deposits. Tax Time is a BREEZE!

I use this very same system in my real estate business since I created it back in 1991. Registered users get free updates for life! You must have the desktop version of QuickBooks PRO. Just a simple one-time investment. There are no recurring monthly fees or subscriptions. I can access it from anywhere in the world as long as I have Internet access. This is POWERFUL and allows you to go 100% paperless.

2. *Investor OnCarrot Website* - FREE with your Gold Membership. This website is an absolute must for your real estate business. Voted America's Best Website for real estate investors. I have partnered with owner Trevor Mauch, and have put a deal together where you can get your powerful Investor Carrot website for FREE! You could go to his website and pay $49 monthly for your website, OR You Can Join our GOLD Membership for the same price. It's only $49 a month and you get not only your Investor Carrot website for free, but a boatload more of Gold Member Benefits. Remember, I use this very same website in my business and you should too! Check it out. Sign up today at www.MikeButler.com/join.

Here are some of the free Investor Carrot websites used by investors all over the country. Check them out and you can see and get a feel about how it will work for you.

Vista Kentucky—www.VistaKy.com
Lewis Baldwin's—www.BregPa.com
Tom Olmsted's—www.PaintedLadyInc.com
Joanne Armstrong's—www.AffordableDreamProps.com
Gary and Lynn Jernigan's—www.JayLaneMgmt.com
Stan Bartley's—www.StanleyHousing.com
Shawn Devought's—www.DevoeRealty.com
Cally Overton's—www.OldHatcheeProperties.com
Shari Frasure's—www.WinchesterHomesForRent.com
Rodney Evan's—www.RodneyBuysHouses.com

3. *Rent Talk* 11-minute video— This is a MUST-Have for Your Rental Business—It does your New Tenant Orientation for you.

4. *LandlordLocks.com*. When I got started, it was a very expensive and royal pain in the butt babysitting door locks, deadbolts, and keys. Now I make money with keys and door locks! TRUE Story! Ernie Riddle's simple system allows you to play "musical locks" (musical chairs) with your door locks and deadbolts. Check out the photos and details on how his locks work. Give Ernie a call if you want to at 1-800-847-8729.

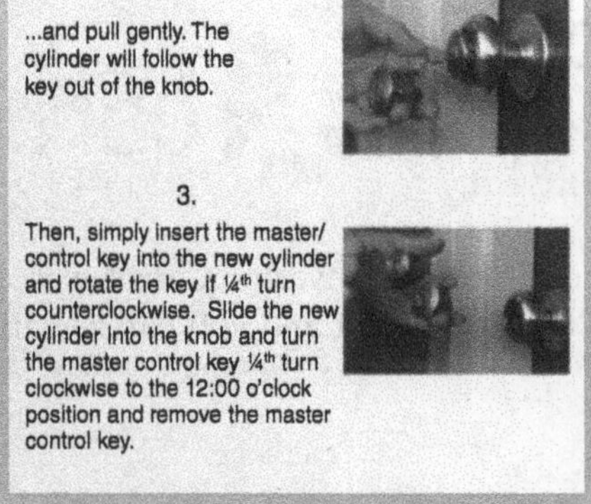

5. Yard signs—David Alexander's www.BanditSigns.com can take care of all of your yard sign and banner needs, at great prices. Depending on the quantity of signs purchased, you can get great discounts the more you buy. I use these 18″ × 24″ corrugated plastic signs and I get many uses out of these signs.

6. *Key Tags*—hard plastic, bright yellow with foiled embedded text on each side. On one side is "We Buy Houses! 896.2595 VistaKy.com"; and on the back side is "We Rent Homes!..." Call John Byron at Prosperity Promotions (502) 416-7812. Contact John to get these awesome key tags. He has over 1,000 different key tags to choose from in different shapes, colors, and more. PLUS he has everything in between and too much to list here. Ball caps, shirts, jackets, ink pens, bags, backpacks, and tons and tons more. I've been using John's company for over 15 years and his products, pricing, and service are incredible. His website is www.ProsperityPromo.com.

7. *Next Up* is a little more expensive, but it is great, especially when using Airbnb or HomeAway. It is my good friend and sharp investor Divyesh Panchal's Key Bot system. This is the most current, state-of-the-art lockbox system I have ever seen. It costs a little more, but well worth it. Here is the link to get all of the details. www.MikeButler.com/KeyPlease. It costs about $9 a month and they give you this expensive

lock for free. It auto-changes the access code after every showing and you can change the code from anywhere using your smartphone. This one is getting new updates all the time. So click the link shown in this section to get all of the details. My friend, Divyesh is a genius.

8. Mike Butler Home Training Systems at www.MikeButler.com.
    - TAX FREE Profit and Income For Life! (your Roth IRA)
    - 5 Minute Trust System—Keeps your name and company name off public records for your real estate and vehicles! Simple fill-in-the-blank Home Training System
    - How To Buy WITHOUT Banks, Money, Credit, Private Lenders, or Partners!
9. Mike Butler LIVE Training Events
10. Invite Mike Butler to Speak at or Train your group
11. MikeButler.com/SMTR – is a brain-dead simple tool to pre-screen applicants, show your vacant unit and collect Rental Application Fee without any phone calls! PLUS, Mike has a special gift for you All for a one time fee of $49 per vacant rental.

APPENDIX B

FORMS and More FORMS

WARNING! You MUST Read the Rules First!

All of the forms found in this book are COPYRIGHTED.

RULE 1

Because you've purchased "Landlording on Autopilot," you have some very special exclusive rights. You have the exclusive permission to copy and "edit" these forms for your personal use and your own real estate business use. You can NOT copy these forms and share them with other investors. You bought this book; you get the exclusive right.

RULE 2

This is very IMPORTANT and is NOT always highlighted in other publications for landlords. Most states have their own landlord/tenant laws. I'm telling you right now the forms I use in Louisville, Kentucky, most likely, will NOT work in California and New York. However, the ideas and concepts can probably be worked into your forms following your local landlord/tenant laws.

For example, I love getting my hands on another sharp investor's lease or rental agreement. I review it in detail. If I find a paragraph or section I really like, I simply take the concept, or sometimes copy the entire section or paragraph and add it to my rental agreement. I've never taken someone else's lease, change the landlord name or use it with my tenants. IT IS DANGEROUS to operate in this manner.

It is YOUR Responsibility to make sure your forms and content are in compliance with your local landlord/tenant laws.

How Do You Ensure Compliance?

Get your own copy of your local landlord/tenant law. Odds are, you can get on the first available computer with a printer and go to google.com and enter "Your State Landlord/Tenant Law." Google should give you a list of websites containing your answer. Just be super careful you get the REAL McCOY and not a TENANT GUIDE. Many tenant associations are creating their Tenant Friendly version of the landlord/tenant laws. Just make sure you get your government version.

I might be a tad bit brutal on these forms; but, just like my parents would crack our butts if it appeared one of us young kids did or would dart out into the street with traffic, I feel the same parental obligation to cause you a little pain now to prevent a huge train wreck down the road.

Examples of WHY to Make Sure

EXAMPLE 1

In my town, landlords are required to disclose the BANK NAME, ACCOUNT NUMBER, and ADDRESS OF THE BANK where their security deposit money is being held. If I used another expert investor's fill-in-the-blank lease, it may not contain this information and I would get clobbered in court if I pursued legal action against a tenant for damages.

EXAMPLE 2

What little bit I understand about Pennsylvania's landlord/tenant law involves language in the landlord's lease. It must be simple, and I've heard comments about being "approved by the Pennsylvania Attorney General." I don't know the details of this, but I promise you if I operated in Pennsylvania, I sure would make it a priority to understand all of this stuff.

EXAMPLE 3

Almost all states require a "Pay or Quit Possession Notice" served to the tenant from the landlord BEFORE a landlord can file for an eviction in court. The danger for you, the investor, is the number of days notice and the language that must be contained in the form, along with how it is delivered to your tenant varies from state to state. Kentucky has a 7-Day letter. Ohio uses a 3-day letter, and so on.

Here's the list of forms available to you for FREE.

1. Key Sign Out Form
2. Rental Application Form
3. Animal Application Form
4. Renters Insurance Form
5. Office ONLY – Move In Checklist
6. New Tenant Welcome Checklist
7. Office ONLY – Move Out Checklist
8. Mike's Move Out Package System
9. Rental Agreement
10. Inherited Tenant Form
11. Receipt of Notice to Vacate Form
12. 159-Point Rent Ready Checklist
13. Door Hanger
14. Holiday Rent Coupon
15. EPA Booklet "Protect Your Family from Lead in Your Home"
16. Resident Reward All-Star Plan
17. Welcome New Resident Checklist Form

Download Your Free Forms

http://www.MikeButler.com/LLAPfreeForms

INDEX

Page references followed by *f* indicate an illustrated figure and page references followed by *t* indicate a table

I

J

K

L

S

T